TRACKING LIONS,
MYTH, AND WILDERNESS
IN SAMBURU

Because Power is a
slippery devil of a
word

TRACKING LIONS,
MYTH, AND
WILDERNESS IN
SAMBURU

Jon Turk

RMB

For information on purchasing bulk quantities of this book, or to obtain media excerpts or invite the author to speak at an event, please visit rmbooks.com and select the "Contact" tab.

RMB | Rocky Mountain Books Ltd.
rmbooks.com
@rmbooks
facebook.com/rmbooks

Cataloguing data available from Library and Archives Canada
ISBN 9781771604734 (softcover)
ISBN 9781771604697 (electronic)

All photos are by Jon Turk unless otherwise noted

Printed and bound in Canada

We would like to also take this opportunity to acknowledge the traditional territories upon which we live and work. In Calgary, Alberta, we acknowledge the Niitsítapi (Blackfoot) and the people of the Treaty 7 region in Southern Alberta, which includes the Siksika, the Piikuni, the Kainai, the Tsuut'ina, and the Stoney Nakoda First Nations, including Chiniki, Bearpaw, and Wesley First Nations. The City of Calgary is also home to Métis Nation of Alberta, Region III. In Victoria, British Columbia, we acknowledge the traditional territories of the Lkwungen (Esquimalt and Songhees), Malahat, Pacheedaht, Scia'new, T'Sou-ke, and W̱SÁNEĆ (Pauquachin, Tsartlip, Tsawout, Tseycum) peoples.

We acknowledge the financial support of the Government of Canada through the Canada Book Fund and the Canada Council for the Arts, and of the province of British Columbia through the British Columbia Arts Council and the Book Publishing Tax Credit.

TO THE SAMBURU PEOPLE

HONOURING THEIR GRACE
AND KINDNESS, UNDER THE YOKE
OF RELENTLESS OPPRESSION.

CONTENTS

PREFACE

On Earth Day 1, in April 1970, I was finishing the manuscript to my first book, *Ecology, Pollution, Environment*. On the 50th anniversary of Earth Day, April 2020, I was finishing this manuscript, the last book I plan to write: *Tracking Lions, Myth and Wilderness in Samburu*. A lifetime lies between those two event horizons: youth to old age, a PhD in organic chemistry, marriage and divorce, wonder interspersed with tragedy, children and grandchildren, a rewarding and lucrative writing career and a life of high adventure in remote landscapes and seascapes all over the world.

But to focus only on the two Earth Days during those spring wildflower seasons, half a century apart, is missing a significant part of the story. On May 4, 1970, 28 Ohio National Guardsmen fired 67 rounds of ammunition at a group of unarmed student protesters at Kent State University, killing four and injuring nine. A week and a half later, in the early morning of May 15, 40 police officers from the Jackson, Mississippi, police department and the State Highway Patrol fired 460 rounds over a period of 30 seconds, killing two unarmed black student protesters and wounding 12. The protests and the killings in both atrocities revolved around the Vietnam War and, in the Jackson tragedy, an ugly legacy of blatant racism.

As I was writing *Ecology, Pollution, Environment*, I was deeply troubled by the Kent State and Jackson murders and I felt that the Vietnam War and racism were so intricately linked with global environmental problems that our book should become more inclusive. But we were writing a college-level science textbook, not a book for general audiences. It was radical enough in its day, because at the time, there were no textbooks about environmental problems or solutions. And it was a science textbook, not an opinion piece. There was no way we could have, or should have, integrated broader social issues with the science of environmentalism. And I didn't see the links clearly enough, so I wouldn't have known how to connect these seemingly disparate issues anyway. The idea languished.

A lifetime passed. I authored or co-authored 35 books, but I never returned to that question that plagued me as a young man. Until now. Jump to spring wildflower season 2020, as I sit at my computer in a small office set deep in the expansive mountain ranges and forest of northwest Montana. The Covid-19 pandemic rages, uncontrolled, and we have no idea how that will resolve. Donald Trump, a racist, corrupt, lying, incompetent, misogynistic, narcissistic, would-be despot, rules the most powerful country in the world. Yes, after I finished the manuscript, he lost the election, but 74 million people voted for him (just slightly less than half the total vote), and to this day he still commands tens of millions of devout and all-too-well-armed followers. Black Lives Matter protests demanding an end to police brutality and social and economic injustices rage across the United States, and finally seem to be penetrating the consciousness of middle America. While some of our environmental problems, such as air and water pollution, have been dramatically reduced over the past half-century, others, including climate change, impending water scarcity and overpopulation, have all become even more severe than they were when I started writing about them in 1970.

Why do people continue to destroy the Earth's ecosystems when the evidence is uncontroversial that humans are living in an unsustainable manner on a finite planet? Why do nations continue to go to war, or otherwise confront one another? Why do we hate, kill and suppress our neighbours over the colour of a person's skin, as we have for centuries? Why can't we just be friendly, loving, co-operative and compassionate?

Perhaps I'm a fool to tackle these questions on this, my last major writing project. There are so many pitfalls, and such a great danger of spouting worn-out clichés and trite overgeneralizations or contributing to the ever-growing litany of Pollyanna mythologies and other self-serving fictions. But fool or not, here I am at the keyboard. I believe that our only hope of making progress toward understanding these essentially unanswerable questions is to start by viewing our Paleolithic selves, and our struggles for survival as a vulnerable primate, weaker than a chimpanzee, slower than a cheetah, with a poorer sense of smell than a hyena, and smaller teeth and claws than a lion. From there, if we follow the arc of history, right up to this Earth Day, with its Trumpian denialists, patterns will emerge that will open insights. And with insights, positive pathways will reveal themselves.

I am a storyteller, not an academic. This journey of discovery must be fun in order to be worthwhile, as any journey must be fun to be worthwhile. So for decades, or a lifetime, I read books, took notes, organized my arguments and waited for a story to emerge that would wrap a complex and controversial topic into a palatable and believable package. Then, in a chance encounter at the Harvard Travellers Club, Tina Ramme invited me to participate in a lion conservation study in Kenya. While the lion research turned into a bust, every event and mini-adventure in Kenya illustrated one of the components of the arguments I had been carefully cogitating and building on for half a century. And then, in an aha moment, as I hid in a maze-like thicket from real or imagined well-armed and murderous antagonists, under the merciless equatorial African sun, with time on my hands, reading Yuval Noah Harari's groundbreaking book *Sapiens*, I realized that this expedition was the narrative I was looking for. The book was born.

To outline a sane and sustainable path forward today, we must start by understanding the strengths and behaviours that gave our *Homo* ancestors survival value on the harsh savannah deep in our Paleolithic beginnings. That doesn't translate into a recommendation that we return to Paleo-Thought, or Paleo-Behaviour, or some such meme. We can't, and won't, all troop back into the forest, live in caves, eat roots and berries, dance in the moonlight to the hypnotic beating of drums, and start over again. And we can't launch ourselves to Mars to start a Paleo-Revival New Beginnings Colony. Both of those extremes are pure foolishness.

But we do need to understand ourselves, and to make peace with our think-too-much-know-it-all brains, and to do that, it might be helpful to broaden our perspective beyond the ever-troublesome, partisan, immediate commotion of the daily news.

CHAPTER 1

THE THICKET

I step gingerly through the narrow passage in the African night, careful not to trip on roots, and stooping low to avoid overhanging thorns. Earlier this afternoon, when it was light enough to see, I noticed that someone had created this path recently, perhaps this morning, leaving fresh machete scars, exposing clear, white wood. I would have expected the cuts to ooze an aromatic sap, but it hadn't rained here in three years, and the drought-stressed bushes had no sap, no water and no energy to release.

For the past few weeks, I've been living in comfortable accommodations at the main camp, in a wall-tent pitched on a spacious stone veranda levelled into an airy hillside, with the forest-savannah stretching in a seemingly infinite expanse below, and Mt. Sabache-Ololokwe dominating the southern skyline. But early this morning, Jawas stopped by and casually told me that it was time to move. He was carrying a tent and bedding, all tied up in frayed string, and indicated that this would be my new home. He didn't explain his reasoning, but he never explained his reasoning – about anything – and I no longer bothered to question him. I stuffed all my possessions into my small backpack and followed him down the hill. As we passed the dining area, I was alarmed to see a burly young Samburu warrior in battle fatigues, lounging seemingly casually around camp, but wearing a cartridge belt across his otherwise naked chest and cradling a menacing, well-worn AK-47. Clearly, the nebulous rumours of trouble that had been spinning around for the past week had morphed into a more immediate and sinister threat.

Jawas led me out of camp, down the hill and across the dry wash to the flat plain where the Samburu herded goats and camels, and where low-budget tourists camped when they came to visit. I expected to pitch my tent near the gazebo where we had partied with the jolly Russians, but instead Jawas veered off onto a hidden trail that I hadn't seen before. Following the trail for a short distance, we entered a small clearing cut into a thorny thicket. Working together, we set up the old Coleman car-camping tent, threadbare and bleached from the sun, blew up an ancient Therm-a-Rest that seemed unlikely to hold air, and spread out a mouldy sleeping bag with a flannel liner decorated with rodeo cowboys. With uncharacteristic sternness, Jawas instructed me to remain here for the rest of the afternoon.

Jawas was one of the Samburu men in their early 20s who had abandoned his traditional vocation herding skinny cattle on the savannah and now worked at the camp. He was the quietest and shyest of the workers, always slipping ghostlike into the shadows with his wry, almost sad smile. He served my meals in silence, moving slowly, slightly stooped, as if he were an old man. But he wasn't an old man, and when I followed him across rugged landscapes, when he was my companion and not my servant, he avoided thorns and entanglements with a subtle quickness that I was unable to imitate. He dressed in traditional clothing, mostly bare-chested, with a broad beaded necklace, a traditional red cloth skirt and a thin checkered cotton cloth that he wrapped around himself willy-nilly. He always carried an ancient knife, the size of a small machete, with a green and black handle made of some local material, which I was curious about, but when I asked about it he just smiled. A small, round plastic pink mirror, such as one might find in a 6-year-old American girl's pocketbook, was strapped onto his knife sheath. When we hiked in the bush together, alert for marauding lions or deadly black mamba serpents, the mirror would occasionally catch stray rays of sunlight that filtered through the foliage and flash pinpoints of light as if they were a signal to some unseen or unseeable entity in the vastness of Africa. At odd, random times, he would stop walking, take the mirror out and groom his curly hair, which was barely a quarter of an inch long, and hardly responded one way or another to grooming. Jawas's English was rudimentary, and my Samburu non-existent, so we didn't talk much, but I found his company relaxing and we spent a lot of time together.

Some days previously, when we first heard rumours of violence in the region, the camp manager, Tina, told me that if trouble ever surfaced, I should escape with Jawas into the mountains, rather than with any of the others. Of course, Jawas. It all made sense. And he was with me now, helping me set up my camp in the thorn-thicket, with a casual demeanour. When we were finished, he backed away with a paradoxically cheery yet sad-looking smile that opened no window into his thoughts or the reality of my present predicament. Then I was alone. I relaxed as best as I could under the circumstances, until dark.

I had memorized the trail we came in on and was certain that I could follow it back out, even at night, but I was curious about the new path, which headed away from the main camp, toward the dry wash. Was this an escape route, like the back tunnel of a rabbit hole? Because, in an emergency, if I could reach the wash, I could link up with the ancient trail where elephants rock-climbed to the summit plateau of Mt. Sabache-Ololokwe on their elbows and knees, to escape the poachers. Poachers, Somali road pirates, rogue government forces. Elephants, people, lions. Everyone around here seemed to be on the run from someone at one point or another. If I could reach the plateau safely, I might be able to slip unseen into that well-hidden cave that Jawas had shown me. When Jawas and I first explored the cave, I thought it was simply a tourist curiosity, but Jawas was uncharacteristically steadfast in his insistence that I imprint in my memory the finger-shaped rock on the far ridge that pointed toward the entrance. Even at the time, when everything was peaceful, I had a vague premonition that Jawas was telling me something important. Now, I couldn't find the cave in the dark, but I wouldn't forget that unique landmark, and the secret passage, if I had enough light to see.

I leave my tent and set out on what I assume is the escape route. After 15 yards, it splits into two paths, and I randomly choose the left-hand fork, but it dead-ends after a few turns, so I return to the junction. Ah, yes, there is one way in, and one route to the back door, with side channels to confuse and delay a potential pursuer, because there are guys with guns or machetes out there somewhere, although no one is telling me the whole story, so I don't know how much danger actually threatens and how much is amplified and imagined by innuendo-based spiralling fear.

I bend a few branches to guide me back toward the tent in the dark, and continue down the right fork. I carry my *rungu* (wooden club) in one hand and a GPS transmitter in the other. I understand that the *rungu* gives scant protection against Somali road pirates who might launch a raid into northeast Kenya, or against Chinese-backed government troops in a helicopter gunship, but my Samburu friends had universally insisted that if I learned how to use Stone Age weapons like a Samburu warrior, not a white man, I would be that much more ahead of the game. Jawas had stolen a lug nut off a long-haul truck headed across the desert to Ethiopia, and armed his wooden club with heavy metal, to up the ante in another ageless arms race. But my club, balanced and smooth in my hand, is simply shaped out of a branch of selected hardwood, with a knot at the end. In my other hand, I clutch the GPS transmitter. Old technology juxtaposed against the new. Out here a person uses every tool available. My nighttime mission is to relay my new position to my wife, Nina, who is home, safe, in the peaceful mountain forest of Montana. It's not that I believe she can helicopter in, Rambo-style, guns ablaze, and whisk me away from a fast-deteriorating emergency, but an ounce of precaution, however sketchy, never hurts.

After a few minutes, the roof of the labyrinth lowers, so I stoop to almost a crawl. Then, suddenly, poof! – I step out into the broad clearing adjacent to the wash. I straighten carefully and view the inky circle of star-studded equatorial desert sky. The nearly full moon is about to rise, creating a faint halo of light on the eastern horizon. If there were no danger, I would simply walk across the clearing – without thinking – careful not to trip on sticks or roots, or step into a pile of fresh camel dung, but otherwise inattentive. But today I stop, stock-still, with my back against the bushes, so I can peer into the crevices of the African night, and in doing so, I feel the sensuousness of the place, log it into my long-term memory, and become richer for this moment. For in my fear, I have, in an infinites-imal small way, become a part of this land. I scan the visual field for

Jon Turk

any movement, listen, smell. Satisfied that I can detect no immediate threat, I relax enough to gaze into the cosmic arc of stars, not to seek either danger or salvation, but simply because it is – as always – full of wonder. "Feel this moment. You will never be here again." Because if I embrace my vulnerability, cherish the danger and hold it dear, I can dispel the wasteful energy of fear and become ever more attentive to detail. Over my decades of adventure, I have learned that in times like this, fear has no survival value, but every neuron-filled nano-increment of alertness will tweak the odds that much more in my favour.

The drought had turned the landscape into a shrivelled mummy of itself, so in the darkness there is little sound and no smells. The moon halo creates enough light to produce faint shadows, but only within a narrow radius, so the world feels small even as the cosmos feels infinite.

I am normally a creature of daylight. But now, as I'm standing under the canopy of unfamiliar stars, the night feels friendly. Not logically, because the darkness might hide me, but just because it feels friendly – this rough clearing hacked out of the thorns for the camels – as all landscapes at all times of day or night, sun or shadow, are friendly if we accept their sentience.

I build a small tipi of sticks to mark my entry back into the labyrinth, then step into the starlight and fix my bearings. Perfect. A lone tree stands shadowy and skeletal in the clearing, with a trunk broad enough to protect my back, and a canopy small enough so it won't block the signal to the communications satellite that will carry my message halfway around the world.

There aren't many lions around, but there is a resident leopard in the neighbourhood. We've met previously and negotiated the boundaries of our territories. I think I'm out of the way down here in the thicket, and not infringing on the leopard's hunting grounds, but you never know when misunderstandings can arise, or when our delicate ceasefire might be broken by a social miscue on my part or her hunger generated from the drought. And leopards hunt at night. So, I walk carefully across the clearing, press my back firmly against the tree, to protect from a surprise attack, and keystroke a short message to Nina: "Possible danger. Have moved camp. Pls note position," and push 'Transmit.'

It's common for me to relieve the tension in times of maximum danger by mentally escaping into temporary humour or fantasy. I don't know whether this behaviour has survival value or not – it doesn't matter – it's the way my mind works, the way I cope. In this instance, I imagine the radio waves taking off – ahhweeee-zing! – at 186,000 miles per second. KaPowEee, bang, clunk. Incredibly, they hit that tiny satellite zooming around up there in space. Bull's eye. "Good shot." An instant later the satellite backs up, takes aim and fires off its own signal. BaZoomOh. Again, "Good shot." Because, from that moving platform zillions of miles away, the satellite finds my house half hidden in the pine and fir forest of the Bitterroot Mountains of western Montana. The signal crashes through the walls without hurting a thing and then comes to a screeching halt inside Nina's silver computer. Because sooner or later Nina will walk across the room to sit down in the big black office chair I bought after her back surgery. I can see her now, a slim woman in her mid-60s, walking with the smooth grace of the fine athlete she is. She looks taller and much younger than she is, because of the way she carries herself over the faded red carpet. She has a thin, angular face, short hair, probably uncombed. When she turns on her computer, does she look up to see the print, hanging on the wall above her desk, of two ravens in flight, against an impressionist blue sky, all mottled and streaky? Or does she look above that to see the original oil of a Bolivian peasant, painted in bright orange, yellow and green, with huge feet and an even bigger left hand, cartoonish, although I have never understood that hand. Does she look even higher to view the photo of a slightly chubby and obviously stoned Elvis shaking hands with Tricky Dick Nixon?

Despite my imagining, the satellite might have been temporarily hidden behind Mt. Sabache-Ololokwe, or perhaps it is overloaded with other people sending out their positions, who knows, but it stalls out trying to relay my simple text. Now, I try to relax, breathe deeply and evenly, to slow my heart rate. Maybe I am exaggerating the danger. Everyone in this small valley is friendly. I have person-ally witnessed no violence, even though there are rumours – and a grisly iPhone video of bullets flying and bodies twitching and bleed-ing in the dust. But that was some miles away, not in my immediate neighbourhood, and Africa is a big place, so maybe the violence won't spread. But then again, someone had shot the engineer who worked on the water tanks in the main camp. But that could have been nothing more than a drunk starting a barroom brawl. But why isn't Tina in hiding? Am I creating an imaginary narrative in my head, joining disconnected dots, to conjure up imaginary adventure and turn myself into a self-proclaimed hero? No. Wait a minute. I didn't assign myself to the thicket. Jawas led me here. Is my tent site in the thicket a hiding place? Or is it a deluxe, quiet, private campsite reserved for me because I am special? There are so many incomplete thoughts and rumours, so many voids in my knowledge and understanding. But the burly guy with the AK-47 is real, not a fictional character in an imagined narrative. So now, out here in the moonlight, under the sprawling canopy of African stars, I can't separate fact from fiction, but all things considered, it won't hurt to tell Nina precisely, latitude and longitude, where I am camped.

"Now, why, again, am I here?" I ask myself.

"Right. I'm on a quest, a journey of discovery, if those words have any meaning. Right. And what is it about this quest that compelled me to leave Nina, our home together and all our friends? Mountain biking in the forest. Hiking in the alpine tundra abundant with wildflowers and sparkling pure water, melting off summer snowfields, bouncing over rocks, dancing rainbows in the sun."

Useless ruminations. Right now, any explanation of this quest that I can conjure up in my think-too-much-know-it-all brain is insignificant compared to the necessity of surviving this moment, or this day, or the next couple of days. And, likewise, I must ignore any fond memories of home and hearth. I am 71 years old; I avoided the Vietnam War, and have lived my entire life in peaceful neighbourhoods, so as far as I know, no one has ever wanted to kill me. Or, if I am only imagining that evil threatens right now, I have never imagined before today that someone wanted to kill me. Either way the fear is real. But what is most disconcerting is that this lethal warrior, whether he is real or fabricated, with an AK-47, or a machete, can't possibly be angry at me, personally, because we have never met. We haven't had an argument, I don't owe him money, and I haven't slept with his wife or daughter. Instead, he is angry at a story in his head about some fictional character that might only vaguely resemble me. And this person isn't simply angry, but so filled with deep-seated hatred that if it came down to a confrontation, I couldn't count on a smile, logic, calmness, imagined leopard-speak, or fundamental human empathy to defuse the situation.

On the other hand, perhaps my fear is nothing more than a story in my own head about some fictional character that resembles an assailant who doesn't exist. Humans, myself included, with interlocking stories spinning through their overactive minds, are just too complex and confusing.

I've faced danger many times in my life – avalanches in the mountains and storms at sea. The inexorable pull of gravity. The leopard on the rock, a few days ago. Each incident was a complex synergy of order and chaos. Predictability and randomness. But even though the end result – injury or death – would be identical whether the calamity were caused by natural forces or human malevolence, I find it disconcerting that there might be conscious people out there, taking time out of their otherwise busy days, when they could be growing a garden, or playing soccer with friends, or bouncing a newborn on a loving knee, to track me down. And shoot me on the spot. Or kidnap me, march me back to their hideout, take out their video cameras, log into their Facebook accounts and lop off my head. Me? Why me? No, it isn't about me. It is about a symbol that I represent. Enough already. I need to remain alert, because only alertness will save me, not floating tendrils of fear or useless stories.

The little green light finally flashes, indicating that my device has sent the message. My task complete, I return to the small marker on the edge of the thicket, toss it into the bushes to remove any artificial signpost, find my way back to the tent and crawl into my musty sleeping bag, smelling of Africa.

Tomorrow might be a busy day and I really should get some sleep.

CHAPTER 2

COFFEE WITH TINA

Eight months before that night in the thicket, I delivered a keynote address about my Arctic expeditions at Harvard Travellers Club, with its warm woods and plush chairs, where everyone is clean-showered and well-dressed, holding sparkling wine glasses and chatting eruditely about adventures in faraway lands, as if everyone had the money and time to leave their jobs and their families, jump on airplanes that spew carbon into the atmosphere and trudge around the planet somewhere. Now and again these days, I earn my living as a storyteller, a travelling minstrel with a PowerPoint rather than a song, couch surfing with kindly members of my audiences, and maintaining sustenance with a fancy dinner one day and a peanut butter sandwich the next.

After my talk, people gathered, and we were chit-chatting – the usual stuff – when I spied a familiar woman working her way through the crowd. My brain jumped into warp speed, "Yes, yes," I reminded myself, "We've met, chatted, had coffee together, last time I was in Cambridge. Kindred spirits. C'mon. Name. Name. Of course. Got it. Tina Ramme."

By the time she reached me, with outstretched arms, I returned her warm hug with a jovial, "Tina. It's so good to see you. Of course, I should have expected that you'd be here."

Tina is short, with a rounded, fair-skinned, Scandinavian face, and a charming, almost innocent, childlike smile, framed by long blond braids that tumble across her shoulders, as if she were just out of high school or even younger, headed into her first-grade classroom with a Tinkerbell backpack, anything other than a woman who has spent a good part of her adult life in remote villages on the African savannah. I'll never understand how she hasn't gotten tanned, burned or wrinkled under the equatorial sun. We had met previously through our shared interest in an NGO called Cultural Survival. She had spent years with the Samburu in northeast Kenya, while, on the other side of the world, and in a radically different climate, I had visited with, learned from and written about the Koryak on the Kamchatka Peninsula in Siberia. We both treasured the wisdoms of our Indigenous friends and teachers and were dedicated to preserving these cultures and fellow human beings.

Tina is a wildlife biologist who had worked with the Harvard Museum of Comparative Zoology and now was involved with the Lion Conservation Fund, integrating her dedication to preserve the Samburu culture with the parallel imperative to preserve lion populations, because culture and local ecology are irreversibly interconnected. While in Cambridge, to keep food on the table, Tina teaches at Massachusetts Bay Community College. I recall bonding to her especially strongly when she told me that she spent so much time in Africa that she only works part-time at MassBay and doesn't even bother to rent an apartment of her own, but couch surfs with friends, moving about, keeping her possessions minimal, so she won't wear out her welcome in any one place. I have a special fondness in my heart for anyone who lives an alternative lifestyle well into adulthood, thumbing their noses at the expected norms of society, intentionally becoming a vagabond, concentrating on their passions.

After exchanging pleasantries, Tina asked if I would help her next field season to study lions among the Samburu people in Kenya.

When I was in high school, I wanted to become a wildlife biologist, but my father convinced me to follow in his steps and study chemistry. So I blasted away at my studies, and was well on my way toward my PhD, until one day I joined my dog, sniffing the cool, fresh, damp spring earth in a Colorado alpine meadow, when all the soil micro-organisms were exploding back to life, and I realized that I'd never wanted to become a chemist in the first place, and that I couldn't spend the rest of my life in the benzene and acetone haze of the chem lab. Despite my resolve to seek new paths, I felt it prudent to finish my research and graduate. But immediately after defending my thesis, I stuffed my diploma in the glove box of a 1964 Ford Falcon, tied a canoe on top and headed into the Arctic to become me instead.

Now, a lifetime later, I faced Tina and wondered, "Why are you asking me to help with a lion tracking project? I'm not a wildlife biologist. I know nothing about the scientific techniques of studying lions. I'm 71 years old, an old man already, and my best expeditionary days are behind me. I'm half-deaf, can't see well anymore, some of my teeth are falling out, I pee too often. Why don't you recruit some ambitious young graduate student?"

As if anticipating my internal doubts, Tina elaborated, "I loved your descriptions of encounters with polar bears on the coast of Ellesmere Island. Clearly, you've learned how to thrive emotionally and physically in company with the dominant predator of the North, which is a skill few people in our modern civilization possess. So, you're just the person I need to help with a lion project in Kenya."

With my curiosity and ego stoked, we agreed to discuss her venture further the following morning. That evening, after all the commotion had died down, and I was warmly billeted in a classic old New England farmhouse, after my friends had gone to bed, I turned on my computer to do a little midnight homework.

The Samburu and related tribes (including the more familiar Maasai) originally lived in the upper Nile valley. They domesticated cattle about 10,000 years ago, at about the same time as, but independently of, the Middle Eastern pastoralists in the Tigris-Euphrates Valley.[1] Later, colourful dhows sporting jaunty tri-corner sails and piloted by sabre-wielding Arab traders brought Middle Eastern and Asian cattle across the ocean to interbreed with the African stock, eventually producing the modern mixed herds. In the second millennium BC, the Samburu migrated into southern Sudan, in the vicinity of the Great Rift Valley, the evolutionary crucible of humanity, and then continued to Kenya between 1000 and 500 BC.

As a young boy, growing up in the woodlots of suburban Connecticut, far from Africa physically and culturally, I sat transfixed

---

1   https://news.nationalgeographic.com/news/2002/04/0411_020411_africacat-tle_2.html.

in front of the TV, watching documentaries that showed stick huts, muscular men in red skirts and lithe, bare-breasted women sporting colourful beadwork necklaces and earrings dangling from stretched earlobes. Those films showed that the herders pricked the neck veins of their cattle to draw blood, which, when mixed with milk, would create a staple of their diet, drawing exclamations of UGH and WOW from those of us who grew up seeing food displayed in spotlessly clean arrays in the supermarkets. But all that was small potatoes compared with the footage of spear-wielding African teenagers battling lions.

Try to imagine the daily life of late Neolithic Samburu nomadic herders. They reached the Horn of Africa, a sub-Saharan semi-desert, before iron tools had found their way into the region, so their tool kit included stone-tipped spears and bow and arrow armament. They are also famous for the use of wooden clubs, called *rungus*, which were (and are) about 45–50 centimetres (18–20 inches) long with a narrow handle and a wooden knot at the business end. *Rungus* were used both in hand-to-hand combat and as a thrown projectile. With this arsenal of spears, bows and clubs, they battled neighbouring tribes for defence and conquest, and protected their cattle from the dominant predators of the savannah. Which is where lions come into the story.

Lions live in Africa and, if given the opportunity, eat cows. So, to survive, the Samburu had to confront the lions. So, how do you excite people enough to give them the courage to confront a ferocious, powerful, lightning-quick lion in hand-to-claw combat, armed predominantly with a long stick, with a piece of bone or, later, a rusted nail lashed on the end of the stick? Well, you do what people have done since the beginning of time: you create a story. You call the battle a 'rite of passage' or an 'initiation into manhood.' Then you equate bravery in the face of a lion with a 'marriage ritual' or some such meme. Potential fathers-in-law must put their collective feet down and require lion-bravery as a prerequisite for marriage. Powerful stuff for amygdala-dominant, frontal cortex–deficient, testosterone-enhanced, adolescent male brains.

It was late, and I really should have shut the computer off and gone to bed, but I had one more search to conduct. Where did Tina fit into this story? Her LinkedIn page listed her as: Founder and Director, Lion Conservation Fund; Professor of Biological

Sciences, Greater Boston Area. Checking the page on the Samburu Lion Project on the Lion Conservation Fund website, I read mission statements such as "Researchers are conducting an ongoing census and survey of the population ecology of free-ranging lions here to establish baseline information about population regulation."[2] That sounded encouraging but generalized. Even after rereading the website carefully, I remained uncertain about the precise details of our present mission.

It had been a long day, so I brushed my teeth, lay down and closed my eyes, but sleep eluded me. Something subliminal was bugging me. I retraced our meeting, watched Tina crossing the room in my mind's eye. Yes, that's what was missing from this story. Tina didn't have the gait, the wiry muscle, the tightly strung sinew to track lions across the harsh savannah. So, I rationalized. That's okay, she will be my conduit to legendary trackers who could walk circles around me without breaking a sweat. But wait a minute. In my admittedly limited research, I didn't see any references to peer-reviewed scientific papers about lion behaviour or lion tracking or lion conservation. That's okay. Perhaps I'm missing the point. There's tons and tons of research papers out there about lions. Their behaviour is well documented. What is my mission, really? Maybe Tina isn't a proficient lion tracker. But she is, was and has been a brave and tireless advocate for the Cultural Survival of the Samburu people. I know from previous reading that she has stood by these tribes in times of peril and potential genocide, exhibiting a steadfastness, loyalty and bravery that I can only vaguely imagine. There is an iron will inside her that isn't readily visible on the surface.

I think about previous travels, and especially about my time spent in Siberia, with Moolynaut the aged shaman and Oleg the robust hunter; I think about blizzards on the tundra, about standing naked in front of Moolynaut, on one leg, in the pose of a crane in flight. By extension, there are mysteries out there in Samburu, just as there are mysteries everywhere, if you open your eyes and heart. So I had a yes or no choice. Tomorrow, I could sip my coffee politely and say, "Thanks for the offer Tina. But I don't think I'll be able to join you." And then that door would close forever.

2   http://lionconservationfund.org/samburu.html.

I don't like closing doors.

Tina and I met the following morning at a trendy coffee shop near Cambridge. I bought lattes for each of us and a muffin for myself, and we sat at a small, spotlessly clean table in the corner, surrounded by all the buzz of urban opulence.

Tina explained that while we think of lions as a resident of Africa, 10,000 years ago they also thrived throughout the Middle East, Greece, Turkey, Iraq, Iran and Afghanistan. It is no coincidence that the Bible talks about "lions lying down with the lambs." Today, outside Africa, there is a tiny population of about 500 lions in the Gir Forest in India, but all the other populations have become extinct. And in Africa, where about a million lions roamed the continent at the beginning of the 20th century, and probably more when the Samburu migrated into their present territory, there are now only about 20,000, living in isolated habitat islands, game parks and zoos. And that number is continuing to drop, rapidly. But the Samburu region holds perhaps the largest truly wild lion population in the world.

The Lion Conservation Fund is dedicated to the preservation of these endangered and critical lion families.

In Africa, today, habitat destruction continues to be the primary factor causing precipitously declining lion populations. If you plow up the savannah, kill off all the zebras and wildebeest, fence the land-scape, plow it, build roads, plant corn and toss in a few Kentucky Fried Chicken franchises, the lions can't make a living anymore. A second factor is trophy hunting from rich urbanites who are happy to pay someone a lot of money, ride around in a Land Rover, blast a lion away with a high-powered rifle and hang its stuffed head in the parlour for friends to gawk at. And then, from the lion's perspective, way down at the bottom of their list of problems are the red-skirted, spear-tossing Samburu with their skinny herds.

But lions do eat cows, and the dollar value of a cow is obvious, so the Samburu have an economic incentive to kill lions. So even though the Samburu have a relatively minor impact on lion popu-lations as a whole, the situation is so dire that we've just gotta pick at all the straws to preserve the last remnants of lion populations struggling to maintain a foothold amid the carnage. As a result, Tina and a few other brave dedicated conservationists have been working throughout Africa to figure out a way for herders, cows and lions to coexist peacefully.

Lion conservation biologists are faced with the challenge of protecting lions without destroying the economic viability and the Cultural Survival of the herders. How do you do that? Switch your thinking, for a moment, from the plains of Africa to the Great Plains of North America as they existed two or three hundred years ago. Among the North American Aboriginal Plains cultures, such as the Sioux, a warrior could demonstrate bravery by killing an enemy in battle. But the greatest demonstration of bravery was achieved by touching an enemy, counting coup, without killing him. In a similar manner, Western conservationists reasoned that Samburu warriors could protect their cattle and simultaneously prove their bravery and complete their rite of passage by counting coup on individual lions in 21st-century style. A warrior would use a dart gun to sedate a lion so he could reach down and literally touch the lion. Pet it, feel its fur, examine its teeth and claws, sense its power and consciousness. Then the warrior would radio collar the lion and initiate a long-lived and intimate personal relationship with it. Over the weeks, months and years, as both the warrior and lion aged, the warrior would maintain a constant vigil of that individual lion's whereabouts and hunting habits. If the lion approached a herd of cattle, the warrior would race to the scene of potential conflict and chase the lion away. If all worked according to plan, the warrior and the lion would form deep emotional bonds so the warrior could essentially train the cat to avoid contact with humans and their cattle. The warriors could maintain their honour, and hopefully win the approval of potential brides and fathers-in-law, all while maintaining the viability of their herds, and without perpetuating the slaughter of the remnant lion populations.

Tina paused. I sipped my latte, bathed in the glow of the healthy urbanites and cheery flow of money around me. My first thought centred on the lion tracking aspect of this proposed journey. "Oh boy. Have you ever tried to train a housecat not to hunt sparrows?" But I said nothing.

Then Tina reiterated her generous offer to invite me to join the project. What, exactly, did she want me to do? Was I expected to wield a spear? A camera? My trusty Walmart notebook? Was I expected to establish a long-lived and intimate relationship with an individual lion? For how long? I have a wife at home. And I love to ski.

Neurologists tell us that the cerebral cortex – that part of the brain responsible for weighing the complexities and consequences of tasks before us, balancing the pros and cons and acting rationally in our own self-interest – doesn't reach full development until sometime in our 20s. That is why teenagers, not elders, are recruited to engage in hand-to-hand combat with lions. But I was an elder, and presumably the logical pathways in my brain had been fully developed for half a century. I should have, could have, gone home, learned a little more about her operation, publications, achievements and failures. I should have, could have, talked it over with Nina. Logic told me to politely thank Tina and ask for some time to think about it. But logic hasn't always been my best friend.

I took another careful sip of my latte, nervously wiped the muffin crumbs off the table onto the floor and waited.

And yes, Tina continued, "Now that I think of it," which I took to mean that she was thinking of it all along, there was another issue, bringing us back, full circle, to our conversations about Cultural Survival when we first met. Tina's facial muscles relaxed – she had finished her explanation of our mission – and then those same muscles tightened again at some memory deep within. Finally, she started speaking again, releasing pent-up energy, sometimes looking straight at me and then staring at the table between us. The Samburu culture and tribal integrity were being threatened. Drought was endemic. People were starving. And after a particularly long time staring at the table, Tina explained that a few years ago the government had launched a genocidal attack on some of the villages with helicopter gunships.

She conveyed her feelings with great commitment and emotion. And left unsaid what course of action – if any were possible – to pursue.

Now it was my turn to look first into Tina's eyes, to connect with this enigmatic person before me, and then to stare at the table where I would be free to journey into my own memories.

In 2000, 17 years earlier, I had paddled a kayak along the remote roadless coast of Kamchatka (far eastern Siberia) with my Russian partner, Misha. Stormbound in the small village of Vyvenka, we met an Indigenous Koryak healer named Moolynaut. We had lunch with her, and then the storm subsided, so we prepared to paddle onward. As we were saying our goodbyes, she held my hand in hers, stared deeply into my eyes and said simply, "Come back. It will be good if you do." On that slim invitation, we made the arduous journey to return the following spring. During that visit, we travelled on the snow-covered tundra with two local hunters, Oleg and Sergei. One day, Sergei's snow machine fell through thin ice into a small creek. As I tried to muscle it free, I slipped on a wet rock and tweaked an old avalanche injury to my pelvis. A few days later, Moolynaut healed me by asking me to stand naked on one leg, left hand behind my back, right arm extended, in the pose of flight, while she journeyed to the Other World to ask Kutcha the Raven to fly to the Woman Who Lives on the Highest Mountain and ask her to realign my damaged body.

I was raised in suburban Connecticut and trained as an organic chemist, and my conventional Western upbringing hadn't prepared me to accept this mysterious shamanic healing. As I told Moolynaut, my mother had never introduced me to Kutcha the Raven. But – undeniably – I was healed. Misha and I returned to Vyvenka three more times over the next four years, not so much to study shamanism, as the word 'study' is used in our culture, but to live among the Koryak people and to travel across the tundra.

I wrote a book about those experiences, called *The Raven's Gift*. But after several years had passed, I felt that I had misrepresented my Koryak friends and my Kamchatka adventures by overemphasizing my healing and the role of shamanism in the daily life of the village. In a sense, that was too easy – too trendy. As the years passed, and I thought about the mysteries raised during my visits in Vyvenka, as I reviewed the words of my friends and the adventures we had shared, I became convinced that shamanism, important as it is, is less vital in the daily life of the tribe than many people in Western society, myself included, give it credit for. The modern Koryak, and by extension our Paleolithic forbears, survived on the harsh savannahs and tundras of this planet through a nuanced integration of a greater whole. They relied on the Shaman, the spiritual leader, who journeyed to the Other World. But the tribe couldn't survive without the Hunter, the pragmatist, rooted in the Real World. Thus, for obvious reasons, the

Hunter was revered as highly as the Shaman. But by far the most important, the basis, the foundation of it all, was the Tundra, Mother Earth. Although every Indigenous tribe on Earth practised shamanism, the defining characteristic of our ancestors was their absolute interdependence with the landscapes around them, their complete, all-inclusive integration with the animistic whole, the air and dust and everything else, that doesn't just surround us, or support us, but is us.

I had used my Western style of thinking to separate, categorize, analyze, and in doing so had given insufficient emphasis to the wondrous wholeness of it all. The Shaman; The Hunter; and The Tundra. The Other World; The Real World; and The World. All one.

And now, sitting in this coffee shop, I knew that whatever I told Tina, or my Facebook friends, or myself, I wasn't going to Samburu to track and radio collar lions. I was journeying to the Horn of Africa, to the cradle of humanity's origins, to the home of one of the world's remnant Indigenous cultures, to hang out with herders and lion tracking warriors; to hang out by smoky campfires while women boiled water for tea; to hang out with the lions; and to hang out under the equatorial sky with the savannah itself. Something would happen – life – and if I arrived with an open heart and mind and no expectations, that 'something' would be just what I was looking for.

There are few remnants of Indigenous cultures left in this world, and with the death of each elder who carries the ancient tribal wisdoms, we lose one more irreplaceable packet of wisdom.

Think of it this way: Humans can't smell as well as a hyena, run as fast as a cheetah or see as well as an eagle; we don't have the teeth and claws of a lion or the strength of a chimpanzee. So how did *Homo sapiens* survive? How did the ancient ancestors of the modern Samburu migrate southward, across the desert, with their skinny cattle, confronting lions along the way? And, in a similar manner, how did Paleolithic and Neolithic Koryak earn a living hunting mammoth with stone-tipped spears on the frigid Siberian tundra? These are complex questions, obviously, and it would be a fool's errand to attempt a quick, one-paragraph answer.

So let's start with what we know. People did those things. We migrated out of Africa, when chimps and bonobos stayed behind, eating fruit and nuts. We crossed oceans, deserts and mountain

Jon Turk

ranges, and moved to every available ecosystem on Earth, from steamy equatorial rainforests to the icebound permafrost. And then we rose to such unprecedented power and dominance that we now threaten our own survival.

Let me start by asking myself a quick question, requiring a 'first thought that comes to your head,' blink-reaction response.

I visited with the Koryak people six times, over a period of a dozen years. What was the single, one-line piece of wisdom that best sums up what I learned in that arctic landscape of harsh winds and soft light? That's easy. In the village of Talovka, an old woman named Marina told me, "If you lose the magic in your life, you lose your power."

She didn't say if you lose the keys to your bulldozer, or the password to your iPhone, or the bullets for your AK-47, you lose your power.

One more question. Rorschach-test-quick, give me an example of a time where you learned the opposite lesson in your upbringing. Again, no problem. When I was in fourth grade, my teacher, Miss Maroney, busted me for daydreaming and sent me off to the principal's office. I remember the incident vividly, because even at that young age I felt the inequity of the charges. Other boys were disciplined for pulling a girl's hair or throwing spitballs. Daydreaming? I wasn't disrupting class or endangering anyone's health and welfare. Why didn't Miss Maroney ask me what I was daydreaming about? Then maybe the class could have taken a break from our oh ... so ... boring endless assault on the Three Rs, reading, 'riting, and 'rithmetic, which are useful enough but seriously limited and limiting. Maybe Miss Maroney could have encouraged my creativity and we could have talked about something fun and interesting for a change. I needed to daydream to find the magic in my life. As Einstein said, "Let us not forget that knowledge and skills alone cannot lead humanity to a happy, dignified, and creative life."[3] In my own way, I was seeking the power to grow up into a happy, dignified and creative adult.

Ah, but we were dutifully following the accepted norms of our Judeo-Christian society, rooted ultimately in the Bible. King Solomon commanded,

---

3   As quoted in Len Barron, *Sensibility: Children, Albert Einstein, and Niels Bohr* (Boulder, CO: self-published, 2020), p. 35.

Go to the ant, thou sluggard; consider her ways, and be wise:

Which having no guide, overseer, or ruler,

Provideth her meat in the summer, and gathereth her food in
the harvest.

How long wilt thou sleep, O sluggard? When wilt thou arise
out of thy sleep?[4]

According to one website commentator, "The ants seem to be very happy, and I think it is because they are so busy. God has put nobody in this world to be idle."[5]

I'm not going to argue whether ants are happy or grumpy when they go to work in the morning, and I'm not arguing God's morality either. But I will argue that if we overemphasize raw labour and directly measurable productivity, we end up with a distorted view of the evolution and creative genius of our species.

In *The Storytelling Animal*, Jonathan Gottschall poses a hypothetical question: You have two groups of people on the Paleolithic savannah, the Practical People and the Story People. The Practical People spend all their time digging roots and hunting zebras. The Story People search for food as well, but they take time off from hunting and gathering to paint pictures, dance and sing. Who wins out? If you were an entirely practical-minded person, you might guess that the people who spent more time food gathering would have more to eat and thus should survive in greater numbers. According to this line of reasoning, you might surmise that our marvelously dexterous tool-wielding hands, coupled with reading, 'riting, and 'rithmetic, are the foundation of human success. But, sorry, this argument ignores the data. Every culture on Earth, from the steamy equatorial rainforests to the frozen North, from the earliest Stone Age rumblings of humanity to 21st-century digital madness, from scratches on stone to streaming videos, has embraced art, music, dance and story. And if we trace history carefully and objectively enough, these paintings, these sculptures, these gatherings under the banyan tree or in the igloo, preceded the next advance in tool technology. Yes, I know that in modern times, local and federal legislatures, with their hands on

---

4   Proverbs 6:6 (King James Version).

5   https://www.biblestudytools.com/dictionary/the-ant/.

the money pots, have constantly and consistently reduced educational budgets for music and art because these activities are deemed to be frilly and unnecessary add-ons to the serious business of science and commerce. But the facts speak for themselves. The Story People survived. The Practical People either never existed in the first place or died out a long time ago.

When I was a young man, I worked as a research chemist because I believed that science, the Three Rs and pragmatism would solve the world's problems. The Practical People. As a much older man, I stood naked in front of Moolynaut, surrendered to a different reality – call it what you will – and peered into windows of human thought and adaptability that defy scientific logic. The Story People.

Break it down, throw all the pieces into the air, and what do you get? The Shaman; The Hunter; and The Tundra. The Other World; The Real World; and The World. All one.

So now, 60-plus years after I got busted for daydreaming, as a fully ordained adult, I was preparing to launch a great adventure, to seek what we all seek, or should be seeking, all the time, whether we wander or stay home, whether we engage in physical or metaphysical adventures – to understand: What makes us tick? How do we become strong? How can I journey into old age with some semblance of dignity and equanimity? How do we, or should we, or will we survive as individuals and a society in this overpopulated, climate-altered, oil-soaked, consumer-oriented culture?

So I asked myself: What insights into those questions would I take home from a journey to the Horn of Africa, where I would sojourn with Samburu and lions, close to the birthplace of our species? That was my quest, simplistic and trite as it may seem once you reduce it down to basics. For that reason, against all Western logic, I decided to accept Tina's offer, travel to Samburu, and see what would happen.

I had a head full of questions, but no rigorous academic outline to follow, no specific agenda, no experts to interview when I got there. You can't hold a microphone out, interview a leopard and by extension the Earth itself, and expect an answer in the King's English. But I had spent decades travelling across remote and frequently dangerous landscapes – tempestuous oceans, avalanche-prone ski terrain, rock walls and deserts – and in those many adventures I had learned to interview the Earth in its own language. Many times, while standing on a snowy ridge, I had engaged in these conversations: "Hey Earth. Jon Turk here. How are you doing this fine, chilly, winter morning? Mind if I ask you: 'Is there a weak layer in the snowpack, below my feet?'" Because if I don't know the shape and orientation of the snow crystals under my skis, I may die. Or, "Good morning, Earth. Do you mind if I ask you a question for our listening audience? What does the shape of that ocean wave tell me about the currents under my boat, and therefore the trajectory of my kayak passage to that tiny island in the ocean vastness?" Because if I miss the island, I die. I know, there are other ways to interview the Earth, easier ways, safer ways. But this has been my way.

For much the same reasons, you can't hold out a microphone and interview Oleg the Hunter, or Moolynaut the Shaman, directly and get the answers that really matter. Your questions are prejudiced by your culture and may be so disconnected from Oleg or Moolynaut's perception of how the world behaves that no one knows what the other is talking about. And then the conversation gets muddled and your conclusions end up being written in your language, not theirs.

I had been trying in my own way to listen to Earth and its inhabitants for my entire life. The only certainty was that if I journeyed onward into old age viewing the world, and myself, only through the narrow window of perception of a 21st-century Ivy League PhD chemist from suburban Connecticut, I would live in a diminished consciousness, because I would be experiencing only the tiniest nano-segment of my own humanity.

CHAPTER 3

THE BIRTH OF MYTHOLOGY

Before we journey into the Samburu nation, on this ill-defined journey to 'see what happens' on the parched semi-desert under the equatorial sun, let's begin by examining the archeological and anthropological record to explain my earlier comments about the adaptations and survival of early hominins. How are we different from our close primate cousins, and how did those differences endow us with the spectacular creative genius and evolutionary fitness that propelled us to dominate the planet? Of course, there is no simple answer. We are guaranteed to find overlapping or contradictory possibilities, and this small chapter cannot be exhaustive and complete. But all those uncertainties should pique our interest, not discourage us.

In 1994, Tim White, a thin, wiry, desert-tanned paleoanthropologist from the University of California at Berkeley, and his colleagues, found a 4.4-million-year-old skeleton of a primitive hominin in the Afar Desert of Ethiopia, just northeast of the present-day Samburu homeland in Kenya. As I now understand so viscerally, the Afar is a potentially dangerous place to work. The scientists must avoid black mambas, scorpions, malarial mosquitoes, lions, hyenas, flash floods, dust tornadoes and contaminated food and water. If that wasn't enough, warring Alisera tribesmen also roam the desert, often trigger-happy with their well-travelled AK-47s. One day, when

Smithsonian journalist Ann Gibbons was visiting the dig site, half a dozen Alisera showed up, dressed in kufi caps and cotton sarongs, carrying their rifles and curved daggers, threatening to kill the anthropologists for trespass. Unfortunately, this is too often business as usual in too many places in the world, now and in our past history. Many human tribes, as well as great apes, lions, wolves and other species, routinely patrol their territories to expel intruders. But we are humans who have the cultural reasoning power to evaluate a novel situation, listen and hold our fire. In this confrontation, Tim showed the warriors how the scientists worked, crawling shoulder to shoulder across the sunbaked desert sands, with small spades, sieves and magnifying glasses, looking for bits and pieces of old bones. The battle-hardened nomadic warriors thought this was not only harmless but humorous as well, so they granted permission for the scientists to continue, with one caveat: if this ridiculous, but physically non-demanding, activity could become a paid job, perhaps the Americans could offer them employment someday.[6]

From the work of White and others, scientists have learned that the earliest human ancestors broke off from the great apes about six million years ago. Whereas chimpanzee feet are specialized for grasping trees, Ardi, the 4.4-million-year-old *Ardipithecus ramidus* that White found, had feet better suited for an upright stance, for walking and running, a distinctive feature to be passed down through the millennia. Despite this critical adaptation, which freed the hands for other uses in the open savannah, *A. ramidus* had a small brain, measuring between 300 and 350 cm^3, slightly smaller than that of a modern bonobo or female chimpanzee. It was an inauspicious beginning, and a visitor from outer space at the time couldn't have predicted that this woman's descendants would someday plow wheat fields and build parking lots that would dominate the Earth's surface, that her great ... great grandchildren would become so successful that humans would invent work-saving machines that made life so easy that we would be threatening to annihilate ourselves. Or, as Harari writes in *Sapiens*, early hominins

6   Ann Gibbons, "The Human Family's Earliest Ancestors," *Smithsonian Magazine*, March 2010, https://www.smithsonianmag.com/science-nature/the-human-familys-earliest-ancestors-7372974/#RrjmqTRQbyooaaPb.99.

were "insignificant animals with no more impact on their environment than gorillas, fireflies, or jellyfish."[7]

A million years later, *A. ramidus*'s descendants, *australopithecines,* represented by the famous skeleton known as Lucy, had brains about 400–550 cm³, roughly 20 per cent the size of the modern *Homo sapiens* brain. Jump another 2.5 million years to 700,000 years ago, and *Homo erectus* had a brain size of about 800 cm³. This trend toward bigger brains continued through the millennia, until *Homo sapiens* artists who painted on cave walls in southern Europe 35,000 years ago had brains the same size as ours, about 1500 cm³, almost double that of *erectus*.

Everyone has seen that iconic illustration of human evolution that shows half a dozen consecutive drawings of hominins evolving in a linear and seemingly inevitable passage from the knuckle-walking ape to the modern *Homo*. In the version that I have pinned above my computer monitor, the erect, muscular, Neolithic, athletic hunter finally evolves into a hunched-over fat man waddling through life with a supersized container of Coke. Regardless of where we will end up as a species, or where we are today, we must ask why we evolved this massive think-tank perched precariously on top of a thin neck above our upright bodies. That imaginary scientist from outer space who showed up a few million years ago might have concluded that big brains were not such an effective experiment in evolutionary adaptation.

Brain tissue consumes roughly 16 times as much energy per unit weight as muscle tissue consumes at rest.[8] Even though our brains represent only 2 per cent of our body weight, they consume 20 per cent of our energy. In fact, brains are so metabolically expensive that as we became smarter, we sacrificed other forms of functionality and became less efficient at survival in other ways. For one, we traded brain size for muscle mass, and we became physically weaker as we became mentally stronger. Have you ever tried to wrestle with a chimpanzee? Don't. The chimp will break your bones, twist your

....

7   Yuval Noah Harari, *Sapiens: A Brief History of Humankind* (New York: HarperCollins, 2015), p. 4.

8   William Calvin, *A Brain for All Seasons* (Chicago: University of Chicago Press, 2002), p. 110.

neck off, bite your face; kill you for sure. Bad idea. In one study, researchers pitted university-level basketball players and professional mountain climbers against chimps in a contest where all participants had to lift weights by pulling a handle. The chimps were about twice as strong as the highly trained human athletes.[9] Looking into the fossil record, our *Homo* ancestors began evolving to become *weaker* around six million years ago, when we split off our evolutionary line from the other great apes and started growing big brains. In fact, human muscle structure and metabolism has changed more in the last six million years than mouse muscle has since we parted company from mice on the tree of life about 130 million years ago. In addition, some researchers contend that our digestive systems also became less efficient as we became smarter, thus requiring more and higher-quality food to nourish our thoughts.[10]

If one individual in a group is born with a slightly larger brain than the others, she or he is presumably smarter and thus more able to locate food and shelter, find a mate and raise their young. On the other hand, she or he is weaker, less efficient at digesting food and needs more food to survive. In addition, big brains require big heads, and our ridiculously large heads increased maternal mortality in childbirth. This mortality curse was amplified because, at the same time, early hominins began to walk upright, requiring a narrowing of the hips, making birth even more difficult. And if those weren't sufficient disadvantages, once we grew up and started walking, our big heads made us more vulnerable to head/neck injury. In a strictly tooth and claw arms race, victory goes to the fastest and strongest, the creature with the biggest teeth, fastest legs and sharpest claws. But human evolution didn't work that way. There was a multi-faceted trade-off over a variety of survival strategies, and early hominins put a huge evolutionary investment on brain size.

Looking at the whole experimental foray into human-sized brains, the jury is still out as to whether all that grey matter will convey evolutionary fitness over long stretches of geological time. After all,

---

9   https://news.nationalgeographic.com/
news/2014/05/140527-brain-muscle-metabolism-genes-apes-science/.

10   Heather Pringle, "The Origins of Creativity," *Scientific American*, March 2013, pp. 36ff.

small-brained crocodiles have been around for 65 million years, while *Homo sapiens* log in at a paltry 200,000 – so far. Given a few hundred million or a billion or so years, and lots of opportunity for random mutation, evolution has tried many diverse strategies. Internal skeletons, external skeletons, no skeletons. Tiny individuals, small, medium, large. Virus, bacteria, dinosaurs, bunny rabbits, octopuses. Each species has a unique strategy for propagation of its DNA. And as far as evolution is concerned – as if evolution had 'concerns' – the propagation of DNA is the only trick in the book that matters. Cities? Agriculture? Religion? Computers? Book clubs? Authors? Bah – only if it keeps the DNA going. Of the roughly five million animal species on the Earth, human-sized brains evolved only once. No one knows how this one will turn out. And you and I probably won't live to learn the answer.

Even though big brains have numerous downsides, as well as upsides and an uncertain future, they did evolve. Which leads to the critical question: What were our Paleolithic ancestors doing with their big brains that made the investment worth the disadvantages?

Before we examine the anthropological data, return for a moment to my 'daydreaming is taboo' childhood upbringing. In grade school I also learned that our ancestors' secret to success was our marvelously dexterous hands, with a thumb counter-opposed to four nimble fingers – a hand adapted to holding and manipulating tools and weapons. Well, chimpanzees have similar hands to humans and they also have a big toe counter-opposed to four little toes, well designed for grasping, so shouldn't they be twice as good at using tools as we are, and hence twice as successful? Smart-ass commentary aside, *Homo sapiens* are, in fact, a tool-using species, so let's start with that.

Most probably early hominins used clubs, much like the *rungu* I carried in Samburu. And we can assume that they used unaltered rocks to crack nuts, as modern chimps do. But wooden clubs and unaltered rocks leave no fossil record, so we have no way of knowing when the first genius hominin or hominoid picked up a rock or stick and used it as a tool. The earliest confirmed manufactured stone tools were sharp-edged flakes, hammers and anvils dating back to 3.3 million years ago.[11]

....

11 Rebecca Morelle, "Oldest Stone Tools Pre-Date Earliest Humans," *BBC News*, May 20, 2015, https://www.bbc.com/news/science-environment-32804177.

They had sharpened edges but were otherwise quite primitive because they didn't have symmetrical cutting surfaces. To an unpractised eye, these earliest tools don't look that much different from a piece of sharp rock that might have been broken off by natural events.

Walk down to a river or stream some day and you're likely to find numerous oval-shaped rocks that were rounded as they bounced along the streambed. Find one that fits nicely into your hand – just palm sized – not too heavy, but not too light. Now take another rock and bash it against your palm-sized stone until a few flakes break off. With time and practice you can form two knapped faces meeting to form a symmetrical edge, like a modern steel axe. You are now holding what is called a hand-axe. A hand-axe has no shaft or handle and no artistically fluted shapes, but it represents the earliest tool with symmetry around its cutting edge. The earliest known hand-axes come from Kenya and are dated to about 1.76 million years ago, over a million and a half years after the first crude stone tools.[12] Hominins probably used hand-axes to slice through the tough skin of scavenged kills, cut meat, break bones to obtain marrow and scrape hides. By extrapolating from modern chimpanzee behaviour, we can reasonably guess that they used the same tools to crack nuts, smash tubers and open fibrous stems. Given our long and violent history, it also seems likely that some aggressive clever fellow figured out that hand-axes would be handy for cracking an enemy's head in battle.

For the next million-plus years, tool innovation was exceptionally slow. While several incremental refinements have appeared in the fossil record, exquisitely crafted stone points didn't show up until 500,000 years ago, and the earliest evidence for the bow and arrow is at 75,000 to 60,000 years ago. Rick Potts, of the Smithsonian Institution, writes of the earliest hand-axe designs: "In our present world of rapid-fire technological advance, it is unthinkable that any single manufactured item could endure for so long.... We tamper with just about everything we create or lay our hands on. The hand-axe people just kept on making hand-axes."[13]

In table form:

---

12 K. Kris Hirst, "Acheulean Handaxe: Definition and History," *ThoughtCo*, January 28, 2019, https://www.thoughtco.com/acheulean-handaxe-first-tool-171238.

13 Rick Potts, *Humanity's Descent* (New York: Avon Books, 1996), p. 139.

YEARS AGO	BRAIN SIZE (CM^3)	TOOL INNOVATION
4,400,000	300–350	
3,500,000	400–550	
3,300,000		Earliest stone tools
2,000,000	600	
1,760,000		Hand-axes
700,000	800	
75,000–60,000	1500	Bow and arrow

Thus, in each instance, brain size increased 200,000 or more years *before* each major advance in tool technology. Yet Darwinian selection, commonly summarized as "survival of the fittest," prepares organisms "only for the necessities of the moment ... not a squiggle more."[14] Every adaptation must provide a selective advantage for the organism *in that generation*. Natural selection doesn't anticipate what will happen 50, 100, 100,000 or a million years in the future.

Think of a bird wing. Clearly, flying conveys evolutionary fitness to an animal, for escaping predators, finding food in treetops and so on. But wings didn't evolve all at once, presto, in one massive mutation. Rather, some bird ancestor evolved its upper body limb into something broader and lighter than an arm, called a proto-wing. According to evolutionary theory, proto-wings had to convey a distinct advantage to the existing generation. If the proto-wings were a disadvantage, then the bird ancestors in that generation would have died out and flying birds would never have evolved. Scientists hypothesize that proto-wings were used for something other than flight, temperature regulation perhaps, until they grew large enough to become useful for a new function, flight.

Countless generations of *Homo erectus* couldn't have spent their whole lives feeding and nurturing a metabolically expensive brain and sometimes dying in childbirth so that their descendants many generations later would manufacture hand-axes, or that modern humans would design computers and send rocket ships into space. It

14   Edward O. Wilson, *Consilience: The Unity of Knowledge* (New York: Alfred A. Knopf, 1999), p. 48.

doesn't work that way. To understand who we are, we need to sleuth out what *Ardipithecus ramidus, australopithecines, Homo erectus* and early *Homo sapiens* were doing with their big brains in that generation, to survive on the harsh African savannah.

The first clue comes from study of teeth size. Modern chimpanzees have large canines, even though they are mainly vegetarian, and vegetarians generally have small canines. Moreover, chimp males have considerably larger canines than the females. This trend is common in many modern primate species, where males possess canines that are up to 400 per cent taller than those of females, even though both sexes eat the same diet. The consensus among primatologists is that large male canines serve as weapons in violent confrontations, such as male-to-male battles for females or intertribal warfare.[15] In contrast, among *A. ramidus*, one of our early ancestors who lived 4.4 to 6 million years ago, canine teeth in males and females are about the same size. This similarity indicates that males were less violent than modern primates. Somehow the males found food and mates without biting each other as often as modern primates do. They formed tribes and learned to co-operate within the tribe.

Big brains enable us to know the people in our tribe well enough to smooth over minor conflicts, maintain harmony and work together efficiently. Think of all the information about your friends and neighbours you store in your brain. Sally borrowed my lawn mower two years ago and returned it out of gas. Joe brought me dinner when I was sick. And then, it is also handy to store indirect information. Maybe Sally never borrowed my lawn mower, but she borrowed Harry's mower and returned it out of gas. We then use this data to identify our friends and enemies, our partial friends and partial enemies, our sometimes friends and sometimes enemies – and then, by anticipating the behaviour of others into the future, we can make important decisions, like whether or not to loan our mower to Sally.

Other animals, primates especially, cheat, lie, help and groom. They know fellow members of their troop well enough to predict the intentions of others from past data; but with our big brains we are

15 J.M. Plavcan and C.B. Ruff, "Canine Size, Shape, and Bending Strength in Primates and Carnivores," *American Journal of Physical Anthropology* 136, no. 1 (2008): 65–84, https://www.ncbi.nlm.nih.gov/pubmed/18186502.

capable of managing more data and more complex data about more individuals. In the 1990s British anthropologist Robin Dunbar quantified a correlation between primate brain size and average social group size. Dunbar's number is the "cognitive limit to the number of people with whom one can maintain stable social relationships," or, more informally, the number of people you could sit down at a tavern with and comfortably engage in conversation without feeling embarrassed that you don't really know that person.[16] Dunbar's number for modern humans is 150. We probably know more people than that, but we don't know them well. As a result, before we had lawyers, police, prisons, rulers and laws, tribes seldom exceeded 150. If we had more than that, we couldn't maintain social cohesion. In contrast, baboons commonly maintain hierarchical tribes of 50. In Gombe National Park in Africa, chimpanzee troops range between 40 and 60 members, but these large communities commonly split into smaller families of between 3 and 15 members. Dogs, elephants, dolphins and any other social animal all have their Dunbar's number, proportional to brain size.

The next pertinent clue to human co-operation, related to the first, comes from the observation that approximately two to three million years ago, our ancestors created the first garbage heaps. Piles of bones indicate that hominins carried their animal carcasses from disparate locations to central campsites that they used repeatedly, for many generations. Bones in the trash piles are scarred with cut marks indicating that the animals were butchered for food. Numerous discarded axes lie near the bones. Many of the axes were manufactured from stones that were collected from sites up to ten kilometres away.

Thus, hominins were transporting food and tools to central locations and sharing. Why didn't they eat the food where they found it, like chimpanzees and bonobos do? It's a lot of work to drag a dead antelope home. Wouldn't it have been easier to camp out at the site where they killed or found the antelope and eat the meat at the site? Apparently not.

Food gathering can't be shared efficiently by the whole tribe. For one, it's often difficult to hunt, scavenge or forage with nursing babies, pregnant women and elders. In addition, there is a certain

---

16 https://en.wikipedia.org/wiki/Dunbar%27s_number.

amount of luck involved in finding food in any given place, on any given day. Therefore, it's efficient to have a home base and then send hunters and gatherers out in different directions. One party heads off toward a water hole to the west, while another party walks north or east. While the hunters and scavengers are out seeking meat, other people in the tribe could be dispersing to dig tubers. Grandparents could stay at the base camp to babysit the kids. At the end of the day all the parties return to the central campsite and share the food they collected. If some individuals return empty-handed, the successful ones share because their fortunes may be reversed tomorrow.

When our ancestors harnessed fire, campsites became ever more central to co-operative survival mechanisms as early tribes congregated around the hearth. It is difficult to pin an exact date on the controlled use of fire. Almost certainly *Homo erectus* used fire 400,000 years ago; perhaps as early as 1.5 to 1.7 million years ago. Fire not only provided a communal gathering place, it also provided a way to cook food, making it more digestible and allowing our gut size to shrink so our brains could grow larger.

During this gradual process of evolution, extending over millions of years, as our brains grew bigger and our stances more upright, one evolutionary adaptation to the problem of mortality in childbirth was that babies were born earlier and smaller. Compared with other animals, human babies are woefully immature – totally defenceless and incapable of caring for themselves for many years. Therefore, tribal cohesion and family unity became essential to nurture our young to adulthood.

When we think about the advantages of co-operation, it is easy to visualize group defence, babysitting and the improvements in the efficiency of each individual with specialization. But perhaps most important, when people work together, play together and hang out around campfires together, they exchange ideas to improve their lives. Invention. This exchange is called cultural adaptation and is orders of magnitude faster than genetic evolution, because an idea can spread throughout a population virtually instantaneously, whereas genetic evolution requires many generations.

No one can go back millennia to document how new ideas arose among Paleolithic humans, but we can look at the behaviour of other mammals to get a sense of how cultural adaptation works. For example, one band of modern chimpanzees has figured out how to crack nuts with rocks, while other nearby bands do not know this trick. The genes of both bands are the same; it's just that one genius chimp in one band figured out this handy trick and taught it to friends, relatives and children and not to his neighbours in competing groups. There are a huge number of examples of this type of learned behaviour among our animal neighbours. For example: One clan of Antarctic orca whales (killer whales) hunts minke whales, another hunts Weddell seals, while a third group hunts penguins. There is almost no crossover in prey preference. The orcas who hunt Weddell seals have learned to swim in unison, creating a monstrous tail wave that splashes the seals off an ice floe and into the water, where they can be easily gobbled up. This is learned behaviour, not instinct, because other clans don't know this trick. And it works well enough so the Weddell seal-hunting orcas flourish. There are two important points here. One, obviously, is that the learned, social hunting technique, like the chimp trick of cracking nuts, has evolutionary advantage. The other is that learned hunting techniques become tribal. If a seal-hunting orca moves to another tribe, his or her new buddies won't know the trick and might not be inclined to learn it, and the seal-hunting orca might not be adept at penguin hunting. So seal hunters stay with seal hunters, penguin hunters stay with penguin hunters.

Using this model of orca-hunting techniques, let's look more closely at the consequences of human cultural adaptation. Without getting into a "which came first, the chicken or the egg argument," we can imagine that as early hominins gathered around campfires, they shared cultural identity through religion, ceremony and storytelling. As a result, they bonded into tribes and survived in a harsh savannah. Although Romeo and Juliet intermarriages almost certainly occurred, most of the time tribes were exclusive. There was simply too much to gain by sticking with your tribe and too great a barrier of admission to joining another tribe. Ideas flourish, leading to evolutionary success. Leading to US vs. THEM – and eventually to all sorts of horror.[17]

---

17   Carl Safina, *Becoming Wild: How Animal Cultures Raise Families, Create Beauty, and Achieve Peace* (New York: Henry Holt, 2020), pp. 79ff.

Of course, we can confidently assume that there were cheaters and intratribal conflicts, just as there are cheaters and intraconflicts in all modern human societies, as well as in chimpanzee and baboon groups. The ability to cheat without getting caught, or catching clever cheaters, and thus maintaining co-operative tribes, is all part of Dunbar's number. The net result is that, all in all, co-operative hominins were successful enough that many subspecies evolved and proliferated.

It's essential to recognize that just as co-operative behaviour maintained relative harmony within each tribe, the same behaviour did not – and does not – apply to interactions between tribes. The US vs. THEM thing. When one tribe confronts another tribe in battles for resources, territory or, as we will later learn, abstract mythologies such as religion, then the gloves come off. God's commandment "Thou shalt not kill" all of a sudden becomes "And God shall smite thine enemies." But I'm getting ahead of myself.

One critical question: Were early hominins predominantly eating the scavenged carcasses of animals killed by other predators, such as lions and hyenas, or were they doing the hunting, and killing, themselves? Henry T. Bunn of the University of Wisconsin–Madison observed that most African predators kill mainly old and young animals, the slow ones. But the bones in human garbage heaps represent much higher proportions of healthy animals in their prime. Thus, humans were obtaining a lot of their meat directly, by hunting. And they were more efficient at taking down mature prey than their neighbourhood lions, who were bigger, stronger and faster. And all this occurred a few million years ago, long before advanced weapons such as the bow and arrow.[18]

How did they do it? The fossil record leaves us no direct evidence, so instead we turn to observing the strategy of the last of the modern Indigenous hunter-gathers on the African savannah, the !Kung (often known as the San, or the Kalahari Bushmen). Although the !Kung use bows, their primitive weapons have limited range and killing power. As a result, they commonly use an even more efficient technique known as 'persistence hunting.' A group of hunters will observe a

....

18   Kate Wong, "The Rise of the Human Predator," *Scientific American*, April 2014, pp. 47ff.

herd, of antelope for example, and select out an individual. Then they will run toward the herd, and when the animals flee and scatter, they will chase that individual. But, you argue, this can't be effective; antelopes are fast sprinters while humans are comparatively slow. True, so the antelope disappears off into the bushes. But it leaves tracks.

A track is a symbol. It is a representation of a thing (antelope) but not the thing itself. From the shape and orientation of the tracks, the hunters can deduce an accurate narrative of what the antelope is doing – and thinking. In the beginning, it is scared and running. But later, it slows to a walk, indicating that it is tired and believes that it has eluded its pursuers. As the noontime sun beats down, it moves into the shade because it is hot and thirsty. Now the slow, persistent humans begin to catch up.

Recall that as hominins evolved big brains, they became weaker. As they moved out onto the savannah and began to walk upright, their foot configuration changed so they became less efficient at climbing trees. In turn, as they became upright, they sacrificed the sprinting speed of four-legged creatures. To survive, they must have gained some other pretty amazing physical attribute or attributes to compensate for all these losses. In his book *Born to Run*, Christopher McDougall imagines a hypothetical fantasy of the birth of the first modern human: "One day, out pops a slow, skinny, sunken-chested son who's barely bigger than a woman and keeps making a tiger target out of himself by walking around in the open. He's too frail to fight, too slow to run away.... By all logic, he's marked for extinction – yet somehow this dweeb becomes the father of all mankind."[19] It turns out that, along with our social co-operation, early hominins evolved 26 anatomical adaptations that endowed us with the ability to run long distances. In a modern 50-mile race pitting Man Against Horse, in Prescott, Arizona, human ultra-runners usually beat the fastest long-distance horse. Part of this suite of adaptations is that with our hairless body and ubiquitous sweat glands, humans are "the best air-cooled engine that evolution ever put on the market."[20]

Returning to our hunt: The antelope's body is covered with hair and panting is an inefficient cooling mechanism. As the afternoon

----

19 Christopher McDougall, *Born to Run* (New York: Alfred Knopf, 2009), p. 218.

20 Christopher McDougall, *Born to Run* (New York: Alfred Knopf, 2009), p. 223.

progresses, the speedy antelope slows down and the hairless, sweating human hunters start to catch up. And, remember, we are also masters of co-operation and communication. From observations of tracks, the hunters can plan into the future and devise a strategy among themselves. They send one runner into the cool, shady thicket to chase the antelope back out to the sun, where it will continue to dehydrate. The modern !Kung send their slower runners ahead to keep the animal afraid and moving, while the best ultra-runners hold back. Finally, the antelope falters as it approaches heat exhaustion. Then the fastest runner, who had been hanging in the rear, takes off. As he passes the slower runners, those hunters pass their half-filled water bottles to the strongest and fastest. And when the moment is right, the well-hydrated, partially rested speedster sprints forward until the antelope finally drops. Presto, he kills his prey with a simple hand-held weapon.

To summarize: Persistence hunting involves tracking (understanding symbols), an accurate knowledge of the habits and relative strengths of hunter and prey, and then the ability to form a narrative, through deductive reasoning, to project an outcome in the future if certain techniques are followed. Thus, hominins learned to collect data, imagine and reach conclusions. The reward was a reliable supply of meat, high-quality food that nurtured our big brains, which were necessary to plan this sophisticated, co-operative hunt. With a little extrapolation, it is easy to see that after some millions of years, the cognitive tools of the pragmatic hunter eventually became the tools of science. In addition, the techniques of the hunt also formed the basis of our inquisitiveness to explain what we can't directly observe in the moment. The hunter projects thoughts into the unknown to deduce the physical and mental state of an animal that it can't see. Later, the same hunter asks questions about the formation of the cosmos, something out of the realm of observation. And presto: myth, storytelling, religion and eventually science are born.

Before we puff up our chests too much, thinking that we, alone among the marvels of creation, are OH! So Special, it's important to emphasize that all higher animals learn, remember, organize, retrieve and communicate environmental data essential to survival in a complex and chaotic world. And many operate co-operatively.

Where can I find food, water and shelter? Where does danger lurk? Who are my enemies? My friends?

Complex animal behaviour is ubiquitous both in the wild and within human experimental labs. An elephant matriarch will lead her herd over miles of open country to arrive at a specific seasonal food source when it is ready to be eaten. So, in some manner, she must imagine food, which she can't perceive, because she is too far away, but which she can remember. Food availability is optimal on different calendar days every year, depending on seasonal changes in weather and rainfall, but the matriarch understands how all these factors interact, makes the necessary calculations and assumptions, and brings her family to the site at the proper time. For example, in the centre of the Samburu nation, in northeastern Kenya, there is a flat-top mountain, Sabache (also called Mt. Ololokwe), with cool springs and lush pastures on the summit plateau, all largely protected from poachers. The trail to this Eden is so steep and rocky that the elephants must crawl upward on their elbows and knees. But they congregate here yearly. How do the elephants decide when it's time to make this arduous pilgrimage, or whether to make the pilgrimage at all? Well, we don't know precisely what goes on inside an elephant's brain. But elephant researcher Vicki Fishlock writes that when the matriarch thinks it's time to make a pilgrimage, even when the herd is far away from the desired destination, she "makes a long, soft rumble, raises her ears and flaps them against her neck and shoulders like a hand clap, and the family sets off as if this was the signal they had all been waiting for." At other times, some family members might disagree and, in Vicki's words, "discussions can go on for hours."[21]

Or, as another example: When game wardens built a fence surrounding the Serengeti, to separate game preserve from farmland, *within a week*, lions learned to position two lionesses along the perimeter of the fence, while a third drove prey toward the barrier. When a terrified antelope or zebra raced away for its life, it would encounter the fence and veer either left or right, into the waiting jaws of one of the pre-positioned big cats. Again, this strategy involves

---

21   Carl Safina, *Beyond Words: What Animals Think and Feel* (New York: Henry Holt, 2015), p. 88.

significant planning, foresight and communication, not unlike the human persistent hunt.

Human reasoning is not categorically different from the behaviour of other mammals. But, again, we are just that much better at thinking, planning and imagining than any other species. Remember, back in the distant Stone Age, human hunters ran down prey in its prime while the lions had to make do with the old, young and sick. And then, no chimpanzee has ever picked up a stick and sketched an outline of an imaginary mermaid in the sand, or built a bow and arrow, or any of a host of things that people have done.

Homo sapiens evolved around 180,000 years ago, roughly 5.8 million years after the first hominins. Another clue to early hominin and *Homo* behaviour comes from burials. Reverence for the dead not only reflects the tribal bonding we felt for our friends and relatives, but also implies that in some manner, our ancestors were contemplating the great mystery: What happens at death, when this mysterious entity we call consciousness departs from the temporal world? About 500,000 years ago, long before *Homo sapiens* evolved, the bones of about 30 early hominins and a few bears ended up in a pit in a cave in Atapuerca in Spain. Archeologists speculate that the bears could have tumbled into the shaft by accident, while seeking a place to hibernate. But what about the people? A single stone hand-axe also lay in the pit, made of a type of stone unknown in the vicinity. According to some scientists, this pit is the first evidence of ritual burial. Others argue that this site is so much earlier than any uncontested burials that there must be some other explanation.

The earliest uncontested evidence for ritual burial occurred 80,000 to 100,000 years ago at Qafzeh, Israel. Archeologists have uncovered the bones or bone fragments of 27 or more separate individuals, all sprinkled with ceremonial red ochre dye. One nearly complete skeleton was that of a child who had suffered a debilitating brain injury as a toddler. Even though this child must have been unable to function normally, either physically or socially, the tribe lovingly cared for it and nourished it for eight years after the injury, and then gently laid it to rest surrounded by deer antlers as gifts for its journey to the Other World.

At about the same time, a person, or more probably a group of people, collected calcite crystals and transported them to a rock shelter in the Kalahari Desert. The crystals were too soft to become functional tools and have no known utilitarian purpose. The only reasonable explanation is that people collected them because they were pretty, or because the play of light inside these minerals led to what we might call spiritual or religious wonder.[22] Thus, in this distant desert rock shelter, we see the early manifestations of our humanity.

Balancing all of our strengths and weaknesses – our big brain, co-operation crystal collections and burials – *Homo* did well enough for a prolonged period of time, but then, starting around 90,000 years ago and extending to 70,000 years ago, extreme and prolonged drought in East Africa altered ecosystems, opening savannah where there had been rainforests, and stressing all animals, causing them to find new sources of food and water, and compete in new ways with their neighbours. *Homo sapiens* were pushed to the verge of extinction. From DNA studies, anthropologists estimate that only about 2,000 humans survived the worst of the drought, about the number of students in a modern urban high school.[23] We can imagine that small bands were scattered around the plains and savannah, hungry, watchful, just hanging on. This evolutionary experiment, the balance of brain and body, seemed headed toward failure.

Gradually, the rains returned, ending the great drought, which had parched Africa for nearly 20,000 years.[24] As might be expected, our population started to recover. But the population increase that occurred was so much more spectacular than that of any other species that climate change alone could not have been the only factor.

In thinking about humanity's phenomenal success at this critical junction, I recall a Bob Dylan quote: "And it dawned on me that I might have to change my inner thought patterns ... that I would have to start believing in possibilities that I wouldn't have allowed before,

---

22   Ruth Schuster, "Somebody in the Kalahari Had a Crystal Collection 105,000 Years Ago," *Haaretz*, March 31, 2021, https://www.haaretz.com/archaeology/somebody-in-the-kalahari-had-a-crystal-collection-105-000-years-ago-1.9670735.

23   "Humans Almost Became Extinct 70,000 Years Ago," *The Telegraph*, April 25, 2008, http://www.telegraph.co.uk/news/science/science-news/3340777/Humans-almost-became-extinct-in-70000-BC.html.

24   Edward O. Wilson, *The Social Conquest of Earth* (New York: Liveright, 2013), p. 83.

that I had been closing my creativity down to a very narrow, controllable scale ... that things had become too familiar and I might have to disorientate myself."[25]

I don't mean to imply that a single individual consciously decided to change his or her inner thought patterns. But somehow, mysteriously almost, there was a giant renaissance in human creativity at this critical junction, when our ultimate survival was on the line.

Between 1992 and 2002, archeologists working in the Blombos Cave in South Africa discovered that approximately 75,000 years ago, Stone Age artists had drilled holes in seashells to string them together, perhaps as jewellery, like a necklace. This discovery proves that, once again, people were engaged in time-consuming behaviour that didn't directly aid their tooth-and-claw survival on the brutal savannah. Alongside the shells, the scientists found 8,000 pieces of red ochre rock, which were deliberately engraved. Two pieces of this ochre rock stand out because they were incised with delicate diamond-shaped patterns, bounded by parallel lines. Archeologists have found several similar carvings in nearby sites. In 2018, archeologists found paintings with similar patterns to complement the engravings, indicating the artists in Blombos were creating art using different media.

It is impossible to know what all this art symbolized in the eyes of its creators. But just as a track of an antelope is an idea of an antelope and not the antelope itself, or a picture of a horse is an idea of a horse, not a horse itself, these scratches and paintings were symbols, representations of something. Undeniably, the people who lived in the Blombos Cave and vicinity were thinking abstractly. An abstract thought, however primitive, is an imagination of a thing or an event. It is a narrative, or a dream that doesn't necessarily exist in the material world. And just as the first sharpened rocks were the precursor to the iPhone, these parallel lines in the Blombos Cave, whatever they represented in the eyes of their creators, were precursors to the development of much more sophisticated ideas, stories, dreams, lies and religions – precursors to the Greek superheroes, Aesop's Fables, the Epic of Gilgamesh, the Tlingit Creation Story and their counterparts in every culture in modern or ancient times. But

---

25 Bob Dylan, *Chronicles* (New York: Simon & Schuster, 2005), p. 71.

Jon Turk

that's only the beginning. I'd like to take the liberty to also include music and dance as forms of myth. Like an oral story, music is made of vibrations in the air, ephemeral, tiny packets of energy that pulsate, expand into space, dissipate and then cease to exist. Similarly, dance is a movement created and disappearing in the instant, except that music and dance create stories in our brain that make us happy or sad, inspired or fearful, and these stories don't disappear but remain in the heart and soul of the dancers and their audiences. A song, the beating of drums, or bodies gyrating to the music are creations that don't have the direct utility, or tangible permanence, of a spearhead or a sewing needle, or even a persistence hunt; but they inspire us to love our neighbours – or to march into battle.

The Blombos Cave geometric patterns are significant, but for me another archeological site, a few hundred kilometres north, in the Kalahari Desert not far from the crystal collection mentioned earlier, arouses deeper evocative emotions. In 2006, Professor Sheila Coulson, from the University of Oslo, was searching for human arti-facts in the Tsodilo Hills in the northern Kalahari. It was a promising place because the region is famous for having the largest concentra-tion of rock paintings in the world and remains a sacred site for the modern !Kung. Coulson and her colleagues found a small cave, its entry half hidden by a fold in the rocks. Within the cave, they found a rock sculpture six metres long by two metres high that resembled the head of a huge python. Tool marks prove that some long-ago person carved the snake's basic features and etched 300–400 indentations in the rock to resemble scales.

Coulson recounted, "You could see the mouth and eyes of the snake. It looked like a real python. The play of sunlight over the indentations gave them the appearance of snakeskin. At night, the firelight gave one the feeling that the snake was actually moving."[26]

From an abundance of evidence in the cave, scientists date the python carving to about 70,000 years ago, slightly after the Blombos Cave beads and carvings, and roughly the time the *Homo* population started to increase.

....

26 Yngve Vogt, trans. Alan Louis Belardinelli, "World's oldest ritual discovered. Worshipped the python 70,000 years ago," *Apollon*, February 1, 2012, https://www.apollon.uio.no/english/articles/2006/python-english.html.

Coulson and her co-workers found more than 13,000 artifacts in the cave, including primitive carving tools and finely shaped spearheads. Many of the spearheads were made from red stone that was quarried hundreds of kilometres away. After ancient people had shaped the stone, they burned the spearheads in a fire, although there was no pragmatic reason to heat those stone points if they were used as tools or weapons.

These ancient people also carved a small chamber behind the stone snake, which is accessed through a back entry, a narrow, sinuous shaft that opens on a nearby hillside. This passage has been worn smooth, indicating that many people wiggled through it over a period of years, decades or centuries.

Coulson writes, "The shaman, who is still a very important person in San culture today, could have kept himself hidden in that secret chamber. He would have had a good view of the inside of the cave while remaining hidden himself. When he spoke from his hiding place, it could have seemed as if the voice came from the snake itself. The shaman would have been able to control everything, and then disappeared from the chamber through the secret exit. It was perfect."

In many archeological discoveries, we must guess what the Stone Age artists were trying to say or depict. But we need no guesswork here. According to the creation myth of the modern !Kung people, humankind descended from the python and the streambeds around the hills were created by the God-snake as it wandered the desert in its endless search for water. Two small paintings in this cave, an elephant and a giraffe, also correlate with modern !Kung myths. In one modern story, a python falls into a body of water and cannot get out by itself but is pulled from the water by a giraffe. In another, the elephant, with its long trunk, is used as a metaphor for the python.

Without any doubt, the serpent cave was a temple, a sacred place in the bowels of the Earth, where people envisioned the origin of humanity through the body of the fearsome serpent. The ancient !Kung expended a huge amount of effort to create this temple – effort that was not directed toward the daily necessities of survival. Imagine the tedious and time-consuming labour needed to carve the giant python, chipping stone against stone, breaking off flakes, crystal by crystal, and grain by grain. Then, imagine a dangerous pilgrimage across barren desert with its prides of lions, to collect the red rock, arduous knapping to shape a tool, and finally imagine some ritual to consecrate the spearheads in fire and to offer these valuable weapons to the Serpent God, rather than using them for the hunt.

Now enter the cave with your family, your tribe, out of the hot sun, crouched low and into the cool dark bowels of the Earth. Once inside, there are no leopards to fear, antelope to hunt, water to fetch or roots to dig. Here, thoughts have no sky to escape into and are reflected off the stone walls back into an emotional place we don't understand, so we name it the subconscious. Out of the still silence, the stone serpent speaks in echoing, eerie and mysterious tones that amplify this journey into the unknown and unknowable folds of the human brain, evoking ecstasy, terror, passion, rapture, rhapsody, awe, euphoria – a passage into the Other World. What do those words mean? Unless the words evoke a feeling that already exists inside you, they are just words: pulses of air, bursts of energy, symbols – a representation of something, not the thing itself.

In an ordinary day, we go to work, hunting zebras or selling insurance, eat dinner, play with the kids and perhaps make love with our spouse. All good stuff. But the ancient !Kung were seeking and experiencing something additional. They were practising religion, telling stories. As Jonathan Gottschall writes in *The Storytelling Animal,* our ancestors "thronged around hearth fires trading wild lies about brave tricksters and young lovers, selfless heroes and shrewd hunters, sad chiefs and wise crones, the origin of the sun and the stars, and the nature of gods and spirits."[27]

Thus, our art, our sculpture, our religion (music and dance?) bonded humans together into co-operative tribes that were able to effectively defend themselves, find food and innovate. But there is one more issue. In his book, *Becoming Wild: How Animal Cultures Raise Families, Create Beauty, and Achieve Peace,* Carl Safina, biologist and animal advocate, argues that the appreciation and creation of beauty occurs so many times in the animal world, and is so recognizable across species, that "evolution is not just survival of the fittest, but survival of the beautiful."[28] Safina asks us to consider

....

27 Jonathan Gottschall, *The Storytelling Animal: How Stories Make Us Human* (New York: Mariner Books, 2013), p. 176.

28 Carl Safina, *Becoming Wild: How Animal Cultures Raise Families, Create Beauty, and Achieve Peace* (New York: Henry Holt, 2020), p. 203.

the familiar example of a peacock's elaborate tail. Logic argues that colourful, showy feathers would be a *disadvantage* because they are metabolically expensive to produce and at the same time make the peacocks more visible and hence more vulnerable to predators. So why did they evolve? The famous evolutionary biologist Alfred Russel Wallace argued that the elaborate tail feathers are a 'fitness indicator' that announces to females that I am so healthy, robust and crafty that I can afford to support the growth of useless feathers and, at the same time, I can elude predators, despite my disdain for camouflage. And the females swoon. Thus, in any generation, the most elaborately feathered males had an advantage in the sexual selection of females. Consequently, over many generations, peacocks' tails evolved to become ever more colourful. Wallace's contemporary, Charles Darwin, believed that there was no need to rely on the complex 'fitness indicator' hypothesis. He wrote, "A great number of animals ... have been rendered beautiful for beauty's sake."[29] I'm not going to step in the middle of a disagreement between two of the greatest scientists of all time. But I will point out that in both arguments the colourful elaborate tail feathers evoked a dopamine response that resulted in a warm fuzzy feeling that led to either desire for sex or appreciation of beauty. Or, what seems most likely to me, appreciation of beauty leading to desire for sex. And the species thrived. When humans see peacock feathers, they aren't stimulated to have sex with the peacock, but they do perceive the colourful array as beautiful. Which implies two conclusions. First, that humans share a similar perception of beauty with peahens, and by extension with other birds and other animals. And second, that there is reason to conclude that a warm, fuzzy, dopamine-releasing awe of beauty endows an individual and a species with an innate advantage in the struggle for survival.

That second conclusion is where we connect this argument with human art. Cultural adaptation is much faster than genetic evolution. Around 70,000 years ago, humans began creating art – beauty – not by slowly evolving elaborate and colourful body parts but by cultural adaptation that led them to create beautiful thing: beads,

29 Carl Safina, *Becoming Wild: How Animal Cultures Raise Families, Create Beauty, and Achieve Peace* (New York: Henry Holt, 2020), p. 210.

drawings, sculpture (and probably music). And the human population exploded. Over many millennia since then, humans have lavished so much energy creating beauty, in all cultures, with no directly observable reward in terms of food gathering, that, whatever the evolutionary explanation, creation of beauty is one of the defining characteristics of our phenomenally successful species.

In roughly the same time period when humans created the first scratches on rock and gathered in serpent caves, our ancestors also improved their tool kit in many ways. In Sibudu Cave, a rock shelter in a sandstone cliff in South Africa, archeologists have found the earliest bone and stone arrowheads (61,000 and 64,000 years old, respectively) and the earliest needle (61,000 years old). Inhabitants of Sibudu Cave mixed plant and mineral products together to produce glue used to attach points to shafts, indicating that they were "competent chemists, alchemists, and pyro-technologists."[30] They slept on cozy bedding made from leaves with insect repellant properties.

When we think about our species, us, *Homo sapiens*, who we are, who I am, who you are, who our ancestors were, we can speculate that we are a pragmatic, tool-wielding species who tacked on spirituality because our more efficient hunting gave us extra free time. Or that symbolic thought opened new pathways in the human brain to initiate the reasoning that led to technological advances and improved hunting efficiency. There is no way to know with any certainty which of these scenarios is accurate, but it seems reasonable to assume that there was no linear pathway in either direction. A didn't lead to B and B didn't lead to A; they both came inside one glorious, complex package. Thus, a Cognitive Revolution of both art and technology occurred, more or less, at the same time. Harari dates the Cognitive Revolution at 70,000 years ago, which is an approximate number, given all the vagaries of the archeological record, combined with the impossibility of fixing an exact onset to a process that undoubtedly evolved gradually. The important point is that this Cognitive Revolution included both art and technology arising together because both are rooted in the same cerebral process: abstract thought.

....

30   Heather Pringle, "The Origins of Creativity," *Scientific American*, March 2013, p. 37.

In *Sapiens*, Harari argues that this proliferation of human genius was sudden, because "something happened" to reprogram the human brain. He writes, "The most commonly believed theory argues that accidental genetic mutations changed the inner wiring of the brains of *Sapiens*, enabling them to think in unprecedented ways and to communicate using an altogether new type of language. We might call it the Tree of Knowledge mutation."[31]

I find this a reckless and unsupported argument in an otherwise brilliant and carefully researched book. Abstract thought is too complex to be controlled by a single gene that was altered by a singular random mutation. There are too many variables to condense it down into one cosmic ray blasting into one corner of one gene somewhere in one individual who just happened to then have a lot of kids, etc.

The other argument against the Tree of Knowledge Mutation is that burials and crystal collections preceded the 70,000-year date for the Cognitive Revolution, indicating that abstract thought and action arose gradually, starting earlier than we originally thought it did, and building incrementally. In addition, the fossil record is woefully incomplete, recording only the indirect evidence of complex social behaviour preserved in rock, shell or artwork; and our information comes only from those sites scientists have happened to find. There is no reason to claim humans started creating mythology, music and art precisely at any specific date you choose, because some archeologist might find an older site tomorrow. And even if no one finds an older site, there can be no fossil record of a father singing a nursery rhyme to his baby, or a shaman talking about her journey to the Other World around a campfire, without the elaborate serpent cave. By the same reasoning, we can never know when our Paleolithic ancestors organized the first persistence hunt, indicating high levels of cognition, logic and communication. And, remember, from the table given previously, that increases in brain size significantly preceded any fossil record of either tool technology or art throughout the early prehistory of humankind. And that increases in brain size had to endow individuals with increased survival potential in that generation that were great enough to offset the disadvantages.

....

31 Yuval Noah Harari, *Sapiens: A Brief History of Humankind* (New York: HarperCollins, 2015), p. 21.

One additional factor that contributed to this Cognitive Revolution and related population explosion must almost certainly be that we perfected sophisticated syntactical language. A monkey can yell, "Lion!" and all the members of the tribe will scamper up a tree. Or it can yell, "Eagle!" and everyone will drop to the ground and hide in the thorn bushes. But only a human can articulate, "I saw a lion this morning and it had just killed a zebra, so it is probably satiated just now and sleeping off its full tummy." Or, "I watched a lion hunting, but the zebra got away, so the lion is probably more dangerous right now."

Stepping back from the specific dates and events, a clear pattern emerges of a weak, slow, bipedal hominin surviving, and then undergoing an explosive population growth within a complex, ever-changing environment through an incremental process of advanced cognition, reasoning, communication and invention. From the earliest stages of our evolutionary history and development, humans evolved big brains that endowed us with the ability to co-operate efficiently within our tribe and to attain group strength greater than the strength of any individual. These big brains also ventured into abstract thought and the interpretation of symbols, perhaps starting with advanced tracking techniques. But then we took a step further, beyond anything observed in any other animal: We created our own symbols, adorned our bodies with ornaments and invented stories that purported to explain events and entities that we had never seen, touched or smelled, and that we would never see, touch or smell. We told stories about death, origins and other mysteries of the universe. These stories, manifest through sculpture, painting and word symbols, are called myth and are universal in every human culture on the planet. During this same Cognitive Revolution, we began crafting advanced tools that made our lives easier and more efficient. Complex syntactical language facilitated the spread of ideas as people shared their inspirations and vaulted creativity into a shared process.

So far, so good. Advanced tracking and communication skills, followed by invented tools, endowed us with the ability to survive on the harsh savannah – to feed ourselves, evade enemies and raise our children. Our mythologies, our storytelling, told in sombre awe-inspiring caverns or around starlight campfires, increased the cohesion of the tribe. Seemingly non-pragmatic activities – art, music, sculpture, dance, ceremony – became a unique and marvelous source of power. Harvard biologist and environmentalist E.O. Wilson wrote that the function of art was to "impose order on the confusion caused by intelligence."[32]

Ah. Wouldn't it be idyllic if our story ended here? But it doesn't. Because our mythologies became the wily serpent that spun around and bit us in the ass. Worry is a kind of story, projecting a narrative of woe into the future. Ego is created by self-aggrandized stories of our own importance. As we will outline in more detail in the following chapters, with the congregation of large numbers of people into cities, and the inevitable creation of central government, some individuals learned that they could manipulate others through the skilful and nefarious creation of political myth. And then the real trouble began. But, again, I am getting ahead of myself.

---

32 Edward O. Wilson, *Consilience: The Unity of Knowledge* (New York: Alfred A. Knopf, 1999), p. 245.

Jon Turk

CHAPTER 4

A MOTEL AT THE
END OF THE WORLD

In July 2017, I flew to Nairobi, met a driver named Anthony, recommended by Tina, and we drove out of the city toward the Samburu outback.

It's normal, these days, to see Mercedes and Lexus dealerships in even the poorest countries, so no surprises here as we speed north on a six-lane highway. I must admit to a double take, however, when Anthony points out the location of an indoor ski area, but I later learned that he was just taken in by false advertising, or simple miscomprehension of the unfathomable habits of the super-rich – or of winter. In any case, we pass the Panari Hotel, whose website boasts a "Unique, Tropical Ice Skiing Field," which, despite its confusing name, is really an ice-skating rink – opulent enough without hyperbole, in Kenya, lying smack on the equator, where the average per capita income is $1,246, about $100/month.

Just north of the Panari, Anthony points to a few men in faded blue jeans and ragged hand-me-down T-shirts who are herding skinny cows along a thin strip of dirt-like stuff covered with a brightly coloured kaleidoscope of plastic detritus, interspersed with a few blades of worn-down, chewed-up grass, all improbably squeezed between the highway and a furniture showroom. We are zooming along at 100 km/hr, within the flow of cars and trucks, each pod of metal and humanity headed somewhere, with no obvious terror or panic. No one swerves, looks, gawks or takes photos, because all this is just another normal day on the outskirts of Nairobi.

But Anthony notices. "Maasai."

Maasai are closely related to the Samburu, and generally more well known in North America.

As Anthony and I zoom along, I imagine that the previously proud and independent Maasai who were eking out a polluted, noisy, parched existence in the shadow of that furniture showroom have their own urban worries, and that lion predation is low on their list of immediate concerns.

I should have ridden a bike to Samburu, taken a week, not six hours. I could have rented some skates and glided around the rink at the Panari, interviewed a few folks and then later in the day chatted with the Maasai herders, played images against one another. But I didn't do that. You see, I was confused or misguided, or blinded by my own romanticism. I thought that I was heading off into the wilderness to commune with lions and Aboriginal Samburu and that this urban story was peripheral to the real action. But I did record a list of images that raced past the car window over the next six hours.

First and foremost, as one notices along any road in any country on this planet today, people are selling things.

There are billboards for high-speed internet and scotch whisky.

Buy 2 Yoghurts and Get 1 Free

Then there are roadside vendors selling produce from their farms. Some have large well-organized stands, like those in a farmer's market in North America. Others stand behind a small rickety table with a pineapple or two, or a few cucumbers looking limpid under the hot sun. At the bottom of the capitalist hierarchy, a skinny shirtless boy is holding a live chicken by its feet, and waving it in the air, its wings flapping and eyes wide open in terror. I want to stop Anthony and buy the chicken, maybe pay the kid a little more than it's worth, and then let the chicken go, run for it, eat bugs, have a sporting chance. But I don't want Anthony to think that I'm crazy.

We pass a darling young girl walking home from church in her white dress holding her daddy's hand. And a lithe teenager with tight jeans and the words "Kiss" and "Me" plastered in sequins, one word on each butt cheek. People being people. Sweet, peaceful images of humanity at its best. Next is a shiny tummy-tuck clinic surrounded by stick and cardboard huts. All this is unsurprising. But I am caught off guard by a billboard that advertises:

Five Star Luxury Wilderness Lodge

3, 5, AND 7 DAY SAFARI EXPEDITIONS

ONLY 15 KILOMETERS AWAY

Is there really a wilderness game park with leopards and rhino so close to the tummy-tuck clinic? Sometimes the Anthropocene sneaks up on me, when I should be more aware of how quickly the world has changed. My mental image of Africa has inexplicitly, and incorrectly, stopped when David Livingstone, in his search for the Nile, was completely out of touch with the civilized world for six years. But wake up, Jon, I say to myself, in my own backyard in Montana Lewis and Clark took 2½ years to wander from St. Louis to Portland and back. I live in the forest on the edge of the Frank Church–Bitterroot–Selway Wilderness (which is nearly the same size as the Serengeti National Park) and would not be surprised to see a tummy-tuck clinic along the paved roadway in the densely populated Bitterroot Valley 15 kilometres east of the Wilderness. I shouldn't have been surprised by the proximity of game parks to modern civilization at its best and worst. Yet I find small comfort in that reality. On past expeditions, in Siberia or the North American Arctic, I've travelled in true wilderness, where you can walk on a transect for several time zones without meeting people or crossing a paved road.

"Okay," I tell myself. "Recalibrate."

Since independence in 1963, Kenya's population has increased fivefold, to 52 million. All these people have to live somewhere and eat something. All these people need roads, houses, power lines, farms and so forth, all of which takes up space somewhere. And some, not many, but some of these people need tummy-tuck clinics, ice-skating rinks and Mercedes dealerships. So who draws the short end of the stick? The lions, rhinos and elephants. So there is a game park only 15 km from this road, with its advertised "wilderness experience."

I have been in Kenya less than 24 hours, and it isn't going to do any good to overthink myself. Now I am in Anthony's car and he is speeding along over, around and through the potholes with the adroit dexterity and practice of a competent professional driver.

We pass west of Mt. Kenya, but the mountain is obscured by low-lying clouds. Rainfall, captured by the mountain, has nurtured rich agriculture in the region. We are surrounded by green fields dotted with numerous villages and the road is crowded with big trucks and modern farm machinery. As early as 1925, the British East Africa Commission wrote that this part of Kenya contained some of the richest agricultural soils in the world.

In the town of Nanyuki, we stop at a KFC, which is located inside a gated mall. I walk past the AK-47-wielding security guard with a nod and a perfunctory wave that announces, "I am a white man, and he is my driver, and that is the only identification I need to gain entry through this checkpoint." Anthony suggests that we each order the "Two Piece Meal" and a soda. Inside the mall, the well-dressed, advantaged kids are laughing as they run up a down escalator. Outside the iron gate, the less advantaged kids are laughing as they give each other rides in a rusted wheelbarrow with a wobbly wheel and a flat tire.

After lunch, Anthony drives us farther north into a drier climate, where the vegetable farms surrender to wheat fields, and baboons pick grain left on the ground after the combines have passed. As we continue, ever farther from the capital, traffic diminishes and the road predictably becomes narrower, bumpier and more potholed. Even the wheat farms can't hang on as we approach Samburu, only flat-topped Acacia trees and yellow-brown sand of the legendary African savannah. Empty space. Carl Safina wrote that, in the 1980s, "Samburu seemed eternal, a true remnant of wildest Africa.... And we lay all night listening to roaring lions."[33] But, as we roll into the small town of Archers Post, instead of lions, antelopes, zebras and giraffes, we pass skinny goats roaming the streets to pick at trash while

---

33 Carl Safina, *Beyond Words: What Animals Think and Feel* (New York: Henry Holt, 2015), p. 114.

Jon Turk

others graze on seemingly non-existent forage on the drought-baked plains. The buildings on the roadside are made of sunbaked mud, while stick and bramble huts dominate farther out on the savannah. Except for the plastic trash on the roadway, everything is soft, even, brown – neutral, relaxing and quiet. People are resting in the shade of the buildings here and there. A few camels plod in the distance, straining to feed on tree leaves. I wonder idly how many years of drought it would take the camels to evolve longer necks to reach the higher leaves, like giraffes.

I expect the pavement to die out and for Anthony to turn onto a rough-hewn dirt track, like I had seen in all the movies. But no. We pass over a nondescript little bump across the road, and from there, north and – poof! – the Africa that I had imagined, even the modern 21st-century, overpopulated Africa, striving to mechanize, even the Africa with ice-skating rinks and five-star lodges in faux wilderness – suddenly vanishes. Anthony's car, which had been bouncing around – rattle, bang, jolt – suddenly glides, as if lifted into the air on a magic carpet. The pavement beneath our wheels is inexplicitly new, smooth and wide, cutting across the desert in geometrically engineered perfection, headed straight toward Ethiopia. Or someplace like that. A monster Mercedes diesel 22-wheel tractor-trailer is parked on the edge of town, but otherwise I don't see a single car, truck, hut, goat, camel or person all the way out to the horizon. The A-2 Road.

Even in the relative cool of the late afternoon, heat shimmers off the coal-black surface. I ask Anthony to stop, and I climb out of the car to stand on the edge of the Kenyan desert, dust devils dancing toward the horizon, nothing green in sight. Infinity. Space that seems empty but isn't. Wilderness. I take a deep breath, slowly exhaling the 20-plus hours in the aluminum tubes of the aircraft, the well-polished bustle of New York and Frankfurt airports, the less well-polished bustle of Nairobi, the long drive. And now, in front of me: Wilderness. The birthplace of humanity.

In the near distance, about 30 kilometres away, a prominent mountain rises out of the parched plain and scrubland. It reminds me of desert buttes in the American southwest with its near-vertical cliffs supporting a broad, flat-topped summit, except that the rock is granitic, not sandstone. Tina calls this Mt. Sabache, but my map lists it as Lolokwe, and most internet sources name it Ololokwe (or Donyo

Sabache or Ol Donyo Sabachi). To avoid, or add to the confusion, I'll call it Mt. Sabache-Ololokwe. Whatever the name, this is a Samburu sacred mountain, home to the gods. A place for pilgrimages – to pray for rain. As a retired rock climber, I notice that the south and east faces are worthy walls of vertical granite, similar to the topography in Yosemite. And, in fact, when I return home and look it up on a popular rock-climbing site, I read the following post: "A massive, big wall in Samburu, Northern Kenya. There are a few routes, with potential for more on the steepest parts. Routes are long (2 days), committing, and often difficult. Be prepared for extreme heat in the day, cold at night, and variable rock quality."[34]

But once I look beyond this prominent, calendar-photo landmark, the overriding feeling is of planar vastness. Out there, far away to the northeast, lies Ethiopia with its mysterious ancient civilizations. To the east, the pirates of Somalia are hijacking ships on the Indian Ocean; to the northwest, the Sahara stretches across the continent. A person could get lost in this savannah-desert, die of thirst, get eaten by lions. Good stuff. But then, I stare at the anomalous A-2 Road, that somehow shouldn't have been here, running in engineered perfection, oblivious to undulations in the landscape, to deserts or mountains, to vanishing human or animal cultures, crossing parched riverbeds that no longer hold water, except in memory.

Anthony comes up alongside me. "Good road? Yes?"

I nod.

"The Chinese built it as part of their Belt and Road Initiative. It's good for us. The Chinese are helping us. I am a driver, and good roads make my life easier." Anthony explains that, in the old days, the 500-kilometre drive to Moyale, Ethiopia, would take two days in the dry season, bouncing over washboard, choking on the dust. During the rainy season, forget it; the journey could take a week as vehicles bog down in the mud, and if you were skilful enough not to get stuck, the road would undoubtedly be blocked by someone else who was mired up to their axles.

Despite Anthony's enthusiasm, I can't help thinking that in under-developed countries, good roads in remote regions are almost universally built by the military, because they are the only organization

34 https://www.mountainproject.com/area/111839600/ololokwe.

with sufficient money and incentive to build a highway that few people use. So why were the Chinese interested in this investment in this place? And then, bingo: Did the road have anything to do with the genocidal attacks that Tina had talked about in Cambridge? Or some other colonial enterprise? This wasn't something to discuss with Anthony, so I put my thoughts on hold. Anthony has been driving all day and he wants to return to his son's house before dark, so we have to keep moving.

Half an hour later we see a small sign, 60 centimetres high, painted on a block of jagged, broken concrete, half hidden by some scraggly bushes, with leaves that are doing their best to become green. The sign is hand-painted with a crude impressionistic blue-sky motif dotted with clouds, hanging over a childish drawing of Mt. Sabache-Ololokwe. Hand lettering announces Sabache EcoCamp, 2 kilometres away, followed by a phone number and arrows pointing toward a rough dirt track.

We bounce off the A-2 Road and enter a tight valley, almost a canyon, clothed in forest scrub that is significantly denser than the vegetation along the A-2 Road. Small granite outcrops protrude here and there. A few dik diks (small antelopes about the size of a dog, but with longer legs) scamper off, darting through the brush, ducking and weaving so fast that it is no surprise that they are the main survivors in this country. The place reminds me of Cochise Stronghold in the Dragoon Mountains in southeast Arizona. Part of the resemblance is that both are rugged landscapes of thick, thorny, desiccated brush interspersed with granite outcrops and spires, producing a maze-like mystery. But more striking is the emotional similarity: Both are landscapes where bandits, fugitives and anyone oppressed for any reason can hide. From 1850 until his death in 1874, the Chiricahua Apache Chief, Cochise, and about 1,000 of his followers, hid in the Dragoon Mountains, raiding the nearby countryside, then escaping into the rugged canyons where the US Cavalry couldn't track them down. Maybe I have too active an imagination, but the canyon we're entering feels like that kind of place, where a local tribe could elude superior forces because they know the country, its waterholes and its hiding places.

After a couple of kilometres, we pass a large dusty clearing with a corral for goats and another for camels. A hundred metres farther, the road drops steeply into a steep sandy wash, which is barely passable now for a good driver, but would be a mud trap for a vehicle when the wash is a flowing river during the rains. Anthony stops, gets out, feels the depth and cohesiveness of the sand with his toe, climbs back in the vehicle and downshifts. We slide and skid down into the wash and then grind up the steep far bank in low gear, wheels spinning and sand flying. After another half a kilometre, we come to a stop at the end of the road, in front of a few buildings.

Several Samburu in their late teens, all male, come out to greet me and introduce themselves. David, Moses and Ian have assumed European names and speak passable high school English, while Jawas has retained his Samburu birth name and speaks in broken pidgin. All are strong, healthy, athletic, beautiful young men, dressed in traditional Samburu style: red shuka skirt, bare-chested, with a cotton cape loosely thrown over their shoulders. They all wear beaded necklaces, with David's being the most elaborate – a broad, intricate, colourful breastplate cascading across his chest. David also sports a flashy pink sash around his waist. These four young men cluster around me and lead me to the centre of the camp, dominated by a large building with a thatch roof that extends beyond the walls to shade a spacious stone veranda. I don't know who in the European world convinced us that houses should have sharp edges, square walls and geometric corners. I guess a house, in some manner, is meant to separate us from our environment, announce that we are different from (better than?) nature. And since nature has no square corners, we can show our superiority by living inside a geometrical and artificial environment. This building made no such announcement. The wooden structural components, posts, roof ridge and rafters, are constructed of desert tree trunks and branches, pleasingly bent and folded, because nature does not produce straight lines and sharp corners. The stone walls are only waist high, so cool evening air can blow through the interior, a luxury permitted only near the equator. And thatch is bundled grass, so if you look at the building from above, as I was to do many times from the flanks of Mt. Sabache-Ololokwe, you had to peer carefully to distinguish a building from a grassy clearing in the forest. This is a dining room for up to 20 people, with a table of dusty Samburu souvenirs that are for sale and a few mostly forgotten tourist brochures in a dark corner.

Twenty-five metres away, I see a second building, which Moses tells me is the kitchen. A fence of thorns, a *boma,* encloses a small corral, with a fire ring and a table for two, next to the dining hall. A little above this protected space, I notice one small stone and thatch building, which is Tina's house, and a half a dozen wall tents pitched adjacent to small stone verandas, which Moses explains are residences for the motel guests.

I am confused. I guess that I had expected some sort of research camp. But no, this is a safari camp, set up for tourism. Had I missed something back there in Cambridge, or in the many emails that Tina and I exchanged? No matter. There are no tourists in sight anyway. I remind myself that I am here, now, and to be patient as events unfold.

David, Moses, Ian and Jawas had made a choice, as we all make, whether we live in Samburu or Calgary, Kamchatka or Detroit, to buy more heavily than some of their peers into the dominant economic structure of their particular time and place on this planet. Thus, they are working as motel staff rather than out on the savannah defending their cows from marauding lions.

Weeks later, after I have gotten to know them better, I ask each one to write down a short autobiography. Ian praises me effusively, and then asks for money. Jawas and David smile and shake their heads sadly, indicating, I assume, that their writing skills are marginal. Because I know nothing about his childhood, I ask David about the symmetrical rows of small scars across his belly, to which he responds, shyly, "They are to make me look pretty." Moses writes a resume of his education and grades (C+ average in high school), thanking Tina for the opportunity. "I was assisted by Tina because my family are soo poor can't make to pay school fees. She cave [save] me and I call her my nutureing mother." Moses's two brothers didn't go to school and are herding the family cattle.

After our introductions, I ask, "Is Tina here?"

Ian, the most precocious of the group, answers, "Oh, she is around."

I can't decipher whether she is "around" somewhere in Kenya, or "around" camp, or "around" somewhere on Earth, but again, no matter. Ian offers to show me to my living quarters, so I grab my day pack with all my stuff, and follow him along dirt paths, and then up a series of stone steps, to an old green canvas wall tent perched on another stone veranda. My tent site overlooks the camp, and I look down at the thatched roofs and tents all melding into the thickets.

A gnu, a small African antelope, with white stripes along its body and short, pointed, curled horns, follows us up the path. Ian explains that after the leopard had eaten its mother, the gnu moved in with the cows, and then adopted itself to the camp. It nuzzles me and sniffs my armpits, then licks my face with its sandpaper-tongue. Welcome to Africa.

Ian leaves, with a promise to return shortly with tea. My wall tent has two single beds, a small electric light powered by a solar panel, and a stone-lined bathroom with a shower that does work and a toilet that doesn't. I go back outside, pull up a canvas chair and relax on the veranda. The main valley, with its A-2 Road, is a few kilometres away but seems farther than that. Mt. Sabache-Ololokwe rises prominently to the south, its flank lifting out of the wash just a hundred metres away. From this aspect, the climb to the summit looks steep and brushy, but you could scramble up, without resorting to rock climbing.

Ian returns with a tray, covered with a white napkin, and a tea service. Very colonial. Now it is his turn to ask questions, about my family and home. I show him photos of our house in the Montana forest and he asks, "How many cows do you have?" When I tell him, "None," he cocks his head with a quizzical look and says, "Sorry," thus opening a simple but revealing window into his culture and his thoughts. With our introductions complete, he tells me that I should come down to the main plaza at 8 o'clock for dinner and leaves me in silence.

I sit quietly, sipping my tea. A few small vervet monkeys scamper about, their dark expressive faces bordered with white, as if they are arctic travellers with a hood trimmed with polar bear fur.

I remind myself, "Okay. I'm in Samburu. I wonder how long it would take to get to know these monkeys as individuals, learn their family relationships and their social structure, as Jane Goodall and other researchers have done." It seems like a daunting task, requiring more patience than I have. "Let's see now. I'll be here for six weeks and I might have a lot of free time on my hands. But ... I have a big fat book in my pack, *Sapiens: A Brief History of Humankind* by Yuval Noah Harari. I guess I'll watch the sunset and then start reading – slowly."

For quite a few years, I've been nurturing an idea to write a book about the role of storytelling in human culture and development, how stories have been our strength and weakness, our path to survival and our passage to destruction. From early reviews, I realize that Harari has much to say on this subject. I reason that, if nothing else happens, this beautiful campsite on this forgotten hillside in Africa will be my writer's retreat where I can relax, read and think in peace and quiet, where I have no access to my skis, kayaks or mountain bike, far from the concerns, distractions and obligations of my life at home.

CHAPTER 5

WE BECOME A
STORYTELLING PEOPLE

The first explosion of the Cognitive Revolution was followed by a second renaissance approximately 25,000 to 35,000 years later. A 44,000-year-old mural painting on a cave wall on the Indonesian island of Sulawesi shows a group of hunters facing off against an array of wild pigs and dwarf buffalo. The hunters, drawn in monochrome red, are disproportionally small compared with the animals they face. Many of them have strangely elongated faces, more like animal muzzles or snouts. One has a tail, and another appears to have a beak. Archeologist Maxime Aubert and his colleagues argue that this is not an attempt to recreate an event that occurred in real life. Instead, the characters are intentionally drawn as therianthropes – human-animal hybrids – representing a fictional narrative, a myth.[35]

Half a world away, artists and shamans in Europe also developed ritual art, and like the older rituals in the Kalahari and in Indonesia, much of this art blossomed in underground caverns. The 38,000-year-old lion-man sculpture, found in a German cave, is a beautifully

35 Kiona Smith, "A 43,900-Year-Old Cave Painting Is the Oldest Story Ever Recorded," https://arstechnica.com/science/2019/12/a-43900-year-old-cave-painting-is-the-oldest-story-ever-recorded/.

apportioned ivory carving of a human man with a lion's head. Clearly, the artist knew that such a creature didn't exist and could never exist; it represented a myth. Or, as another example, a 35,000-year-old panel on the walls of the Lascaux cave in France shows a bison, head down, as if threatening or charging a man who is leaning backward at a 45° angle, either standing on his heels or in the process of falling. The man has a bird's face, and a giant erection. Beneath the man, the artist drew a bird on a stick. A spear crosses the bison's rear flank and its intestines are spilling out in coils. Once again, this is not an attempt at depicting a hunting scene that happened, or might happen, in real life. The artist didn't see, or expect to see, a man with a bird's head hunting a dangerous, charging bison while sporting an erection. Undoubtedly, the artist was creating a complex story, another mythology. These myths were created to evoke the same awe, ecstasy and tribal cohesion that inspired people who carved the serpent cave in the Kalahari Desert, so long before.

Did the artists in southern Africa, southeast Asia and Europe communicate with one another, exchange ideas and discuss the spiritual underpinnings of the myths they depicted? Or did myth arise independently in disparate cultures? We can never know the answer, but given the difficulty of travel across continents and the thousands of years between the creation of these three artworks, it seems logical that myth arose independently in disparate cultures and, by extension, that the creation of myth is an inherent propensity of those big brains that evolved in our crania over time.

The Paleolithic artists who ventured into these dark subterranean caves would have needed torches to see what they were doing. According to a report in *Time and Mind: The Journal of Archaeology, Consciousness and Culture*, these burning flames would have reduced the amount of oxygen in the caves, inducing hypoxia (oxygen deprivation) in the artists' brains.[36] Deep inside the bowels of the Earth, embraced by the cool rock walls, and deprived of sunlight and

36 Yafit Kedar, Gil Kedar and Ran Barkai, "Hypoxia in Paleolithic Decorated Caves: The Use of Artificial Light in Deep Caves Reduces Oxygen Concentration and Induces Altered States of Consciousness," *Time and Mind: The Journal of Archaeology, Consciousness and Culture*, https://www.tandfonline.com/doi/full/10.1080/1751696X.2021.1903177.

oxygen, the artists would have experienced altered consciousness. They were stoned. Clearly, they didn't understand the science of hypoxia-induced hallucinations, but just as clearly, the fossil record reveals unequivocally that our distant ancestors were spiritual seekers, journeying to some impossible-to-define Other World, staring into the mysteries of unknowable wonders.

Along with sophisticated sculpture and painting, burials became ever more elaborate during this period. In 1955, archeologists discovered the 34,000-year-old burial sites of a mammoth-hunting culture on the frigid northern steppe in Sungir, Russia. In one gravesite, a boy, about 12 or 13 years old, lay head-to-head with a 9- or 10-year-old girl. The two bodies had been laid to rest covered with about 5,000 ivory beads each, and the boy wore a hat and belt with 250 fox teeth. Small ivory statues surrounded the skeletons.[37] Scientists estimate that, using primitive tools, a skilled Paleolithic craftsperson needed to work for 45 minutes to prepare a single ivory bead. Thus, some person, or more probably group of people, chipped, cut, ground and polished for a total of 7,500 hours to produce the 10,000 burial beads. In addition, they had to pull the teeth from 60 or more foxes for the boy's adornment. We can only guess at the cultural beliefs that inspired such a tremendous effort. One theory is that this boy and girl were the children of important leaders, indicating a rigorous and well-established hierarchy in the tribe. Another possibility is that these two had been identified at birth as endowed with special spiritual powers, perhaps as the incarnations of long-dead, highly revered ancestors. If this is true, then the Sungir mammoth hunters practised a highly sophisticated belief system incorporating lives in the Real World and the Other World. A third theory contends that these youngsters were victims of ritual sacrifice, again as a reflection of complex religious practices.

Did music and dance accompany these ancient rituals? The only absolute data points we have come from rock, shell, bone and paintings found in the fossil record. If people were singing and dancing, or beating rhythms on hollow logs, or even on more sophisticated

---

37 Lea Surugue, "Why This Paleolithic Burial Site Is So Strange (and So Important)," *Sapiens*, February 22, 2018, https://www.sapiens.org/archaeology/paleolithic-burial-sunghir/.

Jon Turk

drums of stretched hide, these early musical gatherings and instruments would have left no trace. But 40,000 to 43,000 years ago, at approximately the same time European artists were creating lion- and bird-headed men, and the Sungir hunters were burying their dead, musicians in Germany crafted flutes out of bone from vulture and swan wings and woolly mammoth ivory.[38] One of these flutes is well enough preserved that it can still be played today, the musician's breath flowing through the swan wing as air flows over the bird in flight.

All these artistic and ritual endeavours, from the serpent cave to the swan flutes, consumed a massive expenditure of time and effort not focused directly on finding food or creating shelter. Yet humans thrived and their populations flourished during these time periods. Thus, art must have had great pragmatic value in terms of fundamental Darwinian survival value, achieved through tribal cohesion and co-operation. As early *Homo sapiens* became an intensely tribal species, the collective strength of the group became so much greater than the strength of each individual that the cost of creating the art and ritual was more than offset by the gain.

But within the complexities of the human brain and psyche, storytelling is much more multidimensional than tribal cohesion alone. Put the storytelling-art-tribal cohesion connection on the back burner for a moment and consider an entirely different scenario.

People make millions of decisions every day, and our survival is intimately related to the collective efficiency, speed and reliability of all those decisions.

I'm walking in the savannah and see a blurry, dun-coloured form moving quickly in the bushes. Bingo. The movement is here and gone in a fraction of a second, too quickly to identify the object. Nevertheless, I must decide how to respond, or if I should respond. Should I ignore it, run away or chase after it? In *Suggestible You*, Erik Vance argues that the brain is an expectation machine.[39] It builds a repertoire of experiences and past events to predict what will occur in

38 https://en.wikipedia.org/wiki/Paleolithic_flutes.

39 Erik Vance, *Suggestible You: The Curious Science of Your Brain's Ability to Deceive, Transform, and Heal* (Washington, DC: National Geographic Press, 2016).

the future. Relying on expectation is much faster than spending a lot of time analyzing each situation independently. Therefore, expectation is a gift of evolution, a valuable survival tool. To make a decision, I recall patterns from past experience, or patterns related by my peers, and then I construct a narrative of cause and effect. If I am in Africa, even though I may never have seen a lion in the wild, I can shortcut a whole lot of thinking and wondering and cogitating and conclude that the blur of motion could be a lion, so I run away. Simple enough. In these decisions, the sensory information bypasses the thoughtful cognitive cerebral cortex because I don't have time to contemplate and weigh all the possibilities and outcomes. I need to act, right now. In the interest of speed, the brain takes shortcuts. And that's okay as a survival mechanism. If I assume that flash of movement is a lion, and run away, and it isn't a lion, I'm still alive, so no harm done. On the other hand, if I linger to get a second look and stop and scratch my head to think about all the possibilities, and it was a real lion, then I'm dead, which is not okay. Over the course of evolution, our brains have become hard-wired to accept mistakes in the interest of speedy action. But as we shall see, this shortcutting can also lead to BIG TROUBLE.

We use this storytelling decision making all day, every day, both for life-and-death decisions and for everything else. If someone throws a ball into the air, there is no observational data that tells me that the ball will return to Earth. But my memories, my narratives of patterns, assure me that the ball will, in fact, arc upward, reverse course and fall. These narratives are so accurate and useful that, with practice, I can run to the precise place where the ball is expected to be a few seconds from now – and catch it.

Animals have some version of storytelling decision making. Elk know when hunting season starts, dogs know when their masters are supposed to come home. But humans have taken a critical additional step in using language to develop ever more complex stories and to intertwine tribal bonding myths with practical narratives. Consider the Klamath narrative from the Pacific Northwest:

"A long time ago, so long ago you cannot count it ... the spirits of the Earth and sky, the spirits of the sea and the mountains often came and talked with the People."

"Sometimes the Chief of the Below World came up from his home inside the Earth and stood on top of the mountain.... One time when the Chief of the Below World was on the Earth, he saw Loha ... a beautiful maiden, tall and straight as the arrow-wood. Her eyes were dark and piercing; her hair was long and black and glossy."

And – guess what?

"The Chief of the Below World fell in love with her."

And – guess again.

Loha refused to marry the Chief of the Below World.

So he got pissed off and threw a temper tantrum.

"Mountains shook and crumbled. Red-hot rocks as large as hills hurtled through the skies. Burning ashes fell like rain. The Chief of the Below World spewed fire from his mouth."[40]

This myth conveys a record of volcanic eruptions in the Cascade Mountains of northern California, Oregon and Washington and warns the tribe of danger. Violent volcanic eruptions occur regularly, but at infrequent intervals, in the Pacific Northwest where the Klamath lived. Mount Mazama blew its top to form Crater Lake about 7,000 years ago, and since then a violent and potentially lethal eruption has occurred in the region roughly once every 1,000 years, the last one being Mt. St. Helens, which exploded on May 18, 1980. Given the limited human lifespan, that translates into an eruption once in 30 generations. If you want an oral memory device, so people will pass the warning down through the ages, you need a foolproof, long-term method of data storage and retrieval. Story. Cause and effect. If I throw a ball into the air, it will fall. Wait long enough and the volcanic mountain will blow its top.

But wait a minute. Why do we need the beautiful maiden, "tall and straight as the arrow-wood," and the angry suitor in this volcano myth? The Klamath people didn't understand plate tectonic theory and couldn't construct a geologically accurate narrative of cause and effect, so they created a mythological narrative of cause and effect. But now, because we are a social, tribal species, over the course of evolution our brains have become hard-wired to remember narratives of human behaviour. Therefore, the Klamath storytellers anthropomorphized the geology.

....

40 Elizabeth Wayland Barber and Paul T. Barber, *When They Severed Earth from Sky: How the Human Mind Shapes Myth* (Princeton, NJ: Princeton University Press, 2006), p. 6.

This anthropomorphizing is effective because humans are not only hard-wired to remember narrative, we are also especially hard-wired to remember narrative of interpersonal, intratribal interactions. One function of our big brain is to know everyone in the tribe and to understand all the complex relationships among people. Thus, I need to know how I relate to Mary, and how Mary relates to anyone else. Recall also that nearly everyone is honest some or most of the time, and nearly everyone is dishonest, or deceiving, some or most of the time. On a practical level, each person needs to know who will come to the rescue when the lion attacks, who might sleep with my mate when I am away or who might horde (or share) food during famine. Each person needs to discern the hidden intentions of others.

Discerning the intentions of others is so important that humans have evolved 43 different muscles to control facial expressions that can be received, read and interpreted by others, across cultures. A smile, laugh, frown, smirk, grimace, snarl, raised eyebrow or curled lip accurately conveys our emotional state, our mental well-being, our personality and mood, our physical health, our credibility and our intentions.

This whole scenario takes quite a bit of brainpower. Ants, bees and termites, who live in highly co-operative societies but operate with tiny brains, don't deceive, or find some activities joyful and others tedious. On the other end of the scale, chimpanzees do lie and cheat. A deceitful chimp in captivity may hide food from others. In the wild, Jane Goodall observed a chimp to yell, "Leopard!" when it located a tree with a small amount of yummy fruit. Then all the other members of the tribe would run away, and the no-good-for-nothing-rotten-down-liar could relax and feast. Human big brains evolved into a complex arms race. It takes intelligence to invent a lie and deceive your friends and neighbours. And then the non-cheaters need extra brainpower to perceive the intention of the cheaters and thwart their subterfuge. Suddenly, it all becomes complicated.

Paleolithic Billy asks Paleolithic Sally to the *H. hablis* equivalent of the movies, and afterward, "We'll head up to Emerald Lake and watch the submarine races." And from the perspective of passing genes onto the next generation, Sally has a vested interest in discerning Billy's intentions. Later, when Sally becomes a mother, she needs to tell her daughter how the world works, so she tells a story: "Once

Jon Turk

upon a time, in a land far away ... [all kinds of magical things happened] and then the lion-headed man asked the mermaid to watch the submarine races." And because it is so important for people in flexible co-operative societies to discern the intentions of others, that there are heroes and villains, storytellers created narrative to provide examples – lessons – outlining the nuances of human behaviour. And those who listened, understood and remembered had an evolutionary advantage over those who didn't. And then over a few million years this behaviour became embedded in our DNA. As Joshua Greene writes in *Moral Tribes*, "We find stories engrossing because they engage our social emotions, the ones that guide our reactions to real-life cooperators and rogues. We are not disinterested parties."[41]

In any narrative, we run through imaginary scenarios of "if that" or "what then?" If the imaginary husband cheats on his imaginary wife, what social complexities arise? "To be, or not to be." Six-year-old children invent narratives of being lost, kidnapped, bitten by a dog, dying. In all these mental games, children prepare for life as adults, and adults are free to imagine where real life actions might take them. Stories are a consequence-free mechanism of imagining possible scenarios and learning how to navigate a complex world.

Returning to the Klamath volcano myth: The elders wanted to warn the tribe that certain mountains might become deadly at any time. But because the warning must remain within the tribal culture for a long time, the storyteller wraps the geology in a complex narrative full of human-like love, anger, betrayal and bravery that has nothing to do with the volcanic eruptions but everything to do with our hard-wired fascination, critical for survival, with remembering the friendly or nefarious emotional intentions of others. And that is why a modern sportscaster will tell us that such-and-such a player is embroiled in a messy divorce, which has nothing to do with the baseball game but everything to do with holding our attention.

Along the way, in the back-and-forth feedback of evolutionary development, stories became a form of entertainment. *Groundhog Day* is a 1993 comedy film about a fictional character, Phil Connors (played by Bill Murray), a TV weatherman from Pittsburgh who is

---

41 Joshua Greene, *Moral Tribes: Emotion, Reason, and the Gap between Us and Them*, Reprint ed. (New York: Penguin, 2014), p. 65.

assigned to cover the annual Groundhog Day event in Punxsutawney, Pennsylvania. He finds the town, its characters and the assignment incredibly boring. And then, in a fantasy time-loop, he becomes destined to relive the boring day over and over again, for eternity. The film has become a classic because we all live in our personal version of a repetitious Groundhog Day, getting up in the morning, preparing breakfast for the kids, going to work ... and so on. How do we break out of boredom and keep our minds sharp for those moments when we need clarity to survive?

Higher animals have invented play as a means of spicing up their lives. Polar bears slide down snowbanks for no discernible reason, dolphins surf on boat wakes and dogs chase Frisbees, even though these activities require an expenditure of energy without a direct reward in terms of finding food or mates, or escaping enemies. Human children play long before they learn how to read, write or add 2+2. Human storytelling may have started out as a means of data storage and retrieval, linking cause and effect, or a means of teaching about the complexities of intratribal social interactions, but somewhere along the line, stories became an integral part of play-based survival.

As Karen Benzies, a child development specialist at the University of Calgary, explained to me, play is problem-based learning all wrapped up in a hard-to-define concept called fun. Mammalian play behaviour comes with rules, and if you don't follow the rules, no one wants to play with you. Play stories teach us social skills. But beyond that, and harder to quantify, play is a means of entering Storyland, where we relax, allow our thoughts to expand into space – a means of diversion, coupled with the bonding of tribes around the glowing firelight of a savannah evening. It feels cathartic to laugh and cry, to fear and rejoice, with our friends. And in that catharsis, as in sleep, we gather strength for the difficult tasks ahead.

We have shown how storytelling infuses many different types of behaviour. In the solemn rituals in dark labyrinths, and modern houses of worship, people experience something indefinable called spiritual wholeness and, with that, tribal cohesion and co-operation. Hunters following the tracks of a gazelle relied on past narrative to procure food. Throughout our evolutionary history, 'expectation machine' stories have continued to facilitate survival in everyday situations. Myth provides entertainment to the toddler listening to a fairy tale or to the adult watching TV. For all these reasons, fictional narrative has become ubiquitous in all societies, primitive and advanced, from the equator to the Arctic.

But, once again, never forget that there is a dark side as well. To hold together as a group, people need to bond together, to relate to one another peaceably, to co-operate and to identify and punish cheaters. We are all one. Love, peace, bro'. In direct contrast, to survive and thrive during inevitable battles for resources between tribes, each tribal member needs to feel separate from that group across the river and bonded to this group. US vs. THEM. This delicate balance of unity on one hand and disunity on the other hand is critical, because in all too many cases we must convince ourselves that the individuals of our tribe are superior to the individuals of that other tribe, and thus it is just fine to kill those human beings who happen to live over there. Rally 'round the flag, boys. Thus, each group establishes specific markers, beliefs and symbols that create its uniqueness.

Returning to our Klamath volcano myth:

If you believe that the sun rises in the east and sets in the west – well, big deal. Those men and women who live on the other side of the river also believe the same thing. But if you believe that Loha, the beautiful maiden, refused to marry the Chief of the Below World, and *if everyone else in your tribe believes in Loha,* that story becomes significant because those people across the river don't believe in Loha. So the narrative becomes an 'identity marker.' We are different than you. Which naturally leads to: we are special; we are better. Leading to: (you guessed it) we can now declare war on you, burn your crops, rape your women and enslave your children.

War, however terrible it is, can have its evolutionary advantages if our tribe, or pack or pride secures, defends or enlarges a critical hunting ground. Wolves, lions, chimpanzees and many other mammals engage in intertribal warfare, and kill, over territory. But our human skill with language, organization and abstract thought has endowed us with the dubious distinction of engaging in large-scale warfare, involving thousands to millions of individuals. And now another twist: Our ability to tell stories, to imagine things that don't exist, to create identity marker narratives, has opened the doorway to justify warfare that is not about securing something real, tangible and good to eat. Every despot and dictator in the world, from ancient times to the present, every religious fanatic who stands up on a soapbox to call a Holy War and convince me to throw your babies off the cliffs – is or has been a master storyteller. And there have been many despots. And many babies have been thrown off cliffs.

Even the pragmatic side of storytelling can have its downside. As explained earlier, we can speed up our decision making by shortcutting a time-consuming reasoning process with a quick story. Someone reports a robbery and a policeman on beat in the neighbourhood sees a black man in a dark doorway. The man in the doorway stops, reaches into his pocket and pulls out a dark object. The policeman tells himself a quick story linking imagined cause and effect: Black man equals robber – equals danger. Dark object equals gun – equals danger. It's time to act, not time to cogitate. The problem is that the storytelling shortcut mechanism is frequently flawed, and the brain makes mistakes. It will overlook, discount and dismiss peripheral data, or alternate possibilities, to preserve the first story that it believes to be correct – especially when speed is critical, because it is responding to a threat. The officer draws his firearm and: Bam, Bam, Bam. Whoops. There was an alternate narrative. The man in the doorway was exiting the building after bringing hot chicken soup to his sick grandmother. He was taking his phone out to call his daughter to pick her up from her gymnastics class. Whoops. The expectation machine, cause and effect, didn't work this time. Short-cutting through storytelling is fast, but not always accurate.

In summary: We evolved to be a big-brained, social, mostly but not completely co-operative, storytelling animal. Which is where we are today. Your body is fixed in space and time; you are at work, riding the subway, washing the dishes, changing diapers, whatever. But your mind is free to roam into fairyland, or anger-land, to a promising future, or to relive that nasty confrontation with your boss two years ago. On average, each person flashes 2,000 short, self-invented daydreams through their heads every day. Most of these mini-narratives run 10 to 20 seconds before that diversion is diverted by something else – a red light in traffic, a ringing phone, a talking co-worker, a crying baby or the realization that we should be doing what we were doing before the daydream started.

And when we are not inventing our own stories, we are entranced by the narratives that others feed us through books, internet, TV, conversations, sermons, advertisements, politics and any of the above all mixed together: conspiracy theories, tales of good and evil, heroes and villains, lovers and rapists, gods and devils. In 2018, the average American spent five hours a day in front of the TV, 31 minutes absorbing media on tablets and 1 hour 39 minutes on phones. Add in radio and surfing the net, and Americans logged about 10 hours and 39 minutes each day consuming digital mythology. Intertwined with the sheer number of hours spent glued to gizmos, each person is exposed to 5,000 ads per day; that's five per minute, if we sleep eight hours. Each ad is a mini-narrative trying to convince us that we NEED to buy this or that to look good, feel good, smell good, attract mates, find a job, approach nirvana, stay slim or become rich.

Eighty per cent of conversations among adults are tales of other people's lives: gossip. Dr. Nicholas Emler, professor of social psychology at the London School of Economics, argues that "swapping of juicy bits of information is fundamental to being human and separates us from the rest of the animal kingdom. Baboons and chimps have complex societies because individuals know a lot about each other. But because they cannot talk, they rely on direct observations and so they are limited to groups of around 50. The one thing that sets us apart is that we can talk to each other with complex syntax. We exchange social information. We form much larger and more complex societies than other animals because we affectively gossip (tell stories about one another)."[42]

Today, storytelling is so integral to our humanity that a 1-year-old toddler will create the fiction that his teddy bear is tired, put it to bed and gently tuck in the covers. At 2, a little girl will set chairs in a row to represent a car and drive her mom to school. When 3-year-old children gather to create mini-theatre, they pitch their voices differently when playing the king, the queen, the baby or the cat. Starved and half-dead, children play-acted imaginary scenes in the death camps at Auschwitz. When we grow up to become adults, we cry

----

42 Fiona Macrae, "You'll never guess what ... We spend 80% of our time gossiping," *Daily Mail*, September 8, 2009, https://www.dailymail.co.uk/sciencetech/article-1211863/Youll-guess--We-spend-80-cent-time-gossiping.html.

as the screen hero is adrift in the desert, sweat when a heroine faces the bad guy's sword, and become aroused when the two meet and embrace, even though we know that these stories are fiction repeated by speeding electrons and photons. We also buy cosmetics when an advertising executive creates a narrative that we will be happier if we look or smell different, crave gizmos or exotic vacations when told to do so, and follow religious or political leaders who spin all sorts of mythologies about loving, hating or killing people we don't know.

Adding to the negative, the stories in our heads form our often-damaging sense of ego, frequently create marital strife and allow us to amplify existing misery or wallow in imagined misery. Stories remove us from presence, the NOW. So, I googled "How do Zen Masters get rid of the stories in their heads?" And I pulled up pithy stories about techniques to manage and delete the stories in our heads. We can't escape the fact that we are a storytelling people.

It's no secret that humanity's phenomenal success, powered in part by our ability to create myth, and manifest as explosive population growth and technological development, is now turning around, like that snake biting our ass again, to threaten our survival. Clearly, we need to use our big brains to get us out of this new mess, created by our own inventiveness – and arrogance. But where do we search for solutions? Toward the bow and arrow or the serpent cave? Do we need to become the Practical People, or place our emphasis on becoming the Story People? Do we need ever more sophisticated technological fixes to grow more food on less land, sequester carbon and so on? Or are we better advised to listen to Marina from Talovka and find the power through human magic?

It's not a yes-or-no, either-or argument. Technological solutions are always welcome. But the last time we were in this pickle, when our survival was threatened, we took time out of our busy lives to make shell necklaces, scratch messages in ochre rocks and sit for long hours in the darkness to sculpt a serpent. I wish it were that simple: either-or, a wise choice vs. an unwise one. But it's not. As soon as we look at the serpent cave – or any other simplistic idea or image – and say, "Oh boy. Wonderful, excellent, stupendous. That's our path outta here," then whoops, we run into trouble. The Paleolithic storytelling animal that survived on the savannah by congregating in the serpent cave became the storytelling animal that shot, bombed, gassed and incinerated 50 to 80 million people in the Second World War after being riled up by congregating, shouting and raising clenched fists at Nazi rallies. Or, as another example, in the United States, the most opulent country ever in the history of humankind, almost 750,000 people died from opioid overdoses between 1999 and 2017 – yes, because of lost jobs and whatnot, but more directly from the stories they generated in their heads about lost jobs and whatnot. Our think-too-much-know-it-all brains sure know how to spin stories that help us survive on the savannah, or that create wonder and awe, but the same brains are also quite proficient at generating confusion, anger, hatred and misery.

CHAPTER 6

A LION EATS A COW

My first evening in Samburu, I read until dark and then sit watching the stars, wondering what will happen next. Someone starts a fire down at the dining area, and the cheery orange flames pierce the darkness. Ian walks up to tell me that dinner is ready. I follow him down the steps, navigating the well-trodden path without a headlamp, to hone my night vision and memorize this landscape. Inside the *boma,* next to the dining building, Tina is sitting at the small table with a clean white tablecloth, next to the fire. She had to have been here when I arrived. She could not possibly have been unaware that Anthony and I had driven into the compound. In this savannah silence, the noise of a car engine is unmistakable. I let it go.

"Hi Tina, so good to see you."

We chit-chat about the plane flight and then Tina tells me – whoops – I probably should have come a week later. She's just got here and there are so many administrative details to take care of that she doesn't have time for any lion tracking right now. "Oh, and I think that I told you this before, but I need to remind you that an election is coming up." Yes, she had told me about the election before I bought my ticket. But I had ignored the dark clouds; the momentum in my brain had been too powerful for me to slow down and reconsider my plans. But now that I was here, Tina reiterated that violence had erupted during past election cycles. "So you never know." There was no action to take right now, and if I'd had no access to Tina's news, I would have assumed that this valley was one of the most peaceful places on Earth.

The following morning, I walk down to the dining area. Tina doesn't show up for breakfast, but Ian appears and offers me two gifts: a Samburu wooden club, called a *rungu*, and a walking stick.

What do I do with these things?

"Do you know how to kill a charging lion with a *rungu*?" he asks.

I look at my club with renewed interest: a thin smooth handle of a hard wood with a knot at the end. And then I try to imagine a charging 250 kg (500 lb.) lion, yellow mane flowing in the wind, legs churning, teeth bared. I swing my *rungu* tentatively, to feel its weight and heft, its balance and range. Nope. My daddy never taught me how to kill a charging lion with a *rungu*.

Ian shakes his head sadly at my obvious deficiency. "Maybe you think to hit the lion on the head?"

I don't need to make a fool of myself, so I shrug noncommittedly.

"No, you don't," he explains.

Ian takes the *rungu* back so he can demonstrate. "Like this." Then, with a silent, explosive outburst, like an NFL running back breaking through the line at the Super Bowl, he leaps into the air, spins sideways and swings his weapon horizontally at waist height.

I still haven't quite comprehended the lesson until he explains. "You jump up and out of the way, so the lion does not eat you," and Ian looks at me intently, head cocked slightly to the side, to make sure I am listening. "And then, as you are falling back to the ground, you hit him on the side of the neck. Hard. Do you understand? You swing the *rungu* with your falling body and the arm. Together. Break his neck. If you hit him on the head, he will not stop. He will eat you."

"Thank you. Got it." I try jumping, spinning and swinging, and Ian smiles feebly as if to say, "If that's the best you can do, my friend, then I guess that's the best you can do. You are a white-haired white man, after all. We'll have to live with that."

My lessons aren't over. While I am accustomed to using trekking poles in Montana to take pressure off my worn-out, aging knees, in Samburu a walking stick is another weapon, used to defend against black mamba serpents. Black mambas are Africa's longest venomous snake, reaching up to 4.5 metres, although the average is about 2.5

metres. They are also among the fastest snakes in the world, slithering at speeds of up to 20 km/hr. When cornered, these snakes will spread their cobra-like neck flap, open their black mouths and hiss. If the mamba is close, and strikes, you have about 70 milliseconds to get out of the way. And if you can't move that fast, the serpent's neuro- and cardio-toxin is lethal to humans 100 per cent of the time, if no anti-venom is handy. Ian instructs me that, if confronted, I should strike a mamba on the head or flick it out of the way with my stick. "Got it?"

"Got it."

Then, somewhat shyly, Ian, asks, "I teach you to use a *rungu*. Can you teach me to use a GPS?" Seems like a fair trade to me, expanding the breadth and depth of human knowledge.

As an aside: One day, weeks later, an old African hand, a white man who had lived in the bush for decades, showed up in camp to hike up Mt. Sabache-Ololokwe, and asked about my weaponry. When I explained the lessons Ian had taught me, he obviously thought I was some kind of jerk, telling myself a story of going native. I don't know whether I was a jerk or not. But I do know that when I travel in foreign cultures, I try to do as I am instructed, and through-out my stay, if I ever forgot to carry my *rungu* or snake flicking stick, one of the Samburu would always send me back to my tent to retrieve it.

Ian brings me some boiled eggs and white bread toast, and then watches me eat. I ask him about the lion tracking project that I came here for. Huh? He doesn't know anything about a lion tracking project. "Oh, lions are around" (as Tina had been "around" yesterday afternoon), he explains, somewhat perplexed by my question.

I ask him if lions sometimes eat cows.

He looks at me as if that was a dumb question, and answers, "Oh yes. Sometimes lions eat cows. That is bad because cows cost a lot of money." Ian goes on to explain that each individual lion becomes habituated to specific kinds of prey. Once a neighbourhood lioness took a liking to ostrich eggs. She taught her young to eat ostrich eggs and passed the trait down through the generations through cultural learning.

I wait for more. I want to ask, "Is it possible to train a lion that eats cows to stop eating cows?" But I hate to pose two (or three) dumb questions in quick succession. Anyway, in Ian's mind, that part of our conversation is now complete. Actually, he's been waiting for me to finish eating so he can hustle me out of 20 bucks. "Would I like to go for a camel ride?" Not really. But ... Ian reaches into his bag of tricks and pulls out his carnival barker capitalist clincher: "I'll take a photo of you and send it to your wife. My Fakebook name is Ian Fantastic. She will get a photo of you on the camel from Ian Fantastic. Your wife will love this. Only 20 dollars."

I know an obvious con when confronted with one, but I also understand how to leverage a situation, so I pay my fee, ride the camel, and then when Ian feels patient and benevolent toward me because he is flush with cash, I ask about the violence that Tina had spoken about, that was, maybe, somehow associated with the A-2 Road? Ian speaks slowly, carefully, seeming to weigh each phrase against a personal image, telling me perhaps 1 per cent of what he remembers. In a few clipped sentences he explains that clan warfare engulfed the village when he was 14. And then he cuts the narrative short and looks at me without expression. His story doesn't jive with Tina's account of a conflict with government troops. So maybe there were two conflicts. Or, alternatively, someone was confused. Or editing the truth. All I know for certain is that at the time of the conflict, Ian was about the age of my grandkids, Jaimon and Julian. While they played video games with electronic bullets and bloodshed, he had dodged the real thing.

I don't ask for details. He doesn't seem inclined to talk further, and I feel that the story or stories might surface in due time without me barging in right away with probing questions about a deeply personal and disturbing tragedy.

I grew up in a normal Connecticut house – not too big and not too small. My father was a professor of chemistry at City University of New York, in Manhattan, and my mother was a school psychologist, so we had adequate economic means, by North American standards. But by global standards, or Kenyan standards, we lived in opulence. In my adult life, I intentionally stepped down the economic ladder by rejecting a secure, steady job with pensions and tenure, and ended up living in a small cabin in the Montana forest. In contrast, Ian grew up in a stick hut and is working his way up the economic ladder, to seek increased wealth with this job as a motel maid. And he takes his job seriously. The violence we speak of is in the past.

Oh, yes, and now that the camel ride, money transfer and questions are all over and done with, we do have a real and immediate problem. "Did you notice that the toilet in the bathroom behind your tent doesn't work?" he asks. I tell him that I did notice. I checked it out first thing this morning and the float mechanism in the reservoir is broken and lying on the ground. "On the ground?" he asks. "Yes, lying on the ground." "Hmm, it must be the monkeys." With the drought, all the water holes have dried up, with the exception, of course, of the toilet reservoirs. So the monkeys have learned to remove the ceramic tops and drink from the toilet reservoirs. And when the float mechanisms get in the way, they rip out the floats and toss them aside. Ian suggests that we try to fix the mechanism, but after examining the broken parts, I suggest that he bring me a plastic bucket, so I can draw water from the shower and flush the toilet manually. And when I finish, I fill the bucket one more time and set it out in the open, so the monkeys can drink without wrecking things or invading my privacy.

After Ian leaves, I read a little more from *Sapiens*, and then shortly after dark the bonfire starts up and I take that as my cue to walk down for dinner. Tina has reappeared as mysteriously as she had disappeared. She explains that a lion killed a cow in the adjacent valley and asks me to help track it with the regional headman, Dipa. She offers no insight into what we are expected to do if and when we find the lion. Clearly, I'm not privy to all the information around here. And there are too many questions to know where to begin. So, as with my brief interview with Ian, I decide against asking questions. Instead, I resolve to sit back, enjoy the warm starry night, eat my dinner and allow the story to unfold, as if I were a disinterested observer.

Lions see eight times better than humans in the pale illumination of stars and moon, and therefore they frequently hunt at night. No one wants to track a lion through heavy thorn scrub while they are hunting and we are effectively blind, so we agree to convene at 4:30 the following morning for an early start.

When I arrive at the dining compound well before first light, the friendly old night guard is sleeping on a hard, stone bench, but otherwise no one is around. Tina shows up at 5:30, but someone in a nearby village has gotten sick, perhaps cholera. As IV fluids and electrolytes could be the difference between life and death, Tina takes off to the hospital. Mid-morning, Dipa shows up in a battered, right-out-of-the-movies Land Rover. He's in his mid-40s, tall, even for a Kenyan, with high cheekbones and narrow, slit eyes, as if he wakes up in the morning squinting at the equatorial sun reflecting off the yellow-brown desert sand. He sports a short, wispy moustache reminding me of a teenager showing off his first facial hair. Dipa has a warm smile, revealing a few missing front teeth. He wears minimal adornment, just a few small, beaded bracelets and a large, somewhat gaudy Western watch. What you notice about the man is his quiet, assured command presence. It's nothing definable. He speaks softly, slowly, with a guttural, half-purr, half-growl cadence, without attempting to dominate a conversation. But he dominates the space, or the conversation, and you know that he is the leader. And that you are in good hands. According to camp rumour, when Dipa was a young man, he would scoop up a black mamba with his bare hands, break its neck and casually toss it aside, as his quiet, unassuming way of establishing the hierarchy in the neighbourhood.

Tina returns and we finally load up and start driving. No one is carrying a rifle, a dart gun or radio tracking gear. But I have my *rungu* and my snake-flicking stick, and this is what I came for.

Dipa explains that yesterday, a 10-year-old boy was herding the village cows when the lion attacked and killed one of the cows. The boy reasoned that because that cow was already dead, he might as well let the lion fill its stomach, so it wouldn't need to kill a second cow. At least not right away. So the boy gathered the rest of the cattle and herded them back to the village.

Right. At 10 years old, an age when mothers and fathers in North America walk their kids to the bus stop to protect them against even the slimmest possibility of danger, this boy is entrusted with the cows – the wealth of the village – in one of the wildest and most dangerous environments in Africa. And he faces the lion, armed only with a stick. There are no more fears to confront. You can invent problems, but none will compare. You can play video games of good and evil, but nothing comes even remotely close. You faced the lion.

Tina explains that in Samburu society there are four stages in each person's life: child, warrior, leader and elder.[43] If this is analogous to

---

43 In both Tina's and Shakespeare's telling, the stages of life refer to males only.
    What can I say? In these perspectives, women aren't included.

the Shakespearean stages of life, the Samburu skip a few steps that we in Western society, even long-ago Shakespearean Western society, include between child and warrior. What about:

> the whining schoolboy, with his satchel
> And shining morning face, creeping like snail
> Unwillingly to school.

And after that, what about:

> the lover, sighing like furnace, with a woeful ballad
> Made to his mistress' eyebrow.[44]

For the Samburu, there is no safe cocoon where the child can take time out from survival while the bones and muscles harden and the cerebral cortex establishes a full complement of neural synapses. There is no luxury of adolescence where young people are allowed – even expected – to goof off, sow wild oats, chase women and remain dependent on the tribe while slowly maturing. No. The Samburu metamorphose directly from child to warrior. And the boy faced the lion and brought the cows back to the village.

We drive out to the A-2 Road, head north for a few kilometres and then turn westward to follow a rough track into the savannah. The village is a cluster of huts, each one roughly three metres by two metres, bigger than a backpacking tent but smaller than most family car camping tents. The walls are constructed of closely spaced vertical sticks and the roofs framed with curved stick rafters. Each structure is lined with an odd and individual assortment of cardboard, plastic sheeting, cow hide and threadbare canvas to keep out the wind, dust and (now non-existent) rain. These homes resemble the play forts Spiker Feen and I built in the woods when we were 10 years old, but they are permanent residences, not play forts. The *bomas* (corrals) for the animals are constructed of piled rows of sharp thorn bushes, one for the goats and a second for the cows. If you asked an average North American observer to comment on the economics of this village, he or she might say that these huts are an indication of poverty: cardboard walls, no granite countertops. But

---

44 Shakespeare, *As You Like It*, 2.7.144–48.

when we sit down for a warm cup of fresh-out-of-the-nanny goat milk, people speak of poverty in terms of grass. And grass is defined by rain. Rain is defined by climate. And climate on the Ragged Edge of the Anthropocene is controlled largely or partly by people in the developed world, like me, living a profligate lifestyle.

I sip my cup of rich milk as an honoured guest. We pick up the boy, with the Western name, David, so he can lead us to the kill site. He has wide-open, expressive eyes and a broad smile that exposes gleaming white teeth and faint dimples on each cheek. With a reasonably clean red and white striped cotton T-shirt and a thin necklace of green beads, he could be mistaken for any 4th-grade schoolboy anywhere in the world.

We drive up a broad flat valley, with zero grass and no distinguishing landmarks that I perceive. The only organisms alive out here are perennial shrubs and occasional trees with very deep roots. And these are barely alive. The boy must see landmarks, because he guides us with precision, left of this bush, right of that one. We inch along slowly in the Land Rover, getting out periodically to clear a path with machetes. Just when I'm thinking that we're moving a lot slower in the vehicle than walking speed, Dipa shuts down the engine.

We climb out of the car.

"Wait a minute, Dipa. Shouldn't we take the machetes with us?" I ask hopefully.

"Don't need them," he replies, looking at me quizzically as if I were not quite with the program. "We don't have the Land Rover so we can walk around the bushes."

It's not my role to tell Dipa how to survive in this landscape he grew up in, but it does cross my mind that a steel machete might be a more effective weapon of self-defence against a charging lion than my *rungu*. But apparently no one else shares this thought. Dipa carries no weapon whatsoever, just as I don't carry a weapon when I go for a casual walk in the forest that I share with bears and mountain lions behind my house in Montana. I try to calmly evaluate the risk. This is an African lion, after all, and it is presumably close by and I have read my Hemingway. But I have too little information and experience to form an accurate opinion. Well, at least we have The Boy. In my imagination, The Boy becomes a fairy-tale figure. The Boy who held his finger in the dike and saved the city. If a lion comes charging out of the bushes, with a low growl, The Boy will find a way. And if he fails, as they say in Montana, I don't have to run faster than the lion; I just have to run faster than Tina. And I can do that. No. I didn't think that. Did I? If the lion charges out of the bushes, won't I be the first to lead the countercharge, with my wooden club and short lesson from Ian?

The Boy leads us unerringly through what is to me an inscrutable maze of thorn thicket spread across a featureless flat valley floor. We reach the dead, half-eaten cow without incident. Dipa sits on the cow's rear haunch, pulls a knife out of the folds of his skirt, cuts off a chunk of raw meat, scrapes the lion slobber off the surface and starts to eat. Of course, why not. The cow is dead already, food is food and humans have been scavengers as well as hunters since the beginning of time. One of the earliest presumed use of stone tools was to crack bones for the marrow even a lion could not access.

Tina reprimands him. "Don't take from the lion. Let the lion return to eat its fill, so it will not need to kill again."

Dipa looks at her steadily, deliberately slices two chunks of meat off the carcass and offers one to me. When I shake my head, he shrugs and stuffs it in his own mouth, chewing slowly. His cellphone rings, and with a full mouth, he conducts some important tribal business.

When lunch and the phone call are complete, we send Tina and The Boy back to wait in the Land Rover and set out to follow the lion tracks. To sound like a broken record, I have absolutely no idea what we are expected to do if or when we find the lion.

At first, I am really pissed off that we don't have a gun. What is this ragtag operation anyway? Of course, everyone knows there is a lion in the bushes. That's why we're here, right? I think back to that coffee meeting with Tina back in Cambridge, the smells and tastes of fine food and drink, the climate-controlled relaxation and, above all, the safety. How did that meeting, in such a benign and controlled environment, lead to my present predicament?

Suddenly, as a flash emotion: I am genuinely thankful that we are armed only with my Stone Age weaponry. A gun – with its sophisticated metallurgy, geometrically straight rifled barrel, carefully machined bolt and firing pin, with its brass cartridges and deadly lead projectile – this gun would give me the luxury and the permission to relax behind my 21st-century facade of dominance over the planet and all its creatures. Without the gun, I need to be, think, feel and live like an animal. To reach back to our most distant hominin past and embrace the vulnerability of our Paleolithic ancestors. And in reaching back through the coils of DNA, I move through the landscape experiencing a quality of attention that carries me into a time and mentality that existed even before artists carved the lion-headed man or scratched rocks in the Blombos Cave, before even the first *rungu*. And, in that flash, I know with absolute certainty that my analytical cerebral cortex is not my best friend right now. I stop for a moment and take a deep cathartic breath. Control-Alt-Delete. Recalibrate. I race a few steps to catch up with Dipa, who is charging ahead at a fast walk. This is exactly where I want to be.

Dipa moves seamlessly, barely looking at the ground, yet staying on the faint tracks in the sand, as if he knows exactly where the lion is going, what its mood is and how dangerous it is to us. After half an hour we encounter the freshly killed carcass of a warthog. The lion had eaten some of the guts and a few mouthfuls of front shoulder, but after polishing off half a cow the day before, it clearly wasn't hungry. So why did it bother to kill the warthog? Because lions kill warthogs when given the opportunity – this very lion who was to be our pupil in the anti–cow-killing campaign. The blood was barely congealed on the warthog, so the lion had to be extremely close.

We pick up the tracks again and follow them through the thick, scratchy scrub. The bushes protect themselves from animal attack with thorns so long, sharp and strong that they easily penetrate the soles of my hiking shoes, if I step carelessly. But the thorns are no defence against the relentless sun that is drinking all the water from the few emaciated leaves that have survived, and from the roots beneath. The sun has also drunk all the water from the desert floor, and small puffs of dust rise from our footsteps. Today, the thirsty sun drinks the blue out of the sky, leaving behind a pale, washed-out ceiling above us. Nothing seems alive – except that it is. That cow was alive until the lion ate it. The warthog was alive, until it wasn't. The lion is surely alive, no doubt napping now beneath this sun somewhere close by, digesting its belly-full of meat. Does the lion know we are alive and following it? I don't know what the lion knows or doesn't know, what it sees and doesn't see. I do know, from considerable experience with apex predators of the North, that the lion knows that humans are a formidable, lethal and unpredictable adversary. We are not prey, like a warthog. And perhaps that is our salvation: the accumulated experience of a couple of million years of an age-old arms race. The lion has what it needs, a full belly, and presumably won't mess with us unless it feels so threatened that it has no other options.

I am almost running to keep pace with Dipa, and yet trying to remain acutely aware of the situation. Should I try to move through shadows of shrub, elusive and slinky, just difficult enough to see, so the lion will need to think a second before acting? Or should I boldly remain in the glare of sunlight, upright and obvious, announcing that I am a Bad-Ass human, more dangerous than You, Mr. Lion.

On a previous expedition, when I was in Kamchatka, with the highest concentration of grizzly bears in the world, I asked a Russian bear expert, Vitaly, this very question: When facing a grizzly, should I feign subservience, or assume dominance? He explained that it depends on the size, age and mood of the bear. I should act subservient to a dominant bear, and dominant to a subservient bear. Great information, in a way, but missing the critical essence of a healthy, safe and supportive relationship with wild animals – and Nature – in general.

That summer, several years ago, my partners and I spent four months sharing the landscape with grizzly bears, living in a flimsy mountain tent. We saw bears essentially every day, and I'm certain they were aware of our presence when we came to shore in our kayaks, made camp, fished for salmon, cooked the salmon, ate and slept. Yet we never once had a negative encounter with a bear. At the same time, we watched bears feed on the rotten carcasses of whales and walrus washed up on the beach, and we never – not once – hassled the bears to steal their food. Mutual respect. Good neighbours. When I returned home, I visited Yosemite National Park with my daughter, Noey, and I took the bear precautions I was accustomed to taking in Kamchatka. A ranger criticized me for being dangerously careless and cavalier. I told him that I thought I knew what I was doing, having just returned from Kamchatka. He replied, "You may know something about Kamchatka bears, but you don't know anything about Yosemite bears."

The point was well made. A bear's attitude toward people isn't universal across continents and landscapes. Bears learn, just as people do. Bears are products of their upbringing, just as people are. Thus, a bear's behaviour is formed by the sum of all that bear's interactions with all the humans it has encountered, for its entire life, plus the sum of all its mother's interactions with all the humans she has encountered, plus her mother's experiences, and so on. Yosemite bears are black bears, and the dominant Kamchatka bears are grizzlies, but the difference in their behaviour is not primarily because they are a different species but because Yosemite bears have experienced a relationship with humans that has been that much more chaotic and disruptive. Bears have been allowed to eat people food, then people have punished the bears for eating people food, then bears have gotten aggressive, then people have learned to react to bears as a fearsome enemy, and bears have learned to become a fearsome enemy. A negative spiral. Mutual disrespect. Bad business for everyone.

Bringing this argument around to the current situation, the lion we're tracking is a lion who has grown up and lived with the Samburu people, in an ancestry of lions who have co-survived with Samburu people for generations. People and lions are both inherently dangerous, lethal predators. But they coexist because Dipa and his ancestors have treated lions with respect for millennia and the lions, reciprocally, have treated the people with respect. Oh, yes, there are clashes. This lion has just killed and eaten a cow, after all. But it is essential to recognize that the lion didn't kill and eat The Boy, and it could have. And Dipa, who is unarmed, has accepted the loss of the cow without recrimination, and has no intention of killing the lion. We are living in a primordial, respectful relationship with nature. In some way that I can only remotely understand, Dipa has no intention of training the lion as you would attempt to train a housecat not to hunt sparrows. In your relationship with your cat, you are the boss and the cat is the pet. In contrast, Dipa is not out here to assert his ultimate superiority and authority. He's here to remind the lion that we are all living together and to gently establish the need for neighbourly reciprocal respect. Thus, no need for a gun. In that light, I've been romanticizing my own danger, adding a White Man, Hemingway Hero twist to this much deeper, more subtle, more vital, more sustainable and more beautiful harmonious communication. My fear and my weaponry (however feeble) are not only unnecessary; my fear has been creating an emotional and situational environment that might create danger and require fear.

But turning off fear is only the first step. If fear is one extreme of a pendulum arc, turning off that fear merely brings you to the neutral position. To traverse the entire arc, and segue from fear to joy, you must swing to the point of respect – humility – good neighbours – a quiet chat across the hedge. Can I prove in a quantifiable, reproducible experiment that a lion recognizes or senses humility? No. Can you quantify love (or hate) between two people? No. You can show the effects of love (or hate). Person A cares for person B; or poisons his lawn. By the same token anyone who has spent significant time around wild animals knows that they discern the intentions of people. In the summertime, elk near our Montana home come right up to the doorstep and peer in the living room window, leaving the mist of their breath on the glass. But come hunting season, they are nowhere to be seen. The elk know that humans who can be good neighbours in summer may also carry a loaded gun on the third Saturday of October.

Tiger biologist Sooyong Park writes: "Domesticated animals like cats and dogs can look at their human companions' facial expressions and discern their moods and whether the humans like them or not. The same is true for smart tigers in the wild. Why are those humans there? By coincidence or by design? They figure out human intentions based on behavior, expressions, and the energy radiated by people and take precautions or even attack accordingly."[45]

Will neighbourly humility and respect absolutely guarantee me safe passage through lion land, or bear land, or the streets of Toronto? No. There are lions, bears and people who have been damaged physically and/or mentally along the path of life, and, as a result, they may initiate unprovoked violence. But in an ecosystem, or city, that has not had a long history of needless violence, unprovoked attacks are the exception, not the rule. So I watch Dipa. I take stock of my current situation. Fear is not only unnecessary but also detrimental. I am not in control, nor do I need, or want, to be in control. I am a good neighbour, and that is the best energy I can put out there to the

---

45 Sooyong Park, *Great Soul of Siberia: Passion, Obsession, and One Man's Quest for the World's Most Elusive Tiger*, Kindle ed., loc. 763.

world. As Sooyong Parks says, "When I am humble, I can see nature more deeply."[46]

Throughout this book, I talk about how people's relationship with other people, their tribalism, gave our ancestors power, and then, later, when the tribalism became distorted, created mayhem. But that is only part of the story. We must also consider how people's relationship with the lion, the bear, the elk, the tiger, the landscape, the rocks and the very air we breathe gave us power, and how, later, the basis of that relationship changed, creating mayhem.

So, if I were destined to see this lion, how would it reveal itself? My white man's fear and upbringing warns me that the lion would appear as a sudden blur of charging motion, bursting through the scrub, with a growl or roar coming after the first hint of motion, after it was nearly upon me, when the warning was superfluous because those pinpoint oval eyes reflecting sunlight in the subdued colours of the desert were all the warning I would need. But that scenario seems unlikely now that I watch Dipa and take mental control of the situation. Maybe, like the mountain lions I have seen in Montana, this African lion would notice me, pause for a second, flick its tail nervously and sense that I was more likely to be danger than food. And then it would slip seamlessly and silently into the savannah. Space and time would slam shut, leaving only the ever-present thorn bushes and a fleeting memory of an ephemeral image.

An important point to realize is that my relationship to this individual lion, to all lions, and to Nature in general, is prejudiced by the cultural stories in my head. So far in this book, I've spent considerable effort arguing that mythology – storytelling, thinking about things that don't exist – has been a crucial component of the creative human genius. Our population rebounded from near extinction precisely at the same time we perfected the art of storytelling and left evidence of this proclivity in the fossil record. Now I will spend numerous chapters arguing the exact opposite, that storytelling is our biggest flaw, the source of unfathomable misery, mayhem and destruction. How can that be?

....

46 Sooyong Park, *Great Soul of Siberia: Passion, Obsession, and One Man's Quest for the World's Most Elusive Tiger*, Kindle ed., loc. 58.

Personally, my greatest strengths are my most flagrant weaknesses, and I strongly suspect that the same is true for you and everyone else on this planet. Yin and Yang, light and darkness, negative and positive, all complementary, interconnected and interdependent – all part of the whole. According to Taoist teachings, there is no dichotomy, no exclusivity, no separation of an individual, or a rock, or a planet, into its contradictory and oppositional parts. So it should come as no surprise or apparent contradiction that our greatest source of power, our evolutionary leap into becoming a storytelling animal, must also be our deepest darkness. Yin and Yang – an indivisible whole.

Of all the living and dying that is going on out here, I have a strong desire to survive this day as one of the living. So does Dipa, I assume, but unlike me, he appears to be profoundly unworried. I can't fathom what he is thinking, but I know that to prepare myself for this moment, and the next, and the one after that, I must close and open various doorways – synapse pathways – inside my brain. Readjust – not my thinking – because thinking is not my greatest asset right now – but my visceral interaction with this landscape that I walk through.

First and foremost, I must eliminate the extraneous stories in my head. Forget that the stories in our heads gave our Paleolithic ancestors the power to survive, and that today the stories in the collective brains of scientists and engineers created the airplane that brought me here. And when I fly back home, after this is all over, I will be glad that the wings don't fall off that airplane, because all the bolts and rivets are in place, with the proper weight and sheer strength. But right now, all that mumbo-jumbo is irrelevant. My only concern, at this moment, is in the present. Nothing else. I am not concerned with any self-generated stories about my age, marital status, educational history, how many books I have written, how much money I have in my bank account or where I hide my passport so it won't be stolen. All irrelevant. Any story spinning through my brain, about global politics, or what Tina is thinking, about my wife and life back home – any fairy tales about The Boy, or God or Cosmic Consciousness – those are just neurons doing their thing. All interpretations or analysis of my situation are useless and counterproductive, sapping energy from the real business of the NOW, which is to survive this moment, with a real and not metaphorical lion napping in the bushes nearby.

Because I am writing this section, because I am using words that are a representation of those moments and not the moments themselves, what you read on these pages is a story, an explanation of a moment several years ago. But in that moment, all I needed to maximize my survival probability was to open my synapses to pure, uncomplicated, sensual awareness.

I stare into the bushes. If I were experiencing this situation artificially, by watching *Wild Animal Kingdom* on the TV, the landscape would be rendered on a flat screen, with camera angles and lenses designed to convey scale. But out here, I need to sense the living three-dimensionality of where I am. "Is that roundish yellow object close or far, and therefore large or small?" "Is it a dun-coloured rock, or the dun-coloured flank of the sleeping lion?" Or, incorporating my other senses: "What does a lion smell like in this desiccated world where flowers are hiding in their buds, waiting for the rain?" "If it did, in fact, rise to attack, would I hear it rustle as it gathered its feet beneath its body, tensing its muscles, preparing to spring?"

We follow the tracks up a dry wash, until we see that the lion has leapt to the far bank. I scramble clumsily through soft sand, marvelling at the seamless agility of the cat, the agility to jump from sofa to the top of the TV, or from wash to higher ground, and hoping that primordial agility will never be directed toward me and my *rungu*.

I peer into the air spaces between the lacework of shadow and light. The landscape seems motionless, but that is only an illusion. Like the mime artist who turns in a circle so slowly that you never see her move, the lacework is in motion, I am just not tuned in deeply enough to see it. Air. Shadow. Sun overhead. No motion. No lion.

I'll never know whether the lion knew we were here, or not. It makes no difference. Whether I am in real danger or imagined danger, I journey into a wilder world where consciousness is not uniquely human consciousness, where plain old garden-variety reality is sufficient. And once I open myself to this sensual awareness, my breath spills out, and my soul opens. Even though I am tired, hot and scared, or more accurately, *because* I am tired, hot and scared, I have entered a wondrous place of great simplicity, where tired, hot and scared no longer exist – because these feelings are irrelevant throwbacks to an alien reality. By opening this door to uncomplicated, non-judgmental presence, I simultaneously and necessarily close the door to explanation, analysis or myth. Explanation is worse than useless – it is downright dangerous – because it would remove me from my senses, reduce my reaction time should the shit hit the fan.

I've been here before. For all my adult life, I have engaged in dangerous outdoor pursuits. When rock climbing on a plane of verticality, I don't need to calculate Newton's laws of universal gravitation mathematically, or to puff up my ego by spinning yarns about my own heroics. Instead, I intuitively weigh the downward pull of the molten core of the Earth against the upward pull of my muscles. My entire body comes alive with a focus on my precise balance point on the tiny nubbin of rock I am standing on. Without formally articulating the thoughts, I weigh the tension in every muscle – too much tension and I am wasting precious energy; too little and I fall. I attempt to become one with gravity, because gravity is my deep and enduring friend right now. Gravity, body, arms, all become one. In a similar manner, when I am kayaking on a wave, I must become an integral, inseparable component of that wave, flowing with its turbulence, revelling in its chaos, joy riding on its potential lethality. That is the only way to survive. I read recently that many dogs are better at catching Frisbees than many humans. A dog would flunk even the most rudimentary 8th-grade physics test; it could not calculate the trajectory of that Frisbee. Presumably, it never tells stories of its adventures to its friends or potential lovers. But it can follow the spinning disk with its eyes, focus on it with all its senses and then leap, spin and catch. I need to be the dog catching the Frisbee, the squirrel jumping from thin branch to thin branch, the eagle diving for a fish. I need to watch, listen, smell and feel for the presence of this lion. Nothing else.

And that is mindful awareness. A wondrous place to be.

There are many safer ways to reach this thought-free cathedral in my brain than following lion tracks in the scrub with Dipa. But that is an irrelevant comparison, involving other realities of time, place and situation. The fact is that right NOW I am following lion tracks in the scrub with Dipa. If I can shut off my annoying proclivity to overthink this situation with human-like logic and analysis; if I can live in this moment without inventing a story about this moment; if I can become the animal that evolved right here, in this desert, 200,000 or six million years ago, depending on when you decide to click your stopwatch, then I have a decent chance of living through the day. And, along the way, I will become that dog racing across the park lawn after the Frisbee with no cares in the world other than the pure joy of its own sensual body.

Once I shut down the stories in my head, open my senses and close my ceaseless explaining, then all the accompanying corollaries fall into place. Yes, I want to live, but as I walk behind Dipa, staring into the bushes, alert to every perceivable nuance in the landscape, there is no extraneous energy in my brain that can be channelled into imagining my death sometime in the future. My fear, my sense of vulnerability, vaporizes into the ether. And if I truly feel this clarity – even for a nano-instant – and then the lion charges out of the bushes and I fail to stop it with my club, and I end up dead: You know, that's okay. It's not the trajectory I would have chosen, but it is one possible trajectory: And it's okay. As David Abram said in his inspiring book *Becoming Animal*, "Only by welcoming uncertainty from the get-go can we accelerate ourselves to the shattering wonder that unfolds us."[47]

If you go way back in time, before *Homo sapiens*, before *Australopithecus*, before roundworms, back to the first separation of structure in the earliest multicellular organisms, the brain didn't evolve to understand itself. It didn't evolve to separate itself from the natural world, to examine energy and matter from a cool, detached pedestal apart from all other sentient neighbours. It didn't evolve to invent heart surgery and atomic bombs. From any evolutionary perspective, all that came later, as a distant add-on. The brain evolved to see the lion in the bushes. And then, by coincidence almost, it just happened to turn out that our brains opened the Pandora's Box and created pathways to invent philosophy, religion and science and to create and believe in a fictional narrative that we are 'Oh so special' and separate from the natural world.

Out here in the hot sun on an afternoon in July, on the Horn of Africa, I am not thinking about the broad arc of human evolution. I am stepping carefully to avoid impaling my feet on thorns and I am staring into the bushes. And when I become awareness, I am no

---

47 David Abram, *Becoming Animal: An Earthly Cosmology* (New York: Pantheon Books, 2010), p. 8.

longer happy, sad, scared, hot or anything. I am too busy looking, listening and smelling to fritter away my essential cognitive power on a purely human, meaningless self-evaluation of my mental condition. The stories in my head have become useless. It's such a chore being a human; it drives me crazy sometimes.

The bushes, sand, rocks and sky come alive. Not in the sense that I expect them to talk to me in the King's English. But in the sense that, by looking at them, into them, by stripping myself naked before them, I join them. My skin remains, as always, a thin impermeable barrier to hold my blood and guts inside and the desiccating desert air outside, but in moments of ultimate clarity, I feel that there is no skin, no clear demarcation between me and everything else. Out there in the people-speaking world there is a name for this: Deep Ecology. Here in the lion-tracking world, we are not using words right now. For this moment, I have become animal. Borrowing, again from the words and wisdom of David Abram, "It no longer falls upon me, alone, to make things happen as I choose. Since I am not the sole bearer of consciousness, I am no longer on top of things, with the crippling responsibility that that entails."[48]

Dipa stops suddenly and holds up his hand. My alertness intensifies, if that were possible. I dart my eyes back and forth. And even though awareness might have trumped fear a moment ago, my reptilian brain has a strong bullshit meter and knows better than to pay attention to the think-too-much-know-it-all cerebral cortex. So, fear prevails. The adrenaline fires off, like an airbag on a crashing car. Poof, bingo, bzzowee. Ready for action.

Dipa turns and says matter-of-factly, "I think we will go home now."

Poof, bingo, bzzowee. Let down. Did Dipa just see the lion? Or sense the lion's presence by some means of communication I don't comprehend? Or did he know all along that we had no endgame if we caught up with the lion, and was just leading me on this quest out of politeness to Tina? Or me? And now it was time to be sensible animals and shade up against this relentless sun, like the lion, and take a nap. I'll never know.

....

48 David Abram, *Becoming Animal: An Earthly Cosmology* (New York: Pantheon Books, 2010), p. 131.

Jon Turk

No lion. As the afternoon shadows form and grow, we turn back toward the Land Rover.

Thank you, Dipa, for leading me deeper into the scrub. Thank you, Tina, for bringing me to Samburu. But most important: Thank you, lion, for sharing your consciousness with me today. Even though we never met in person, I feel that we became friends, of a sort, this afternoon. Not friends like I am friends with my neighbour's goofy dog Ranger who runs up the hill every morning so I can pet him and toss his slimy tennis ball a couple of times. It's different out here. I can't fathom or articulate what the lion felt or thought; I don't even know if the lion was aware that we were tracking it. But I bonded to this lion, or more plausibly to the essence of this lion, because it was an inexorable and essential component of this landscape, along with the cow, warthog, bushes, rocks, sun and desert soil. Together, we shared this day of drought, embraced by this desiccated thorn scrub, on this overheated, overpaved, overfarmed, overindustrialized planet dominated by an overpopulation of undercaring humans. And because the lion could have eaten me, and because after all my fine words I do want to live till evening, the lion gave me the gift of awareness, acceptance and unity with all the wonder around me. Thank you, lion.

The moment we turn around, the bubble bursts and I lose that purity of uncomplicated oneness. But that's okay. It is comforting to know that my animal self is in there and retrievable whenever I turn off my thinking brain and give my feeling brain unfettered freedom to surface.

CHAPTER 7

A COW DRINKS WATER

I'm thinking we'll return to the Motel at the End of the World and I'll take a nap, have dinner and relax. But Dipa has another agenda. The remaining cows are thirsty and there is no water. An African, desert-hardened, camel-emulating Samburu cow can live for five days without a drink. Then it dies. The village herd hasn't been watered for four days, maybe a bit more. Most of the young men are in a distant valley where the bulk of the herd is surviving near a few persistent springs. With the tribe thus short-handed, Dipa asks if I will help bring water to the few dozen cows remaining in the village. Of course, I agree. Maybe that's why we turned back so suddenly from tracking the lion. We had a much more important task ahead. Dipa explains that he will drop Tina, David and me off at the village and he will fetch the water in a truck.

David charges off to do chores while Tina and I sit on small stools outside the huts, by a small fire, to watch the sun set and stars emerge. One of the women brings us bowls of milky rice. After an hour or more, the peaceful darkness is pierced by the sharp glare of automotive headlights and the grinding rumble of a diesel engine churning up the rough track.

On a casual glance around this village of stick huts, 21st-century technology mainly manifests in the form of plastic water jugs, metal cooking pots, cotton cloth, decorative beads and a jumble of ragged cardboard, disintegrating plastic sheeting and remnants of canvas tents that have long ago passed their expiration date. The cows couldn't be worth much in the outlying cash economy. So: Who paid for the truck? In this land of ancient *rungus*, who has the cash for gas, oil, parts and repairs, which, however hodgepodge and ragtag, are still products of modern technological society and supply chains?

Anticipating my question, Tina tells me, "I paid for the truck, out of my tax refund from last year."

"And what would happen if this village didn't have a fairy god-mother with a job in Cambridge and a tax refund?" I ask.

"The cows would die."

An ancient but functional army green tank truck rolls out of the darkness and squeaks to a stop. A few of the young men who have remained in the village drag out a watering trough from behind one of the *boma* thickets. Dipa unties a hose from the side of the truck, connects one end to the drain outlet, hands me the other end and explains that my job is to fill the trough, making sure it doesn't either overflow or run dry. It seems like a simple enough task. But the hose isn't quite long enough. To my way of thinking, we could easily resolve this problem by moving either the truck or the trough, or both, so they are a little closer together. But I am an old man, half-deaf, everyone around me is speaking Samburu and no one else seems to think that there is a problem. Okay, I don't want to appear stupid and incompetent, so I pull the hose as tight as I can – and it almost reaches. But if I kneel and pull, bingo, I'm there. How did those guys estimate the distance precisely, to the centimetre?

I fill the trough with warm tepid water, smelling of algae growth, drawn from some languid seep that has survived this horrible regional desiccation. Dipa stoops down next to me and explains that the cows are panicky for a drink, and to avoid confusion, the herders will release six at a time, let them drink their fill, and then release the next half a dozen.

I kneel, holding the hose, and at a signal from Dipa a young man cracks open the *boma* gate. Six cows ramble out, look around and smell the water. I live in Montana, and although I'm not a ranch hand, I know a little bit about cows. I know that range cattle can be squirrelly, rough-and-tumble and unpredictable, a little closer in temperament to wild animals than to domestic ones. I also know that these Samburu cows have long, sharp horns, and suddenly, they are running toward the water trough at full gallop. They are not charging. Charging is a description of intent, and these cows have no intention of hurting me. All they want is a drink of water. But with heads lowered, white horns glistening in the starlight, they appear to be charging, as in the Running of the Bulls in Pamplona, Spain. I do what any sensible person would do: I pinch the hose off, so I won't spill any precious water, and step aside, so I won't get gored. The Boy runs up, grabs the hose from me and kneels just as the running-but-not-actually-charging cows arrive, and he calmly continues to fill the trough. The cows body check one another for access to the water, like hockey players fighting for the puck along the boards, but mysteriously and miraculously, no horns impale The Boy or poke out his eyes.

The Boy signals that he has a more important and difficult task somewhere else. This is my job, and an easy one at that. So I kneel down and take the hose from his hands. We are shoulder to shoulder, in the sand, with the smell of cattle and African water. I listen to the cows sucking up the precious water and then look into his eyes again: soft, round, aware, set inside a face polished by youth. The Boy has already faced the lion. And now he is teaching me that there is no unemployment or food stamps out here, on the Ragged Edge of the Paleolithic. Bring water to the cows. Or they die. And then you die. He smiles innocently. I smile back. For the second time today, there is no story, no mythology to complicate this moment.

I kneel and take the hose. A small thorn lying on the ground jabs me in the knee, so I shift position. A white-faced cow with a brown spot on her forehead jostles into position, its horn a few centimetres from my eyeglasses. For the second time today, one of our animal neighbours that we share this planet with doesn't harm me. I wonder, without any way to answer the question, whether this cow has a precise spatial awareness of my face and its long, protruding horn. Or am I just lucky? Does she see me as a friend who is bringing the life-saving water? Or am I a nonentity and she perceives only water and an opportunity to survive another day? Idle thoughts and useless ruminations.

The cow drinks with a loud sucking noise. Her nose wrinkles up, almost like a pig's nose, and she swallows with a gentle heaving of her throat. Wrinkle, swallow, wrinkle, swallow. Water is life. I smell the water and feel the light brush of her warm grassy breath that blows against my cheek and neck like a lover's whisper. The savannah is silent except for the slurping of the cows, and the stars shine brightly against the blackness. The lion didn't eat me today, and that is good. The Boy became a man today, and that is wondrous. There is no water in the watering holes, but the cows are saved because there is water in the truck and gasoline in the gas tank, and all the spark plug wires are intact; and that is good. Another cow pushes the white-faced cow aside. Neither of them takes notice of me, but, intentionally or not, neither of them pokes me with their horns.

My mind speeds away from the perfection and wonder of this moment toward distant landscapes where polar bears are hungry because they have no ice to hunt on, and where cute little koala bears are burning to death in the bush fires in Australia.

— — —

We live in an era of catastrophic and ongoing climate change. The newspapers will tell you – correctly – that any single extreme event such as this drought in Samburu, or a specific hurricane in Florida, may be the result of a random fluctuation of weather and not the inexorable change of the Earth's climate. Therefore, it is impossible to prove with any conclusive scientific certainty that this drought, out here in a land that is semi-desert anyway, is directly linked to climate change. But when the entire planet experiences repeated extreme, often highly improbable, weather events, repeatedly, with increasing frequency, coupled with measurably rising temperatures, coupled with alarmingly rising carbon dioxide concentrations in the atmosphere, we can no longer retreat behind vague and limp excuses that these are random, unrelated events. When two 1 in 500 year rainfalls deluge a community in Delaware within a two-year-period, and similarly repeating improbable events occur in Houston, when Australia and California are on fire, when hurricanes become more frequent and more intense, when saltwater fish are swimming over roadways in some coastal cities at full-moon high tides, when major cities with half a billion people in India are running out of drinking water, threatening even the most basic essence of human survival, when the temperature soars to 38°C (100°F) north of the Arctic

Circle, statistically a 1 in 80,000 year event, when the arctic ice cap is melting and the Antarctic ice shelves and glaciers are deteriorating at rates much faster than the 'worst-case scenarios' predicted by scientists only a few years ago, and on and on – then this is catastrophic and ongoing human-caused climate change. My story of these cows drinking water is just one village, a couple of dozen cows, one water truck burning a few litres of diesel and pumping a tiny bit of carbon into the air. And The Boy, who perseveres and becomes a man. There are an uncountable number of tiny personal vignettes of the effect of climate change on people and communities around the world. I can't list them all. So start with this simple image, of Tina, Dipa, The Boy and the thirsty white-faced cow with the brown spot on her nose.

I flew home at the end of the summer of 2017, but the drought continued. Two years later, I googled "Drought in Kenya" – and got 13 million hits. I chose the first reference, reported by *Al Jazeera*'s Catherine Wambua-Soi on August 8, 2019:

Kenya Drought: More than a Million People Face Starvation

Below this apocalyptic headline the editors posted a video that opens with a shot of two Samburu women with beaded necklaces and shaven heads against a backdrop of a parched savannah that looks essentially identical to my photos near the villages along the A-2 Road. No grass. The scattered acacia trees in the background are coated with brownish dust and their leaves show only the faintest hint of green. The video shows people on the move with their possessions piled onto skinny burros while they herd emaciated cows and goats.

The printed byline reads: "Drought has left more than a million people on the brink of starvation in northern Kenya. Communities of herders are competing for water and pasture in many of the affected areas."[49]

My first thought is: "Thank you, Tina, for the water truck that saved those cows in the village that I visited, with the woman who offered me a warm glass of goat milk. You must start somewhere. Thank you."

....

49 Catherine Wambua-Soi, "Kenya Drought: More Than a Million People Face Starvation," *Al Jazeera*, August 8, 2019, https://www.aljazeera.com/news/2019/08/kenya-drought-million-people-face-starvation-190808101756682.html.

As I was putting the finishing touches to this manuscript in the spring of 2020, a year after I read the article on the continuing drought, I went back to the internet and learned that the pendulum had swung a full 180 degrees. Now excessive rains, up to 400 per cent of normal, had provided perfect conditions for locust eggs, buried in the soil for decades, to mass-hatch into adults that were voraciously consuming the new bloom of lush vegetation sprouting in natural grasslands and farmers' fields. As a result, northeastern Kenya was suffering under the worst locust infestation in 70 years. In one village, journalists reported that the whole community rose early, shaking bottles filled with pebbles, banging on pots and pans, blowing whistles and honking motorcycle horns to chase off the ravenous flying flocks. But to no avail.

I pull up a May 5, 2020, feature in the *Washington Post* and scroll through the photos of locust horror. They look scary in the impersonal manner of scary articles of human misery that pop up in the news every day. Then, stop. Recalibrate. Look at the photo more closely, Jon. Oh. I have a good memory for landscape. Isn't that Mt. Sabache-Ololokwe in the background? I pull up a photo from my computer library and compare the two. Yes, that's Sabache-Ololokwe in the *Washington Post* article. I am positive of that. Look again. Stop. Recalibrate. That's the A-2 Road in the foreground. No question about that. I'm already afraid of what I will see, but there's no stopping now. The photographer was standing north of the mountain on the east side of the road. Right. He was only a few kilometres from the village where we watered the cows. Where The Boy lives. Where I drank warm milk. Where we brought water to the cows with the truck from Tina's tax refund.

The article states, "With tens of millions of people already dependent on food aid, a humanitarian crisis, or even famine could happen quickly.... Weather conditions are expected to be favorable for locust breeding over the next three months. There are 18 swarms in Kenya right now. But, with government attention almost totally consumed by the covid-19 pandemic, locusts have tumbled down the priority list."[50]

....

50 Max Bearak and Luis Tato, "They're Back. Trillions of Locusts Descend
    on East Africa in Second Wave," *The Washington Post*, May 5, 2020,
    https://www.washingtonpost.com/graphics/world/2020/05/05/
    locusts-africa-swarms-kenya-ethiopia/?itid=lk_inline_manual_9.

My fingers freeze on the keyboard. I don't have words in my vocabulary for this. I don't have pithy metaphors. This isn't 'like' that or 'like' the other thing. Now I pull up a photo of The Boy, with the Anglo name David, with his innocent smile, broad eyes and slight dimples. That photo was taken three years ago. He's 13 now, a young man in body, whereas he was already a full-grown warrior when he was 10. "How are you doing, David?" I ask rhetorically. "Remember how you showed me not to be afraid as the cows were running toward the watering trough?"

The village, already devastated by drought when I was there, is now doubly devastated by the locust plague. No. Triply devastated, because the ongoing Covid-19 pandemic has sickened and killed many Kenyans and also devastated the tourist economy that many depend on.

As if it were possible to be more dead than dead.

I email Tina and ask if there is any way I can send help, assistance, money. A day later she writes:

> A weather phenomenon occurred that had never happened in recorded history there – or in the memory of even the eldest elders: it rained torrentially in Samburu for nearly 18 months, causing massive flash floods with many human and wildlife casualties. The rains were followed by the locust invasions, which wiped out the new grasslands needed by livestock and wildlife as well as crops in the agricultural regions of Kenya. The locust[s] eventually receded but, shockingly, more rains led to a second and then finally a third invasion of locust[s] – both worse than the historic levels of the first invasion. Because this was widespread across much of Kenya, most crops in the agricultural district of Kenya as well as the grazing lands throughout Kenya, including Samburu, were destroyed.
>
> It's been a rough year for the Samburu – now the Covid has further [exacerbated] their situation as all food and medical supplies – those few that were available including aid supplies – were cut off from the region due to travel restrictions, further pushing them into even deeper famine. If the virus does eventually reach that area, it's likely to have devastating impacts given their lack of available medical care,

cultural living practices, and fragile physical state. Needless to say, the camp has been shuttered as all businesses were ordered closed, so even that small income source was lost. I've been doing my best to live very frugally and retain just the barest minimum of my salary so I can share the rest of my own income with them in the meanwhile.[51]

I write back immediately asking if she can put me in contact with Dipa directly. Does he have a bank account? Can I wire money? Tina sends me his cellphone number, along with additional logistical information – followed by:

If there's difficulty getting through, please let me know. He's a bit elusive to connect with at times – always on the front lines of every emergency, as usual. In fact, when a flash flood suddenly swept through the A2 at the Lerata junction on the way to the camp, a UN land rover was carried away in a massive wall of water. As chance would have it, Dipa was traveling just a few minutes behind them and witnessed it. Thankfully, his own car wasn't swept away. He was able to rescue the UN team, their driver and security guard using the winch on his beat up land rover and his belt, of all things, and a few other useful bits he found in the back of the car to jerry-rig a rescue line after the winch snapped. It was a harrowing rescue. He was not able to save the $75,000 Landrover, however, but no lives lost. I think I have a few photos of them somewhere, shouting for help on their overturned vehicle and of Dipa pulling them to safety. I'll try to locate and send them.

I hope you are safe, healthy and well, and at peace in the crazy world around us.

All the best and much love and admiration,

Tina[52]

Okay, regroup. I go for a short walk, take a leak in the forest outside my office. It's been raining lightly, and the new grasses are

---

51 Email from Tina Ramme, July 7, 2020.

52 Email from Tina Ramme, July 7, 2020.

wet, droplets hanging off the leaves in the early morning summer chill in the Montana mountains. The wildflowers are blooming. The elk have recently calved and are starting to herd up again. I am one of the fortunate people to live in a modern paradise. Okay. I'm going to town later to get some welding done on my trailer. But I really need to get in touch with Dipa. I try. Enlist contacts in Nairobi. Try again. Emails back and forth. Dead ends. Eleven days later I get another email from Tina.

> Sorry Dipa and I have been out of touch. Shit sort of hit the wall with the famine and other crises this week. There were 12 deaths due to starvation in 5 days, among other things. He's been putting out a new fire hourly = exhausted = diminished communication.[53]

You can't multiply zero by something and get an answer more consequential than zero. In a similar manner, if there were no words for this situation before, there are really no words now. Really, zero is still zero. Way back in May, which seems like such a long time ago, the *Washington Post* article predicted that a "famine could happen quickly." Now it's July and people are dying of starvation.

I do a little more research. It seems like a contradiction, but the same global warming that can cause drought can also cause excessive rains. Ocean currents, temperature and wave systems are immeasurably complex. When you alter the temperature of the ocean, the epicentres of warm and cold water move in chaotic patterns, altering local weather over nearby land masses, sometimes this way and then that way. Due to a phenomenon called the Indian Ocean Dipole, severe drought and brush fires in Australia are part of the same meteorological event that caused torrential rains on the Horn of Africa.[54] When I was in Samburu, the pendulum had swung toward drought; three years later, it was rain. Rick Overson, a research coordinator at the Global Locust Initiative at Arizona State University wrote, "Locust outbreaks are expected to become more frequent and severe under climate change.... Locusts are

---

53 Email from Tina Ramme, July 18, 2020.

54 https://www.bbc.com/news/science-environment-50602971.

quite adept at responding rapidly and capitalizing on extreme rain-fall events."[55]

I ask Google some more questions. Turns out that the severity of the locust plague is not only linked with global warming but is also tied to the war in Yemen. When governments are stable, infra-structure in place and resources available, nascent locust plagues can be controlled by aerial pesticide spraying. But in war-torn Yemen, people are too busy killing and being killed with bullets and bombs to worry about dying from locusts. So the locust clouds rise, eat all the food left in Yemen and head on over to Ethiopia and Kenya for their next meal.[56]

To summarize: The current famine in Samburu, and throughout the Horn of Africa, is a complex tragedy caused by three interlock-ing catastrophes: global warming, Covid-19 (which not only causes sickness and death directly but also exacerbates the problem by reducing tourism dollars to near zero) and war. I ask: "How did we, as a species, bumble into this mess, where we have all the knowledge to send rocket ships into space, but we can't manage our own sur-vival?" And the important corollary, "Can we turn this ship around, so the savannah pastures support both wild and domestic grazers in Samburu (and elsewhere), so The Boy grows into a wise old man bouncing grandchildren on his knees? Can we turn this ship around so human population and consumption once again conform to the carrying capacity of the Earth?"

Don't expect me to supply absolute answers, and please don't ask for a checklist of "Things to Do to Save the Earth" – (a) recycle your plastic bags; (b) defund all global militaries; (c) and so forth. Those checklists are very nice, and we need them, but they only skim the surface of the problem. After a million such checklists, the problems keep getting worse.

....

55 David Herbling and Samuel Gebre, "Locust Swarms Ravaging East Africa Are the Size of Cities," *Bloomberg Green*, February 18, 2020, https://www.bloomberg.com/features/2020-africa-locusts/.

56 Linda Givetash, "A Plague Amid a Pandemic: East Africa, West Asia Combat Surging Locust Outbreak," *NBC News*, June 22, 2020, https://www.nbcnews.com/news/world/plague-amid-pandemic-east-africa-west-asia-combat-surging-locust-n1231669.

Enough mumbo-jumbo. There are starving people out there who need to eat. After a few emails back and forth, Tina sends me a protocol to wire money to Dipa. The friendly wire transfer agent at Fidelity Investments has instructions to be on the lookout for money laundering, especially, apparently, if I am wiring money to someplace like Kenya. He asks why I am sending the money. I tell him the whole story. He googles me, googles Tina, then checks that the books listed on my website are real, i.e., that they are also listed on Amazon. He's a busy man, but he takes time to ask what *The Raven's Gift* is about. I tell him it's about the wisdoms of a Siberian shaman and about Cultural Survival, which is what this wire transfer is about. He okays the wire and keys in the routing numbers to send Dipa $500 to buy food. Long term, the Samburu need help with basic infrastructure, akin to the water truck Tina bought during the drought. But right now, they need to eat to stay alive. How is David, The Boy, doing this instant?

Along with the wire transfer of $500 I ask Tina to explain that I am prepared to send another $500. But I need some documentation. So could Dipa please photograph the purchase and distribution of food? Perhaps the most educated of the young Samburu I met, Tiepe, would take on the task of providing feedback information for me. I would pay him a generous wage. If all that works out, I could start something on Facebook, or GoFundMe, and crowd-source a bunch of money to feed the villages. I am here to help.

I get the following email from Tina:

> Hi Jon,
>
> I have spoken to Dipa early this morning and the funds have arrived!
>
> Thank you! He will travel to Isiolo today to get them from the bank and pick up supplies for the villagers. I'll be sending information, messages and photos as they arrive. "Kei supat oleng oleng," to quote him directly. (Thank you very, very much)

In the meanwhile, here's a brief synopsis of some of Dipa's comments and the situation on the ground and some photos I had from just before the lockdown.

Dipa said he is so grateful for the funds. The first thing he'd like to do is emergency intervention to bring food and medicine to those affected by the locust massive invasions and famine. Some children have been attacked by locusts, so he plans to bring medication for open wounds and infections. If there are future funds, he may use them for other projects, but they are in crisis mode at the moment.

He is so happy that you're doing this to help the Samburu! He knows it's way beyond what I can do on my own, try as I might.

Blocking food and medical supplies has been a strategy used in the past by the gov, which we've termed 'passive genocide'. I'm not sure if it was intentional this time or just neglect, but the Samburu are quite invisible nation-wide and one of the most marginalized and oppressed tribes in the Horn of Africa.

Thankfully, Dipa has found an unconventional source to get supplies through but is very limited by resources. This is why it felt like a miracle from the universe when you stepped in! At least he's connected with a group who can legally travel across closed borders and is willing to make an occasional delivery whenever he can find the means to get these critically needed supplies.

I, too, am personally grateful for this help, Jon! It really means a lot to know you care enough to try to help them in this way.

Much love,

Tina

I respond:

Okay. Thank you for this note, Tina:

It brings tears to my eyes.

Next time you speak with Dipa please tell him this:

I am very happy to send these funds under these terrible circumstances.

Please keep up the news and photos, and I will send another $500 in a few weeks, when I can gather the money. That is a promise. As I said, I am happy to do this.

And yes, of course, I fully expected that Dipa would use the current money for emergency food and medicines. Perfect. We will worry about the future in the future.

I only spent a few weeks in Samburu, but as I write this book and relive my experiences, I realize how much richness of spirit I witnessed, how much I learned, how meaningful my friendships had become.

So, as I just said. I will definitely send another $500 in a few weeks. Dipa can count on my word. It will take a little more work and effort to build a web page and launch a social media campaign, and the outcome of that is uncertain. But let's take this one step at a time.

Much love to you, Dipa, and all those people he represents and is helping.

Jon

Over the next few days, I feel like a teenager waiting for a call for a prom date, or an author waiting to receive a hoped-for acceptance of a manuscript. I reason that my follow-up information from Samburu will be delayed at least a week, so not to worry. When I don't hear anything in two weeks, I feel deflated. What happened? Why or where did our communication falter? I reread my emails and, yes, I was clear that at least another $500 would be forthcoming if we could establish a conduit for communication. A photo or two of food purchase and distribution in real time, and not from Tina's archives, would put my mind at ease.

I wait until I am convinced that no response will show up. Okay. What are my options?

I am reminded of an aphorism often repeated by a dear friend in China. "You may travel in China, study Chinese history, and you may even write about China. But you know nothing about China."

In parallel, I know nothing about Kenya, I know nothing about the Samburu culture, I know a little about Dipa, or maybe a lot, that he is a straightforward, honest, likeable, generous, caring human being, and I enjoyed his company immensely. He had a power that is impossible to describe. So. There has been some cross-cultural failure in communication. But if there is no reliable communication, is it wise to send more money anyway? Certainly, I can't do a crowd-source thing and solicit other people's money, unless I have absolutely bomb-proof documentation accounting for every penny. My romantic self tells me I could jump on an airplane with a pocket full of $100 bills and buy and distribute food myself. But that's ridiculous for many reasons: First, even if I wanted to take a temporary absence from my wife and my life, and even if I could rationalize burning up a whole bunch of fossil fuel for an airplane trip, and even if I could sort out all the complex logistics of finding Dipa and distributing food effectively and fairly, and not get robbed along the way, I would spend way more than $500 on travel expenses. In this modern age, this is not a viable and efficient way to achieve a given task. And, anyway, even if none of these hurdles stood in my way, Covid is raging and the border into Kenya is closed. The airplanes are grounded.

I read in the news that a second wave of locusts has descended in Samburu, a third wave of disaster (counting the drought), or a fourth, or a billionth, depending on when and where you draw the starting line. This is tragedy beyond anything I have experienced in my life: not merely the death of an individual, or 100 individuals, but the destruction of a culture. Am I as powerless as I think I am?

In his great novel *Heart of Darkness*, Joseph Conrad describes a British warship firing cannonballs in some crazy war on the coast of Africa. Bang goes the cannon. Puff goes a small cloud of smoke from the muzzle. Whizz, kerplunk goes the cannon ball, landing in the rainforest. And then silence. Nothing. No screams. No return cannonballs, or arrows. No village aflame. No village in sight, period. Nothing. Shooting a cannonball into a continent. I feel as if my $500 was one of those cannonballs, a benevolent cannonball, but just as inconsequential. Did it really happen? The money left my bank account. Tina tells me that Dipa received it and bought food with it, and I have no reason to doubt that. But I would love to have some feedback. Did the money stave off hunger for someone for a day? A week? A month? Did it save a child's life? Could I see a face? Bang. Puff. Kerplunk. And then silence. Five hundred dollars landing amid a continent of misery. I know there are physical and cultural barriers to communication, but there is too much uncertainty, so I don't call the friendly broker at Fidelity to wire another $500.

How do you attach an emotional image onto this catastrophe? In an op-ed piece in the *New York Times*, Nicholas Kristof wrote that an injured or sick child will cry to communicate his or her distress. But starving children don't cry. They can't spare the metabolic energy for tears. They lie, inert, breathing – barely – nothing else – waiting until either food or death arrives.

I'd like to think that human beings, with our big brains and all, altruistic within our tribe, so capable of surviving on the savannah and building rocket ships to the moon, should be able to feed a few hungry kids whose lives are upended by the global warming caused by all of our affluence. But 'I'd like to think' or it 'seems to me' are not the same as a bowl of rice and a glass of milk delivered and distributed to a Samburu village.

We need to feed hungry children now; they can't wait for some pie-in-the-sky global consciousness shift. I weigh my options, fret and worry.

I write a draft of an email to Tina: "Dear Tina; I am trying to follow up on sending more money to Dipa...." And so forth. But I know nothing about Africa.

I see photos of people suffering. That is real.

But I know nothing about Africa. I have good intentions. But locusts know nothing about my good intentions. I delete the email to Tina. And then I write a cheque to Doctors Without Borders. The medical personnel who travel to ravaged lands are brave beyond comprehension, and the charity administration has infrastructure in place to convert money into help. I google around and then send more money to the UN Refugee Agency (UNHCR) and to the Bill and Melinda Gates Foundation. This isn't the same as helping my individual friends who were kind to me, but I am guaranteed that I am helping needy people, somewhere in the world, who desperately need help.

As I said in the preface, I have been trying to make a positive contribution for my entire life. I can't evaluate my own effectiveness (or hopelessness). So, in addition to these few cannonballs of money, I write this book, hoping that these words will make some minuscule additional contribution to a much-needed, much-discussed and much-dreamed-about global consciousness shift.

Words – not rice and milk. Don't overthink this. That is what I have to offer right now. I write with a heavy heart sometimes, but I continue to write.

— — —

You must ask why humanity has allowed itself to create its own problems. Why have we stopped listening to the Earth? Why have we allowed our power to render us powerless? Why are we altering the climate that sustains us? Why do we allow people to starve when there is ample food on the planet? Big questions. Perhaps too big to answer with any precision. But to understand the depth of the problems we face, I believe we must transcend the politics and economics of the immediate situation and look at the human condition holistically, from our evolutionary beginnings. And to do that, let's return to our history of storytelling.

The size of traditional Paleolithic hunter-gatherer communities is limited by two factors. The first, and most basic, is the availability of food and water. In most environments, if you are hunting with primitive weapons, the density and availability of both plant and animal resources in the surrounding ecosystem limits your tribe to about 20–30 people. Thus, most Indigenous groups live most of their lives in small family bands, and then gather into larger groups and tribes for festivals. People visit and party, and teenagers have an opportunity to select potential mates from outside the immediate family before the bands disperse again.

In other instances, enough food is available to support larger bands. Coastal communities draw their food from the vast ocean, and, for example, salmon-fishing cultures have the luxury of relying on a food source that concentrates reliably at a predictable time of year. But even in these cases, where food availability is not a limiting factor, a second limit arises. As discussed in Chapter 3, our brains are large and clever enough to store a reasonably intimate knowledge of about 150 people. Within this group size, we can co-operate effect-ively with our neighbours, enforce order and punish or discourage cheaters. But if the human group size grows much larger than 150, we can't keep up with all of the cultural complexities of the group.

Despite these two limitations, starting around 12,000 years ago, *Homo sapiens* began to congregate in groups that were much larger than 150 individuals. The traditional argument is that people learned to increase the yields of natural seed-bearing plants by discovering agriculture: plowing, planting, removing weeds and adding water. When food became more concentrated, people congregated in greater density and number. Then they became better farmers, so the food density increased even more, so the density of humans increased even more ... until large settlements and then cities spread across the region. The problem with this simple explanation, as with most intui-tive explanations of human history and behaviour, is that it doesn't quite jive with the data in the archeological record.

In 1995, archeologists unearthed an 11,500-year-old site in south-east Turkey called Göbekli Tepe. In the deepest and oldest layer, they found the ruins of ten temples that in their ancient glory were sup-ported by elaborately carved pillars five metres high and weighing up to seven tons. Yet the scientists found no relics of permanent human housing in this old layer of soil: no city, and no farms. The best guess is that thousands of hunter-gatherers collected here, in temporary camps, co-operated over an extended period of time and expended a tremendous amount of group time and energy – to create a place of worship – in response to some elaborate mythology. This is the Paleolithic serpent cave in the Kalahari Desert on steroids. Further evidence indicates that the cultivation of wheat came *after* all these people gathered to build the temples and pray in them. In this chron-ology, temples came first, followed by cities, and then agriculture, rather than the other way around.

Recall our earlier discussion, that during the Cognitive Revolution, technological advancements such as the bow and arrow and the sewing needle did not come first, paving the way for art and mythology to tag along later. Rather the whole assemblage evolved as different expres-sions of the same mental and cultural awakenings. Here we find that elaborate mythologies were the catalyst to jump-start unprecedented tribal co-operation, involving almost unthinkable effort by a huge number of people, over many generations. The next great pragmatic discovery, farming, came after the first cities, giving rise to the Agricultural Revolution. As farmers congregated and stayed tied to their land, populations concentrated, so the Agricultural Revolution became the Agricultural-Urban Revolution.

The great enigma is that cities and agriculture diminished the quality of life, considerably, in many ways.

The work week got longer. In many hunter-gatherer societies, people work 15–20 hours a week; in harsher environments that total may jump up to 40 hours per week. But now you add the effort to build a temple, and that cuts into your free time. And it didn't end there. Jumping into the present, in North American affluent societies, with an unprecedented array of time-saving gadgets, people average 40–45 hours on the job site per week, and that doesn't count doing dishes and mowing the lawn during your time off from work. And in the developing world today, people commonly work 60 or even 80 hours a week before they stagger home to do domestic chores.

Second, the work week got boring and repetitive. In hunter-gatherer societies, there are a multitude of different tasks that need to be accomplished every day. Climb a hill and scan the horizon for antelope. Pick some yummy fruit off a favourite tree. Move camp to a new location. Knap arrowheads. It is an interesting and varied life. In contrast, early farmers dug, hoed and carried water under the hot sun. And when tomorrow came, they dug, hoed and carried water again. Although in the developed world, robots have assumed many repetitive tasks, in many parts of the world, even today, factory workers repeat mind-numbing tasks over and over, for years and decades – for an entire lifespan.

Repetitive work in fields, and later factories, led to serious chronic use injuries. The farmers of the Agricultural Revolution and many workers in the more modern Industrial Revolution and Scientific Revolution have endured and continue to endure bone-deforming injuries of the spine, neck, wrist, ankles, elbow and whatever other part of the body takes the brunt of the trauma. Hunting and gathering activities, while hard in many ways, are varied enough so repetitive use injuries are much less common.

While the Agricultural Revolution led to an increase in the total quantity of food, it simultaneously led to a dramatic *decrease* in the quality of nutrition. Hunter-gatherers eat a variety of roots, berries, fruits, seeds and meat that supplies a complementary mélange of vitamins, minerals, starches and proteins. While members of affluent 21st-century societies have an unprecedented variety and quality of foods displayed lavishly in local grocery stores, the field workers in both primitive and modern, but impoverished, agricultural societies ate (and eat) monotonous and unhealthy diets with high concentrations of a single starchy grain: wheat, rice, corn or other calorie-rich seeds lacking a full complement of nutrients. Due to inadequate diets, average height for men decreased from 178 cm (5'10") during the hunter-gathering period to 165 cm (5'5") after our ancestors took up farming, while women's height decreased from 165 cm (5'5") to 155 cm (5'1").

And that was during the good times. While hunter-gatherers are certainly no strangers to occasional hunger, farmers are reliant on monoculture that is particularly vulnerable to drought, pestilence, plague, fungal infestation and locust attack. And if you lose your crop, you starve for a year, not a day, a week or a month.

Any time individuals of a single species, whether it be wheat or humans, congregate in densely populated communities, the threat of pathogenic disease epidemics increases dramatically. Just as Neolithic farmers had to contend with pest and disease outbreaks in their crops, and later of their cattle, they simultaneously suffered from disease epidemics that proliferated in their often fetid, closely crammed cities. The bubonic plague, often called the Black Death, ravaged cities in medieval Europe, killing between 25 and 50 per cent of the population. In 2020 and 2021, the Covid-19 pandemic raged across the globe. As I sit at the computer today, in late April 2021, vaccine development and dispersal gives us hope, but exploding caseloads in India and portions of South America, coupled with the evolution of new variants, remind us that the pandemic is not over.

Finally, while hunter-gatherers have engaged in tribal warfare in almost every culture on the planet, because farmers relied for their survival on the crops planted in their fields, they had far more incentive to defend their territory than did hunter-gatherers, who often could avoid violence from interlopers by moving on. When you put a tremendous amount of effort into growing a crop, and then need to store this wealth until next harvest, you become vulnerable to attack. As a result, agriculture led to an increase in warfare. In primitive agricultural communities in New Guinea, intertribal violence accounted for 35 per cent of male deaths, whereas in South America, 50 per cent of all adults, of both sexes, met a violent death at the hands of other humans.

The Biblical story of the ten plagues of Egypt documents both the ubiquity and severity of the trials and tribulations facing Neolithic farmers and city dwellers: water turning to blood, frogs, lice and gnats, wild animals, pestilences of livestock, boils, thunderstorms of hail and fire, locusts, darkness. And, finally, the clincher, death of the firstborn. As the Bible tells us: "Every firstborn son in Egypt will die, from the firstborn son of Pharaoh, who sits on the throne, to the firstborn of the slave girl, who is at her hand mill, and all the firstborn of the cattle as well. There will be loud wailing throughout Egypt – worse than there has ever been or ever will be again."[57]

How do you convince people to move out of the forests and savannahs, from an exciting and varied life of relative ease, longevity and health, and toil for the rest of their lives chipping and moving rocks to build the temples of Göbekli Tepe, or the pyramids of Egypt, to hoe fields and haul water, repeatedly, day after day, year after year, generation after generation? It's a wild and crazy question. Sometimes you simply enslave half the population by force of arms. But that's only part of the answer. A more essential component of this transition out of paradise begins with our deep-seated, genetic, sometimes species-saving propensity to gather around the campfire and build tribal unity by telling and listening to stories.

So ... we moved out of the Garden because someone told us a story that God ordered us to. And who can argue or reason with a good story loaded with the word *God*?

"And out of the ground made the LORD God to grow every tree that is pleasant to the sight, and good for food."

But the serpent convinced Eve to eat the cursed apple from the Tree of Knowledge.

And God got pissed off. So....

---

57 Exodus 11:4–6 (New International Version).

"In the sweat of thy face shalt thou eat bread, till thou return unto the ground; for out of it wast thou taken: for dust thou art, and unto dust shalt thou return."[58]

Harari argues that all religious and political manifestos outlining who we are, and how we should lead our lives, are documents that construct, not reality but *imagined orders*. The Bible, the Code of Hammurabi and the Constitution of Canada are all imagined orders. The laws of physics are immutable. Gravity is gravity; it's not going to change and there is nothing you can do about it. In contrast, imagined orders are inventions of the human mind, based on myths, which are also inventions of the human mind. Our leaders assure us that our systems of government rest on intrinsic principles of human behaviour, coupled with political and economic science, but these principles are not immutable, like gravity. Instead, they change all the time, depending on the whims of whatever leader is in power. For example, the Koryak elder I have spoken about, Moolynaut, was born into an immediate, observable, reality of life in a skin tent clustered together with a small tribe of reindeer herders on the remote frozen tundra. But the umbrella *imagined* order, imposed from afar, was that Czar Nicholas II was the Great Father whose wisdom and iron-fisted discipline extended from the streets of St. Petersburg to the Pacific coastal tundra of Kamchatka. Then, by the time Moolynaut was a teenager, whoops, that imagined order was wrong. Now, the Soviet Socialist government, made up of the collective minds and hearts of the workers, created the rules to live by. Well, not exactly. Stalin co-opted the basic Marxist doctrine and tweaked it into a dictatorship, which you'd better believe in, or off to the Gulag with you. The imagined order changed again and became something called a democracy, which was effectively a bandito-capitalist kleptocracy, until it became a bandito-capitalist de facto dictatorship under Putin.

The ancient cities of the Middle East, which formed between 11,500 and 9,000 years ago, had populations of a few to several thousand. But remember, when a community enlarges beyond 150 individuals, the management techniques of egalitarian societies, where everyone is my friend, or at least a well-understood antagonist, break down. Now you needed a hierarchy, a ruler, a command structure,

---

58   Genesis 2:9 and 3:19 (King James Version).

Jon Turk

police and standing armies. As a result, the new cities gave us kings on a throne to rule and pass judgment, to reward and punish.

And then: It's no coincidence that Abraham threw the old idols out of the temple. The Paleolithic hunter-gatherer's animistic spiritual beliefs that honoured the sentience of everything – people, cows, rocks, acacia trees – had no hierarchy. The new religions gave us God on a throne to rule and pass judgment, to reward and punish.

It shouldn't be surprising that kings rose to power and maintained their power by becoming master storytellers. And that's where the trajectory of human history takes an abrupt turn. As I explained earlier, whereas non-human primates developed rudimentary storytelling and consequent cheating, humans, with much bigger brains and sophisticated language, developed more sophisticated storytelling as a means of drawing people together in small bands, to bond into a cohesive, co-operative unit around ancient campfires and to protect the tribe from hyenas. Then, during the Agricultural-Urban Revolution, kings, priests and dictators hijacked storytelling within the new cities into a means of separating people and, all too often, controlling them. Humanity was already hard-wired to be enthralled by tales of serpent gods, lion-headed men, or bird-headed men with giant erections. People seeking power and riches simply had to tweak these stories into fictions that convinced their subjects to believe in what the leaders wanted them to believe in – imagined orders – frequently not for the common good, but for the good of the few.

In a provocative opinion piece in the *New York Times* titled "Why Fiction Trumps Truth," Harari writes: "Many people believe that truth conveys power. [You would think that] If some leaders, religions, or ideologies misrepresent reality, they will eventually lose to more clear-sighted rivals. Hence, sticking with the truth is the best strategy for gaining power. Unfortunately, this is just a comforting myth."[59]

He goes on to argue that there are two kinds of power. Scientific power, the ability to build computers and atomic bombs, requires adherence to data, to telling the truth. Social power, in contrast, is

---

59 Yuval Noah Harari, "Why Fiction Trumps Truth," *The New York Times*, May 24, 2019, https://www.nytimes.com/2019/05/24/opinion/why-fiction-trumps-truth.html.

the ability to "manipulate people's beliefs, thereby getting people to cooperate effectively."[60] If you have a city full of people who are not closely related to each other, and may not even know each other, the only effective way to convince them to coalesce and co-operate around a common goal is to create common stories. But these stories don't need to be true. In fact, the more outrageous the story, or the myth, or the lie, the more effective it is.

Harari again: "Humans know many more truths than any other animal, but we also believe in much more nonsense.... Rabbits don't know that $E=mc^2$.... But no rabbit would have been willing to crash an airplane into the World Trade Center in the hope of being rewarded with 72 virgin rabbits in the afterlife."[61]

But why does convincing people of outrageous falsehoods work? Why do these stories convey power to the rulers, benevolent and evil, who create them? As I stated above, truth is essential for science and technology. When people migrated into the Arctic, they needed to know that bone is stronger than wood, and can be used to make sewing needles, to produce warm clothes. They also needed to know that wood burns more efficiently than bone to produce life-saving warmth. The sun rises in the east, summer comes after spring. All these facts are universal and essential for survival. The people in my tribe know them and the people in that other tribe across the river know the same facts. If you believe in an alternate reality, you die. But social power requires the opposite. If someone invents a story of the Chief of the Below World, or virgin rabbits in the afterlife, or Adam and Eve, then that story projects a collective, bonding memory – an identity common to my tribe, city state, nation or religion. Our stories create a discernible difference between US and THEM. And then THEM turn into those infidels across the river who think that our stories are a bunch of hogwash. Followed, naturally, by: we are better. Followed by: actually, you are scum. Followed by: it's okay, or

---

60 Yuval Noah Harari, "Why Fiction Trumps Truth," *The New York Times*, May 24, 2019, https://www.nytimes.com/2019/05/24/opinion/why-fiction-trumps-truth.html.

61 Yuval Noah Harari, "Why Fiction Trumps Truth," *The New York Times*, May 24, 2019, https://www.nytimes.com/2019/05/24/opinion/why-fiction-trumps-truth.html.

it's my right, or my obligation, to kill you. Collective group stories are so powerful that, today, two people of the same group, a religion for example, who live on separate continents, who will never be within 10,000 kilometres of each other, who have no relatives in common, will co-operatively support a charity, or a war, based on fictional characters and events that cannot possibly exist.

When people congregated into cities, they needed leaders to unite them and administer practical needs. These leaders intuited that truth was a poor vehicle to unite people around common causes. Harari continues, "Socrates chose the truth and was executed. The most powerful scholarly establishments in history – whether of Christian priests, Confucian mandarins, or Communist ideologues – placed unity above truth. That's why they are so powerful."[62]

People find it easy to believe that so-called primitive Indigenous tribes in some forgotten desert or rainforest coalesce around the campfire on the summer solstice, drumming, dancing and singing strange tales of ghosts and spirits. But listen, with an open mind, to politicians on the evening news, or corporate lawyers, or any advertisement anywhere, and you will hear far stranger tales about people, places, events and fantasies that do not, never did and never will exist.

Find it hard to accept that our super-sophisticated brains, with their 100 billion neurons, the product of eons of evolution, which insured our survival on the harsh savannah, capable of inventing all the marvelous gadgetry of the 21st century, could be so hood-winked to rally 'round the flag, boys, and march into death over a myth invented by some evil king, intent on concentrating power for himself? Yeah, it is hard to believe. Because there are no beautiful maidens in this story. Because it is the truth.

And if it weren't bad enough that our engaging, playful stories within the tribe about fair maidens and virgins in the afterlife eventually gave us permission – or encouraged us – to commit intertribal or international murder, to rape and enslave fellow humans, we have to face the fact that these same mythologies initiated a long, twisted path of human history that has given us permission to alter the planetary

....

62 Yuval Noah Harari, "Why Fiction Trumps Truth," *The New York Times*, May 24, 2019, https://www.nytimes.com/2019/05/24/opinion/why-fiction-trumps-truth.html.

climate, which has inexorably led to those skinny, thirsty cows on the parched desert with no grass, followed by the locust plagues and The Boy out there, starving, struggling to survive.

The Agricultural Revolution brought us misery, toil, pestilence, war and disease. Malnourishment stunted our growth. But we sure learned to produce a big pile of calories. And it was easier to raise a bunch of babies in a central house than in nomadic camps. As a result, despite all the negatives, the human population exploded. As we gathered into unified cultures, people exchanged ideas and innovation flourished. Welcome to the Industrial Revolution. The lives for many people improved dramatically. But not for the men who dug the coal out of the earth. They worked long hours underground, frequently died in mine accidents and almost universally succumbed at an early age to black lung disease. Not for the garment workers who sat in front of a sewing machine at the tender age of 14 and then worked 12 or 14 hours a day at that machine, six days a week, coming home to eat a meagre meal and sleep until the alarm rang the next morning – for the rest of their too-short lives. And then we kept getting so much better at thinking about things that don't exist that we entered the Scientific Revolution, and the 21st-century Computer Revolution. A lot has changed. And nothing has changed. Today, the wealth disparity between the haves and the have-nots is at least as great as it was way back when the ancient kings of Babylon ruled the earliest nations in the Fertile Crescent. How did that happen? Why don't the 99 per cent rebel? Throw off the yoke? I've already told you the answer. Because the 1 per cent have been and continue to be really, really good storytellers. As *New York Times* columnist David Brooks writes, "Political viewpoints are not explorations of truth; they are weapons that dominant groups use to maintain their place in the power structure."[63]

I've made my living as a mid-level author, not a hedge fund guru, and I have no particular fame beyond a few thousand readers scattered about willy-nilly, here and there. Yet I own two houses, two cars and the best skis and mountain bikes money can buy. Every time I go to the grocery store, I buy produce and grains from all over the

---

63 David Brooks, "America Is Facing 5 Epic Crises All at Once," *The New York Times*, June 25, 2020, https://www.nytimes.com/2020/06/25/opinion/us-coronavirus-protests.html.

world, and when I am in need, my health is cared for and broken bones set in gleamingly clean hospitals by highly trained health care workers aided by machines unimaginable a generation or even a decade ago. Yet there's a fundamental imbalance here. Just step into a Samburu hut and open your eyes. Or open your eyes wider and view a global landscape, hydrology and climate so severely altered that we have entered a new geological epoch, the Anthropocene: the age where humans have become a global geological force to alter the planet in dangerous and nefarious ways. Or welcome to 2020 and step into a physical and economic world torn apart by Covid-19.

If you could pack 100,000 chimpanzees, shoulder to shoulder, in Times Square on New Year's Eve, pandemonium would break out. They would bite, tear, gouge, strike and kill one another in droves. When 100,000 people collect in Times Square, there are pickpockets and drunks, and fist fights here and there, but in general, people bump and jostle with strangers, smile, get drunk and celebrate. Except for ants, bees and termites, and despite uncountable wars and pogroms, humans are the most successful co-operative species on the planet. The fundamental, inescapable dilemma is that, even though our stories frequently cause Big Trouble, there is no alternative way to manage the uber-complex industrial global society of close to eight billion people without imagined orders – stories – mythology. Governments and religions establish laws and creeds to mandate peaceful coexistence, promote art, justice, philosophy, charity, trade and law enforcement, and to build infrastructure. At the same time, governments and religions have been at the spear point of warfare, ruin, destruction and persecution. Yin and Yang, good and evil, all one.

Harari argues that, throughout history, no king, dictator, prime minister, president, priest, rabbi, imam, sage, poet, songwriter, philosopher, madman or saint has ever succeeded in removing the facade of imagined orders from human societies and cultures. Societies frequently morph from one system to another – from democratic to dictatorial, peaceful to belligerent, unjust to just. But all systems, and all changes from one system to another, are either based on an existing mythology or generated by exchanging one mythology for another. There is no such thing as a management system based on fundamental immutable laws of nature, like gravity. Real (non-mythological) management systems went out with the Stone Age when government was a council of grandparents, parents, uncles and aunts, when food was shared because my fortune in hunting today will undoubtedly be followed by your fortune tomorrow.

As an extreme example, and I apologize in advance for going here: In the United States in the late 20th and early 21st centuries, the Republican Party created a mythology that our imaginary government needed to balance its imaginary budget – and they won elections. Then they realized that, whoops, they needed to reward themselves and their supporters for winning elections by creating such a clever mythology. So they created a new mythology that we needed to give tax cuts to the rich. Incredibly, enough human worker bees were so committed to a mythology called the Republican Party that they said, "Oh, what a good idea. Let me give you great sums of my money." "Let me work hard while you take away my health care." "Let me vote for you."

You can't calmly and logically figure this system out. That's impossible. Paradoxically, our monstrously huge, human, think-too-much-know-it-all brains make us too gullible. You see, money is imaginary as well. If you turn on your computer, enter your username and password, pull up your account summary, and learn that you have $1,000 in your bank account, what does that mean? Of the $1,000 that the computer screen tells you that you have, only 10 per cent, or $100, is backed by currency. The other $900 is something else that economists assure me that they understand, but to cut through a lot of mumbo-jumbo, I'll call it a mythology. A representation of something but not the thing itself. Now, what about that ironclad $100? It's upheld by currency, which is paper money, which consists of promissory notes, which can be printed or shredded at the whim of central bankers. Yes, this system has been working well enough for me, because I live in a country where the central bankers can print money with impunity, so I own fine skis and all that stuff that I talked about a page or two ago. And I know that no one has come up with a viable alternative in this oil-soaked, overpopulated, consumer-oriented, supply chain dependent, climate-altered, Covid-19-wracked society, but you have to admit, at least, that it's funny. Or scary. Or oppressive. Depending on which side of the bed you woke up on this morning. Or which culture you were born into.

So ... the imaginary tribe called the Republican Party became head of the imaginary entity called the United States government and

Jon Turk

scarfed up most of the imaginary money. And then Covid-19 came along, so the imaginary government needed more money, which they didn't have, so they decided to borrow it. But they couldn't find enough money to borrow. So ... the one arm of the government created a whole lot of money out of thin air and used that thin-air money to buy the bonds that another arm of the government across the street were floating because they didn't have enough imaginary money. So ... poof, a few trillion extra dollars of imaginary money became reality (in a sense), and thus the government was able to boost something called the economy.

I have intentionally worded this paragraph to make it sound goofy, but if you think I'm joking, you can read this same information in academic language, in a policy manifesto published by the prestigious Brookings Institute.[64]

Goofy or academic, the system works. As I said above, we're not likely to return to the gold standard. Well ... the system works for most people most of the time, or some of the people some of the time. In any case, in this instance, imaginary money did help millions of people pay their rent and go to the store to buy carrots and milk.

I'm not an economist; I didn't even take Econ 101 in college. It doesn't matter what I think about global economic policy, or what you think either. But I do believe that it is important to understand that money isn't real. As a result, your physical reality – the food you eat, the gas you put in your car and the skis you wear on your feet – are all conditional on someone's imagined reality. If you're poor, the ravages of poverty are real, not imagined. But the underlying reasons for the unpaid utility bills on your desk and the hungry children in your kitchen are primarily the policy decisions (imagination) of those in power. In a similar vein, if humanity's excess consumption is destroying planetary ecosystems, this devastation is real to the polar bears who can't hunt on thin ice and all the other plants and animals (including people) under stress. But, again, this destruction stems largely from all the aggregated policy decisions (imagination) that are implemented by the people we have installed on the top of this human hierarchy we happen to live in at the moment.

....

64 https://www.brookings.edu/blog/up-front/2020/03/25/where-is-the-u-s-gov-ernment-getting-all-the-money-its-spending-in-the-coronavirus-crisis/.

And all those policy decisions, regarding poverty or environmental destruction, or anything else, are – at least in theory – subject to change if we collectively care enough.

And while we're at it, don't forget that at the same time the less privileged people went to the grocery store to buy non-imaginary carrots and milk with their Covid relief money, a whole bunch of the imaginary money ended up boosting the imaginary stock market so the rich got to buy non-imaginary yachts, mansions and private airplanes. While fossil fuel emissions took a little breather and were reduced temporarily during the Covid pandemic, eventually the whole system created a continuation of the burning of fossil fuels due to these yachts, mansions and airplanes, which has led to a continuation of global warming, which causes drought and locust plagues for The Boy – who knows how to protect his cows from a non-imaginary lion but has little understanding of, or access to, imaginary money.

———   ———   ———

So, for 11,000 or 12,000 years our leaders have been lying and cajoling and fooling us into a cascading tower of imagined orders leading to a concrete, observable, verifiable reality where I eat kiwis for breakfast in the middle of a northern winter and The Boy is out there on the savannah banging pots and pans in a tragic, futile, doomed effort to scare the locusts away so the grass will grow, so the cows will live, so he will live. How do we, how do I, make sense of that reality in any cogent, functional way? Well, earlier I promised not to offer up a checklist of "Things to Do to Save the Earth." Now I promise not to explain in clear and simple, well-crafted paragraphs how to make sense of the world we live in. Because I have absolutely no idea what I might say in those fictional, well-crafted paragraphs. But I can step out of the world of imagined orders and myth, put on my old science writer's thinking cap and address one question that should be on everyone's mind.

Because imagined orders have created this oil-soaked, overpopulated, consumer-oriented, supply chain dependent, climate-altered, locust-plagued society, let's ask: How bad is this climate change crisis – really? As you would expect, there's a wide range of opinion:

On September 23, 2019, 16-year-old climate activist Greta Thunberg told the United Nations Climate Action Summit:

> This is all wrong. I shouldn't be up here. I should be back in school on the other side of the ocean. Yet you all come to us young people for hope. How dare you! You have stolen my dreams and my childhood with your empty words. And yet I'm one of the lucky ones. People are suffering. People are dying. Entire ecosystems are collapsing. We are in the beginning of a mass extinction, and all you can talk about is money and fairy tales of eternal economic growth. How dare you!
>
> For more than 30 years, the science has been crystal clear. How dare you continue to look away and come here saying that you're doing enough, when the politics and solutions needed are still nowhere in sight.[65]

To which Donald Trump responded several months later at the World Economic Forum in Davos, Switzerland, "To embrace the possibilities of tomorrow, we must reject the perennial prophets of doom and their predictions of the apocalypse."[66]

To which billionaire investor Anthony Scaramucci commented in an interview with the *Washington Post* (over a quadruple espresso): "I would say that in the last 50 years, collectively, we're having a frat party with the environment. Now Greta and her children and my grandchildren and great-grandchildren are going to be living in the frat house on Sunday morning after we destroyed the place on Saturday night. And so the problem is: When you are an impermanent person on Earth and you're enjoying the frat party, it's very hard for you to stop the frat party."[67]

---

65 https://www.npr.org/2019/09/23/763452863/
transcript-greta-thunbergs-speech-at-the-u-n-climate-action-summit.

66 Dan Zak, "Will Davos Save the World or Put It Out of Its Misery?" *The Washington Post*, January 24, 2020, https://www.washingtonpost.com/lifestyle/2020/01/24/will-davos-save-world-or-put-it-out-its-misery/?arc404=true.

67 Dan Zak, "Will Davos Save the World or Put It Out of Its Misery?" *The Washington Post*, January 24, 2020, https://www.washingtonpost.com/lifestyle/2020/01/24/will-davos-save-world-or-put-it-out-its-misery/?arc404=true.

In my previous career, as a college-level science textbook writer, I reported on climate change for 40 years. I would have to write a different book if I were to attempt to document the careful work of the IPCC (Intergovernmental Panel on Climate Change) and other learned scientific individuals, groups and commissions and to outline all the fundamental changes to planetary systems related to climate change. And looking into the future, we can postulate a dizzying array of scenarios, predictions, possible outcomes. However, we do know that, as of early 2020, human burning of fossil fuels has raised the global atmospheric carbon dioxide concentration from 300 ppm to 412 ppm (parts per million), which, in turn, has raised the temperature of the planet a little over 1°c above pre-industrial levels. The rest is prediction and best- and worst-case scenarios, tied to both scientific calculations and guesses about what human societies can do, or will do, in the future.

Back away from detailed predictions of what will happen or might happen five or 50 years from now and view climate change from a holistic, planetary perspective. Our solar system evolved out of a cloud of gases and dust particles rotating in the vast emptiness of space. Originally, this cloud was homogeneous so that the concentration and composition of matter was more or less the same throughout. In our immediate neighbourhood in space, Venus, Earth and Mars were all formed from the same basic stuff. Today, Venus is surrounded by a dense, carbon dioxide-rich atmosphere. Caustic rain falls from sulfuric acid clouds onto a surface hot enough to melt lead. No life, not even the organic molecules that constitute the basic building blocks of life, could possibly survive there. In contrast, Mars has a thin atmosphere, only 0.6 per cent of that of Earth, and its surface is frigid and dry. To date, roving and orbital spacecraft have not detected any living organisms, and if life does exist on Mars, it must be buried deep underground or beneath the dry ice polar caps. Meanwhile, on Earth, flowers bloom, giraffes make love in the moonlight and dogs play Frisbee. How did originally similar worlds become so different? The answer is that Venus is a bit closer to the Sun, Earth is in the middle and Mars is a bit farther away. The masses of the three were all initially a bit different. And in this complex, chaotic world of sun, gas and rock, small initial differences in mass and solar radiation amplified dramatically into huge differences in outcome. This geologic and planetary history is a vivid reminder that, here on Earth, small changes of the present environment can, or could, cause cataclysmic changes in the near future. How do I dare say this? Because it has happened out in space and also because it has happened here on Earth – many times before.

For the past 9,000 years, as humans built cities and farms, global climate has been more stable than it had been for several million years previously. Looking at the 4.6 billion years of Earth history, there has been no such stability. Our planet plunged into a deep freeze at least five times. Between 700 and 600 million years ago the oceans froze from pole to pole and glaciers covered nearly every square metre of land. At other times, the planet has been hot and steamy, with coal forming in Mesozoic swamps. At the end of the Permian period, 250 million years ago, a dramatic increase in atmospheric carbon dioxide led to the mass extinction of up to 96 per cent of all marine species and 70 per cent of terrestrial vertebrate species.

Closer to the present, between 35,000 years ago and 9,000 years ago, there have been at least 30 events where the global temperature has risen or fallen by more than 5°C (compared to 1°C, so far, for the present warming event). About 32,000 years ago, the global temperature rose by 8°C in a period of years or a decade or two, followed by a rapid cooling of the same magnitude. At the end of the last ice age, 11,700 years ago, the global temperature rose by 10°C, then fell for a brief time by the same amount, then rose again to current levels. As an interesting aside, primitive, non-technological humans survived all these ravages of extreme climate change.

Every warming or cooling event was driven by its own unique sequence of mechanisms. But the speed and magnitude of all these climate fluctuations were certainly amplified by what is called threshold and feedback effects. A threshold effect (also called a tipping point) is an event that occurs suddenly, after not occurring for an extended period of time. Ice melts precisely at 0°C, and not a tenth of a degree before. How does that affect climate? Clear sparkling ice reflects 50–70 per cent of the incident sunlight, like a mirror; this is called the albedo effect. Therefore, ice cools the air above it. Melt the ice to water and the water only reflects 6 per cent of the sunlight. When greenhouse warming causes the temperature of the air and hence the temperature of the ice to increase, at the magic number of o°c, the ice melts. Then the change in albedo causes the air temperature above the ice to rise suddenly and even more dramatically than in the original warming event. When the air temperature rises, more ice melts, which causes the air temperature to rise further, which melts more ice, so one effect feeds another which turns around and adds to the original.... That's a feedback mechanism, a spiralling loop of A causing B and B causing A, that can become exponentially more acute than the original problem.

There are many feedback mechanisms ongoing in the climate regime on Earth today. The arctic sea ice is only two metres thick in most places, so it doesn't take that many warm days, or seasons, to melt it. Antarctic and Greenland glaciers are much thicker than arctic sea ice, but when meltwater or sea water seeps beneath them, the ice can float on this basal water and cascade rapidly into the ocean. Masses of ocean water rise or sink when their density becomes greater than or less than the density of the surrounding ocean, thereby altering ocean currents. Johan Rockström, former director of the Stockholm Resilience Centre, lists ten climate feedback mechanisms already in motion in the world today: permafrost thaw, loss of methane hydrates from the ocean floor, weakening land and ocean carbon sinks, increasing bacterial respiration in the oceans, Amazon rainforest dieback, boreal forest dieback, reduction of northern hemisphere snow cover, loss of arctic summer sea ice, melting of the Greenland and Ellesmere ice sheets, and reduction of Antarctic sea ice.[68] To that impressive list, I add one more: potential abrupt changes in ocean currents from changes in temperature and/or salinity of surface water. Any one of these, or more troublesome, a cascading effect of a combination of two or more, could lead to a global temperature change of magnitude and speed that would be utterly unprecedented within the history of civilization. In such a "Hothouse Earth" scenario, large swaths of our planet would simply become uninhabitable to humans.

In text and trade books, I have been writing about climate change for 50 years. Climate scientists are reluctant to predict apocalypse – and then be caught with their pants down if the apocalypse doesn't

---

68 "Planet at Risk of Heading Towards 'Hothouse Earth' State," *Stockholm Resilience Centre*, 2019, https://www.stockholmresilience.org/research/research-news/2018-08-06-planet-at-risk-of-heading-towards-hothouse-earth-state.html.

Jon Turk

happen on schedule. So they build models, run the assumptions through a computer and then output a best-case, a middle-case and a worse-case scenario. Over my half-century of reporting, time and time again: Uh-oh, the worst-case scenarios have become reality. Uh-oh, the arctic sea ice is melting so fast. Uh-oh, the Antarctic ice shelves are breaking up so fast.

To cherry-pick one example of many. For decades, scientists have known that as the ocean warms and as melting Greenland glaciers pour fresh water into the salty North Atlantic, ocean parameters will change, leading to a best-case, a middle-case and a worse-case scenario. The worst-case scenario has always been that the Gulf Stream current *could possibly shut down*, leading to a catastrophic effect on climate. Measurements of paleoclimate parameters show that the Gulf Stream *has shut down* in the past. But, as a scientist and a writer, I have not gone out on a limb and said that the Gulf Stream *will shut down*. Because I don't know. No one knows. A model is a model, not fact. But, uh-oh. In the spring of 2021, measurements showed that the Gulf Stream *is starting to slow down*. So ... we've upped the ante. But the Gulf Stream has only slowed down. *Not stopped*. So ... we're okay, right? Let's worry about it, later? No, of course not. So ... today, I write that we're that much closer to apocalypse. And that it will happen in a thousand years, or in your grandchildren's lifetimes, or next summer.

To make matters even more complex and alarming, human and cultural threshold effects and feedback mechanisms are initiated by meteorological phenomena, compounding the impact of climate change on human societies. From a recent article in the *New York Times*:

> The farmer stood in his patch of forlorn coffee plants, their leaves sick and wilted, the next harvest in doubt.
>
> Gradually rising temperatures, more extreme weather events and increasingly unpredictable patterns – like rain not falling when it should, or pouring when it shouldn't – have disrupted growing cycles and promoted the relentless spread of pests.[69]

---

69 Kirk Semple, "Central American Farmers Head to the U.S., Fleeing Climate Change," *The New York Times*, April 13, 2019, https://www.nytimes.com/2019/04/13/world/americas/coffee-climate-change-migration.html.

So what happened?

> Last year, two of the farmer's brothers and a sister, desperate
> to find a better way to survive, abandoned their small coffee
> farms in this mountainous part of Honduras and migrated
> north, eventually sneaking into the United States. Then in
> February, the farmer's 16-year-old son also headed north,
> ignoring the family's pleas to stay.[70]

So what happened?

Triggered partly by the failure of the coffee crop, compounded by multiple other political, economic and social upheavals, thousands of Central American poor banded into groups and took off on arduous journeys northward, across Mexico, to seek refuge in the United States. The American press called these groups migrant caravans, while in Spanish-speaking countries they were called the Via Crucis del Migrante (Migrant's Way of the Cross), defining the mission as a result of religious persecution and hope for redemption. The Via Crucis del Migrante numbered thousands of people and caused a huge political commotion in the United States.

But what would happen if the Via Crucis del Migrante contained not thousands of people, but hundreds of thousands, or a few million, or half a billion?

The hottest temperatures that the human body can cope with vary with the ambient humidity, the duration of the heat exposure and the activity level and initial health of the individual. But, as a broad guideline, in the temperature range between 38°C (100°F) and 50°C (120°F) the human body cannot regulate itself anymore and people start dying. Above 50°C, forget it. In May 2016, Phalodi, a city of over 50,000 in northern India, recorded a temperature of 51° Celsius (123.8° Fahrenheit), while the thermometer in the nearby state capital of Jaipur, with 3.7 million inhabitants, soared to 46.5°C (116°C). Today, associated with extreme heat waves, and augmented by ever-rising population and demand, 21 Indian cities, with a combined population of 600 million, are facing severe shortages of water. According to a

....

70 Kirk Semple, "Central American Farmers Head to the U.S., Fleeing Climate
    Change," *The New York Times*, April 13, 2019, https://www.nytimes.
    com/2019/04/13/world/americas/coffee-climate-change-migration.html.

report released in the summer of 2018, all or most of these cities will totally deplete their groundwater reserves by the summer of 2020.[71] So, now, as I write this, it's spring of 2021. And guess what? The situation has gotten worse. Yes, deeper wells and ambitious emergency water diversion projects have kept the cities alive. Barely. But overall, according to the Circle of Blue water watchdog, "Dirty aquifers and water scarcity are destabilizing the world's second-largest country and seventh-largest economy. As its water reserves get dirtier and smaller, India is losing the capacity to safeguard public health, ensure farm productivity, grow the economy, and secure social stability."[72]

You can transport water to a few dozen Samburu cows in a truck – if you have a benefactor like Tina. But you can't transport water to 600 million people in a caravan of trucks. And even if you could bring in enough water to keep them alive, what would they eat when their crops wither and die? And even if you could bring them food in a truck, all those trucks burn gas that exacerbate global warming. And when it gets too hot, people would have to stay indoors during the day and turn on their air conditioners (if they could afford them). But the air conditioners pump warm air from the inside to the outside, which makes the outside air even hotter, so your neighbour's air conditioner has to work that much harder, which means that the coal-fired electric power plant pumps more heat and more carbon dioxide into the air. This is called a cultural feedback mechanism – spiralling out of control.

What happens if half a billion people in India can no longer survive in their traditional homes and initiate a Via Crucis del Migrante? Where do they go? Turkmenistan? Belgium? The social, political and human consequences are unimaginable.

Incredibly, most, or nearly all, the post-industrial, climate-altering human impact on Earth has occurred in one generation – my

....

71 Bhasker Tripathi, "Bengaluru, Delhi, Chennai Among 21 Cities to Run Out of Groundwater by 2020," *Tech 2*, July 9, 2018, https://www.firstpost.com/tech/science/indias-water-crisis-bengaluru-delhi-chennai-hyderabad-among-21-cities-to-run-out-of-groundwater-by-2020-4590221.html.

72 https://www.circleofblue.org/indiawater/?gclid=CjoKCQiA-aGCBhC-wARIsAHDl5x-K_6E_Ee7Cakz46C1UXn5GeUQ6AgyfgvoHroHH_-9fnV-kZJEvpE4aAhp8EALw_wcB.

generation; under my watch and the watch of my peers. I was born in 1945, essentially before computers and television. During my lifetime, the human population has more than tripled, from 2½ billion to over 7.8 billion. Global petroleum consumption has increased 18-fold since I was born; tropical rainforests, which once covered 14 per cent of our planet, have been chainsawed, bulldozed and burned until they now cover only 5 per cent. Between early 2003, when I was already a white-haired 57, and 2020, when I was 74, the annual economic output of China multiplied more than eightfold, from $1.7 trillion to nearly $14 trillion. I could run games with these numbers until the Moon comes home. For example, in two more lifetimes of runaway population explosion, will we have to feed, clothe, house and share our space with 70 billion fellow inhabitants of this fragile planet? Or, if global petroleum consumption were to increase as fast as it has during my lifetime, then in 6½ lifetimes, people would be burning as much petroleum every year as there is water in all the Earth's oceans. It can't happen. Something must change. Big time.

—   —   —

I have been an environmentalist my entire life. As a young, idealistic chemist, I worked in my father's air pollution laboratory. Later, in graduate school, working on my doctoral thesis, I did research that we thought might lead to the development of cheap, organic solar cells that could be used to produce pollution-free, solar-powered electricity. Our theoretical work never quite made the engineering leap to commercial products, but the idealism was there. When I realized that I didn't have the emotional framework to spend my life in the laboratory, I collaborated with my father, sister and brother-in-law to co-author the first environmental science textbook in North America. Our dream was that if people understood the severity of our environmental problems and gained insight into the scientific foundations of both the issues and solutions, then, presto, truth would prevail, and solutions would emerge.

But – no surprise. Truth did not prevail.

Jon Turk

If we combine all our arguments, starting with the observation that in the real world fiction prevails over truth, then it follows that if you want to change the minds of large numbers of people, and therefore change the status quo, telling the truth (writing textbooks) won't work. Instead, you need to create an alternate mass movement based on new mythologies, cleverly created from a different array of fictions. Therefore, our economic and political systems are doomed to follow an endless progression of charismatic and convincing spinners of mythologies and imagined realities.

I find that prospect terrifying. But then, maybe we shouldn't even try to fight logic with better logic. Maybe we need to play the game by a different set of rules. As Einstein reportedly said: "The significant problems we face cannot be solved at the same level of thinking we were at when we created them."

Fifty years ago, when I was still a graduate student in chemistry, one spring day I watched my dog dig holes in an alpine meadow and smell the earth. At first with hesitation, and then with unbridled enthusiasm, I stuffed my nose in one of the dog's holes, smeared wet dirt on my cheeks and drew the essence of spring soil into my nostrils. For a few glorious moments, the world of logic dissipated, replaced by raw, canine, animal sensuality. And the experience of those moments changed me forever.

In the half-century since then, my life has been a constant give and take between logic and sensuality. Back and forth, up and down, it's been quite a joyride. But I can assure you: whenever my think-too-much-know-it-all brain charges off on a logic tantrum, or spins useless stories in its head, I end up in a dark place. A more peaceful alternative exists. Sniffing the earth. Tracking a lion. Bringing water to thirsty cows. I understand the argument that you need to fight one mass movement with another. Or, to reword this statement into a more tribal manifesto: I understand that the only way to overcome evil mass movements is to generate benevolent ones. But, personally, that makes me nervous. I feel so much more comfortable with Joseph Campbell's words in *Hero With a Thousand Faces*:

> Like all who have elected to follow, not the safely marked general highways of the day, but the adventure of the special, dimly audible call that comes to those whose ears

are open within as well as without, she has had to make her journey alone.[73]

Travelling through life alone means that you have enough faith and trust in yourself, so you don't need to follow the stories that others put in your head. Because those stories will almost certainly benefit the storytellers, but they probably won't benefit you, or society, or the planet.

Tina bought the truck to bring water to a few dozen cows, not all the thirsty cows in Samburu, or all the thirsty people in India. You do what you can do. And hope that goodness becomes contagious. I am compassionate to you and that makes you feel good, so you are compassionate to two people, and so on, until goodness explodes across the planet like an atomic bomb. I laugh and smell the flowers with enough conviction that two people laugh and smell the flowers, and so forth, until no one has the time or inclination to promote or to perpetuate evil anymore. We talked like that when we were stoned out of our minds during the peace-love-bro' days in the late '60s. May I talk like that again? Or will you shake your head, call me crazy, call the men in white coats and rush me off to the nuthouse?

---

73 Joseph Campbell, *Hero With a Thousand Faces*, 3rd ed. (New York: New World Library, 2008), p. 21.

CHAPTER 8
CLIMBING
MT. SABACHE-OLOLOKWE

My first task the following morning is to flush the toilet, but the toilet doesn't work, and now, unfortunately, the shower has stopped working as well, so I don't have any water to fill my bucket. I explore around and figure out the water system for the entire camp. Dipa brings water to the Motel at the End of the World in the truck. A gasoline-powered pump lifts the water from the parking area to a large storage tank perched on the top of a hill above my tent site. Once the tank is filled, the daily needs of the camp operate on a gravity system. I hike up and tap the tank; it is about half full. I follow the pipe that runs over the ground from the tank, downhill to my tent site, and detect no obvious leaks. Hmm. Gravity is not a mythology; it never breaks. Following this logic, one of the valves must be clogged, or something, and I don't have the tools, authorization or inclination to take the system apart. I grab my bucket and traipse down to the kitchen for some water. But wait a minute. Have I totally forgotten the white-faced cow with a brown spot on her forehead? Just last night, I was kneeling in front of the watering trough with the cow's breath touching my face and its horns menacingly a few centimetres away. Have I totally forgotten that we are in the midst of a cataclysmic, ecosystem-shattering drought? People, cows, monkeys and lions are all starving and/or dying of thirst. But someone has reasoned, or created a mythology, that because Jon Turk is a white man, he needs to take perfectly good water, trucked in at great expense, poop in it and then flush it to somewhere. I fill my bucket in the kitchen area and carry it up the hill. First I take a sponge bath, being careful to spill as little as possible. Then I do my laundry, and finally use the same water a third time to flush the toilet. Can all our problems be solved so easily?

Mission accomplished. I have time on my hands, so I take out my camera to photograph the monkeys. No monkeys appear on cue, so I set the camera down. A raven swoops in fast and low, black wings glistening. It passes at head level, we make eye contact, and the raven caws mischievously. Then it grabs my camera and takes off with it. Either because I shout or because the camera is too heavy, she drops it – bing – on the stone veranda, breaking my wide-angle lens but not the camera body. I'm bummed. But, then again, Raven has been my special friend since she flew to the Other World to speak to the Woman Who Lives on the Highest Mountain on my behalf several years ago in Kamchatka. Thank you, Raven, you are both Creator and Trickster. Joke's on me today.

Tina goes to town on an errand and when we meet for dinner, she tells me that yesterday, between here and Nairobi, in some sort of apartheid-like battle, police shot 15 people. She shows me a grainy iPhone video, but after watching one bloody body twitching in the dust as a policeman calmly pumps bullets into the obviously dead man, I turn my head. Sorry, Tina, I can't watch the rest of it. Then: Wait a minute. What's going on here? Who is shooting whom, and why? And, more germane to my own selfish self-interest: Am I in any danger in this seemingly peaceful camp that nevertheless reminds me of Cochise's last stronghold?

Tina doesn't have much information. But there is an upcoming election next month. And a decade ago, during the 2007 election, over a thousand people were killed in the streets and thousands more displaced from their homes. And then Tina tells me that just the other day, in case you haven't heard, the opposition leader, Raila Odinga, told his supporters that he would lose only if the election were rigged and the vote were stolen. In which case, he suggests, maybe an uprising wouldn't be a bad idea.

No, I hadn't heard; I was tracking lions and watering cows with Dipa the other day.

Life goes on, uninterrupted, at the Motel at the End of the World. Tina has another important errand to do in town the next day but suggests that Jawas and I hike to the top of Mt. Sabache-Ololokwe. To pique my interest, she reminds me, again, that it is a Holy Mountain. Fine, but I don't need a carrot at the end of a stick to induce me to scramble up a mountain. And, anyway, it's the wrong carrot, because I am naturally suspicious of Holy Places. You take a perfectly normal mountain, tree, rock, city or whatever, and create a mythology around it and call it 'Holy,' and suddenly people get riled up about this piece of real estate and wage war over it. My Universe is a lot more fulfilling and peaceful to me if every mountain, tree and rock is Holy. Like it was when I was tracking the lion.

But, Holy or not, I grab my *rungu*, stick and a water bottle, and then go into the kitchen to nab a couple of oranges. The cook has already been forewarned about our little expedition and has prepared a small lunch for us. Jawas shows up, quickly checks his visage in the pink mirror and we're ready to go.

We walk through the gate at the camp boundary, cross the wash over a concrete dam to hold water when and if it rains, and start upward on a well-worn trail. Without consciously thinking about it, I inhale fully and then slowly exhale. It feels so good to get out of camp, even though everyone is nice to me there and they feed me. I always feel this way when I step into the woods. My brain almost instantaneously assumes a different rhythm; it thinks about different things, awareness changes, sense of time takes on new dimensions, senses respond to different inputs. It's as if I become a newly invigorated person. An extreme example of this metamorphosis occurs every time I step into my skis. The Jon Turk who once walked across the surface of the Earth disappears on cue at the audible click of my bindings as the springs snap into position. I lower my goggles over my face and my vision changes, muscle memory springs into action, so my brain is no longer in charge, unneeded. It's the flow that rules now. These familiar feelings, of walking into the woods or preparing to ski, embrace me like an old friend, who is always welcoming but doesn't talk much. Wild places are extremely complex and extremely simple. Complex because so much is going on – so much breathing, so much moving about, so many interwoven interactions. And so simple because there are few humans. I like people and enjoy my friends, don't get me wrong, and I understand that our big brain–inspired tribalism provided the bedrock of our survival strategy. But the problem is that sociality is fundamentally dependent on telling stories and reading the intention (stories) of others. And that's exhausting sometimes. At its inescapable essence, any story, given or received, removes us from this place and this moment into a place that doesn't exist. Which is the exact antithesis of being mindful, which is all about living wholly in the moment. Yes, I'm a social, storytelling animal, just as you are. But it's not easy being a human all the time, so I need a break from all the commotion, to switch gears, and to open up the animal inside.

In Chapter 3, I argued that peacocks and humans, each in their own way, create beauty, and the appreciation of beauty evokes a warm-fuzzy, dopamine-releasing feeling that endows an individual and a species with survival value. Nature did not evolve to be beautiful to humans. But why is it that just about everyone perceives Nature as beautiful? Again, I borrow from a Carl Safina argument. Humans survived because they were deeply observant of Nature and learned to recognize its dangers and offerings. If stepping into Nature evokes a warm-fuzzy, dopamine-releasing feeling – i.e., if we perceive Nature as beautiful – then our joyfulness will heighten our observation, which heightens our alertness, which heightens our survival. That feeling of awe, wonder, beauty, whatever you call it, when I stepped into the forest with Jawas, when anyone steps into a forest, or a desert, or a city park, is deeply ingrained in our DNA.

Jawas and I start up the path. In an instant, my life simplifies. I concentrate on moving forward with smooth efficiency, watching for thorns both beneath my feet and overhead. And while I am looking upward into the branches, I should also watch out for black mamba snakes hiding in the brownish leaves that have fallen on the ground. And lions. Have we forgotten about lions? How do you communicate respect to a lion that you don't see and that might not even be in the neighbourhood? Fear has a smell. Start the respect without the smell of fear. And as long as I am concentrating on neutralizing potential dangers I can imagine, what about the dangers I don't know about so I can't imagine, but which are dangerous anyway, so I need to react to them, even though I don't know what I'm looking for. If this sounds confusing – it isn't. Just the opposite. Go for a walk someday. Shut out what you have just read because these are just words. Stories. Symbols. Take a deep breath. Put one foot in front of the other. Don't talk to anyone. Just go for a walk.

I have two litres of water and a little food to last the day. So, drink enough to stay hydrated, but ration at the same time. And it's a good idea to remember the path back to camp. Not that Jawas would ever get lost, but even with a competent guide, it's ultimately my responsibility to take care of myself.

The trail climbs steeply, and I enjoy the strain of my quad muscles against my old friend gravity. The deep breathing helps me forget about spinning stories in my head, or retelling stories that someone else spun into my head. Jawas moves quickly and I resolve to keep the pace. The trail gets even steeper and the long-ago rains have eroded all the soil off, exposing a slab of bare rock. I scramble up, touching my fingers lightly against the speckled grey granite for balance. At the top of the slab, I find a large pile of elephant poop, or what looks to me like elephant poop.

"Hey, Jawas. Is this elephant poop?"

He looks at me like he thinks it's a dumb question but confirms that it is.

"Are you sure? I didn't know that elephants could climb rock. That slab was a little tricky, even for me."

"Yes, siree! Elephants do climb anything that peoples do climb." Jawas goes on to explain that elephants scramble up the granite on their elbows and knees because at certain times of year the pastures on the top of Mt. Sabache-Ololokwe contain nutrient-rich grasses. And then he adds, almost as an oh-by-the-way afterthought, that the top of the mountain is generally safe from armed and dangerously lethal poachers who roam these scrublands and savannahs.

Poachers? Bad guys with guns? I want to ask Jawas about Tina's video of the already dead man twitching in the dust, but I don't know what he knows, or maybe I'm afraid he knows more than I think he knows. Or the language barrier is too great. Or he sees me as a tourist and he is doing his job as a motel employee, so he'll hide what he knows.

A long time ago, I was travelling by snow machine with some Inuit friends across the sea ice in the Canadian Arctic. We carried a 55-gallon drum of gasoline, but the drum had a pinhole in it and leaked gas. At one rest stop, one of my companions sat on top of the leaky drum, smoking a cigarette. I commented that maybe he shouldn't be smoking while sitting on top of a virtual bomb. He looked at me, took a slow, thoughtful drag on his cigarette, flicked hot ash onto the ice, and replied dryly, "White men worry too much." Now, many years later, in a vastly different environment, I wonder if all of us here at the Motel at the End of the World are smoking a cigarette on top of a leaky, explosive drum of fuel. It seems that Jawas is not as concerned as I am. Or if he is, he is handling his fears in a different way. I decide to soak up as much information as possible, and to remain hyper-aware, but not to ask him a bunch of questions about bad guys.

Jawas has more to tell me. "Elephants do have special feet." He points to a small dirt platform packed down above the rock. "They stand up here. On the foots." He pauses. "Elephants do hear on the foots."

"Hear? Through their feet?" I quiz him. "I thought elephants have big ears. I thought they hear through their ears, like we do."

Jawas shakes his head sadly, again, at my ignorance. "Yes, siree! Elephants do have big ears." Then he pauses and speaks assertively. "Elephants do hear on the foots."

I have learned from long experience not to question an Indigenous person's knowledge of his or her environment. I let the matter drop. But, when I get home later that summer, I look up the structure of elephant feet. Elephants, being the heaviest terrestrial animal, have fat-lined, columnar legs and feet with a unique bone structure. They walk with their toe bones pointing downward, so in essence they are walking on tiptoe, even though they don't look like ballet dancers. Large subcutaneous cushions on the bottom of their feet distribute the weight, absorbing impact and allowing them to pass through the forest silently. They also have ridges on the soles of their feet that help them get traction when climbing steep slippery surfaces. And if you believe Jawas, which I do, they don't use their marvelously dexterous feet while rock climbing, because they get better traction using their elbows and knees. And, yup, there it was, right there on the internet, in addition to using their large ears, elephants also hear by picking up sound waves in the soil through sensitive nerve endings in their feet. Estimates of how far elephants communicate through the soil vary considerably, but according to Elephant Aid International: "Elephants produce low frequency rumbles known as seismic or infrasound, which are inaudible to the human ear. The rumble sends infrasound signals through the elephant's feet into the ground and can carry underground and be heard by another elephant for as far as 30 miles (50 km)."[74]

Jawas was right, as I expected. Of course, elephants also hear air-borne sound waves just as all mammals do. But that's not all. They have an expressive vocabulary of body language; they touch each other frequently and their long noses are among the most sensitive of any mammal. Elephants use smell to keep track of family and friends and they can also use scent to identify specific individuals who pose a threat. They can smell an approaching rainstorm from 250 kilometres away.[75]

As we continue up the trail, I fantasize about what it feels like to listen to vibrations in the soil – to hear Mother Earth speak – to talk with her, or at least through her. Perhaps then we wouldn't drive so many bulldozers over her skin. But maybe that's just wishful thinking. Humans listen to vibrations in the air and certainly have no compunctions about spewing poisons into our atmosphere.

We reach the ridge top, a 300-metre climb, in a little over an hour, drink some water, catch our breaths and continue onward across a landscape of hot, rolling, yellow meadows, dry stream beds, and the ghosts of springs, now parched by the drought. Abundant cow dung mixes with the elephant droppings. I ask Jawas if the cows climb up here on their elbows and knees, and he shakes his head in resignation at my ignorance but offers no clue as to how they got here.

We follow the trail to a well-used campsite in a grove of trees growing in a protected hollow that must be fed by a persistent

....

74 "Elephant Facts," *Elephant Aid International*, https://elephantaidinternational. org/elephant-facts/?gclid=CjwKCAiA1fnxBRBBEiwAVUouUqouhQ_RHOIFPYwYH9oLDkrecLoOscD1Hr_8d8nCBxl5Yfxha4FbixoCwAoQAvD_BwE.

75 "Elephant Facts," *Elephant Aid International*, https://elephantaidinternational. org/elephant-facts/?gclid=CjwKCAiA1fnxBRBBEiwAVUouUqouhQ_RHOIFPYwYH9oLDkrecLoOscD1Hr_8d8nCBxl5Yfxha4FbixoCwAoQAvD_BwE.

source of groundwater that collects even here, high on the mesa. The shade and the coolness beckon after our hot walk, so I sit down with my back against a downfall log, and Jawas relaxes a short distance away. Looking upward into the canopy, I realize that I have never seen trees quite like this before. The trunks resemble pines, and the green tops resemble palms. Later, Tina tells me that this is one of the last standing virgin forest tracts of cycad trees remaining in East Africa, perhaps the continent. During the Jurassic period, when dinosaurs ruled terrestrial ecosystems, cyads made up almost 20 per cent of the forest, but today they are almost extinct in their original range.

Plant life is abundant here in this small oasis, and I savour the multitude of sweet fragrances floating through the air. The forest plants are talking with one another and with their animal neighbours. Simple communication that we are all aware of, like, "Hey, heads up. I'm a flower, and I'll give you some yummy nutrient-rich stuff to eat, if you don't mind carrying my pollen from place to place." But it's so much more complicated than that. Scientists are only beginning to decipher the full richness and complexity of the multiple conversations going on around us every time we step into a forest. For example, when certain caterpillars chew on the leaves of certain trees, the trees sense the caterpillar saliva and fire pheromones off into the air. Parasitic wasps smell the pheromones and follow the airborne scent trail to the trees, where they quickly find the caterpillars, pierce their bodies with their stingers and lay their eggs inside. And when the eggs hatch, the baby wasp larvae eat the caterpillars from the inside out. It's a busy world out there.

A hundred million years ago, Pterosaurs, winged dinosaurs, swooped among the cyads nibbling on their yellow seed pods, spreading their DNA and ensuring their survival long after the Pterosaurs died out. I can't understand the language of the forest; I can't distinguish the smell of caterpillar spit from that of tree pheromones. But if I pay attention, I can tune in to the living richness of it all, feel it in some indescribable way, like listening to a lullaby sung in a foreign language, and become enriched.

"Hey, Jawas, are we in a hurry? Do you mind if I lie down and close my eyes for a moment?"

"No hurry."

Jon Turk

I lie on my back to smell the air, but become aware of a new mélange of smells from the earth beneath me, so I turn over and sniff the soil, as my dog taught me 50 years ago. Again, my nose is neither sensitive nor well-trained enough to decipher what's going on down there and I don't know enough adequate adjectives in the English language to convey the wonder I feel. But down there, beneath my nose, hair-like tree root ends are intertwined with hair-like fungi, called mycorrhizal networks, which are, in turn, intertwined with roots of neighbour trees. They are communicating and exchanging nutrients, water and sugars. Adults, with their canopies high in the sky, absorb abundant sunlight to synthesize sugars, and then feed young saplings who would otherwise starve in the darkness of the forest floor. Forest biologist and best-selling author Peter Wohlleben anthropomorphizes this interaction to say that 'mother' trees 'suckle their young.'[76] My high school biology teacher, Mr. Follensbee, would have flunked me if I had said something like that, but I tell you: "It's happening, whatever terminology you use to describe it." So, with my abysmally poor nose and equally inadequate knowledge of what is going on around me, I smell the munching and chewing, living and dying, eating and farting.

Jawas interrupts my reveries to remind me that it's time to move on toward the top of the mountain. We hike gradually upward over gently undulating terrain until the visible trail ends at the boundary with a nearly horizontal rock slab that stretches toward the southern prow of the mesa. When we reach the edge of the mesa, I drop onto my hands and knees and peer down the cliffs that I had looked at from below, when I first drove into this place – cliffs, incidentally, that people can climb, but I am certain that elephants cannot. Jawas announces, "This is the top of the mountain." It doesn't look like the top of the mountain to me, because we could keep meandering up the slabs if we cared to, but I am happy to call it quits and sit in the scorching African equatorial sun, watching vultures spiral on thermals rising from the hot rock. Down there in the brown desert, too far away to see, herders are guarding their animals who are trying

---

76 Peter Wohlleben, *The Hidden Life of Trees: What They Feel, How They Communicate Discoveries from a Secret World* (Vancouver, BC: Greystone Books, 2016).

to stay alive on close to zero food. Farther to the south, beyond the horizon, hidden by a dust haze, friends and family are mourning their recently murdered brethren – over some mythology no one understands, not even the victims or the perpetrators. Certainly, the children don't understand, even though they have lost their fathers, and with that loss, their sense of emotional and economic security has been shattered irreparably, forever.

I follow the geometrical scar of the A-2 Road as it slices across a non-geometrical landscape. Off to the southwest a short distance, I see a short, wide, straight, road-like dirt structure set apart from and not connected to the main highway. Jawas tells me it is a "place where airplanes come down and go up." I store that information. Whenever you travel, alertness is so important; you never know what idle piece of chit-chat might become critical someday.

We share an orange, enjoying the sweet, tart juiciness of its flesh as a reprieve from the oppressive heat. Jawas tells me to leave the peels in plain sight because the baboons will eat them. I ask Jawas about the religious significance of this 'sacred mountain,' but this question doesn't make it across the language barrier. Either he doesn't understand, doesn't know the answer or chooses not to tell me. I change the subject and simplify my query: "Tell me about your family." He explains that he has four brothers and two sisters, and the family owns ten cows.

Now it is his turn: "How many cows do you own?" he asks. Apparently, this is a common Samburu conversation starter because Ian asked me the same question before. When I tell him, "None," he shakes his head in pity, or wonder. Then a thought lights up in his face.

"Goats?"

"No goats."

Hmmm.

"A dog?"

"No dog."

Left unspoken is the question, "How are you so rich, that you can buy an airplane ticket, if you don't own any cows?"

I want to explain North American economics, you know, the whole rap about imaginary money. But I've been in this conversation before, in other remote locations, and have found that it is devilishly difficult to put these concepts into sentences that make sense to someone who has not grown up listening to the mythologies, or fairy tales, or economic theory that I grew up listening to. I once told a herder on the Mongolian steppe that in the North American economy, I produce something that is not good to eat and that my neighbour doesn't need anyway, and my neighbour produces something that is also not good to eat and that I don't need, and I buy his stuff and he buys my stuff and we both get rich. And end up with plenty to eat, and plenty of stuff we don't need. The herder thought I was pulling his leg and grew angry with me.

While I'm thinking about what to say next, Jawas, who is clearly curious to understand how the world economy (or at least my economy) operates, asks: "How much did your watch cost?"

It's a Casio from K-Mart, and I tell him the truth. "$20."

He shakes his head in wonder. How could a person be simultaneously so poor that he owns no livestock, not even a dog, and so rich he squanders the ungodly sum of $20 on a watch? Jawas tells me that he owns a Casio watch that keeps perfectly good time and sells for only $2. He also owns a cellphone and is on Facebook. Now it's my turn to shake my head in wonder that he could be so connected with the digital world, and so simultaneously disconnected that he equates wealth with cows and goats. But his logic makes sense because his wealth is real while my wealth is merely a mythology. But, once again, that mythology works well enough for the time being, because, as a matter of fact, I have ended up owning a bunch of stuff that isn't good to eat and that I don't need anyway.

So Jawas and I share this orange, and the intimacy of this day, while at the same time a broad cultural divide separates us. No worries. Every person's childhood informs their adult personalities.

When I was in Siberia, my dear Koryak friend Lydia apprenticed under Moolynaut, to learn her skills as a shamanic healer. She learned to recognize medicinal herbs and to prepare them as tinctures and teas. She memorized chants and incantations, but she could never acquire the power of the older woman. Certainly, part of the difference is personal; every person's power is expressed differently. But, in addition, even though both women were Koryak and were raised in the same village, they were born two generations apart. Moolynaut grew up in a skin tent. She listened to the wind blow every night, as a lullaby or a ferocious blizzard. She knew the sound of gently falling snow, or of driven snow, or rain, the long darkness of winter and the equally long sunshine of summer. She sat on hillsides for endless hours, from her earliest moments of life, watching reindeer eat grass. And when she was older, she learned to listen for the padded footsteps of wolves muffled by silent snow in the long winter darkness – because reindeer were life and life was reindeer. In contrast, Lydia went to a Russian school, and spent her formative years sitting at a desk learning reading, 'riting and 'rithmetic. In the process of learning these essential skills of Western civilization, she lost the ability, forever, to become animal, to learn Moolynaut's Indigenous skills, power and perception of the world. Lydia explained to me that no one – zero people – who grew up in a Russian school had been able to dig deep into her DNA to become the person that she would have been if raised in a skin tent. Thus, no modern Koryak have acquired the shamanic healing powers of their ancestors. And now, with the death of Moolynaut and the rest of her generation, that ancient wisdom is gone, forever. Irretrievable.

I grew up in suburban Connecticut and went to Park Avenue school, where we all lined up, shortest to tallest, and marched down a concrete block hallway to the lunchroom. Jawas grew up in a stick house and herded cows and goats while hungry lions lurked in the bushes. And today, despite his cellphone, Jawas equates wealth with living, breathing livestock. Despite all my time in wild places, I equate wealth with an imaginary entity called money. So, what's the take-away? I need to learn from Jawas to connect to the Earth and to build a sustainable future. And because there is no way to turn back the civilizational clock, because the planet is so overpopulated that humans can no longer afford to be hunter-gatherers, Jawas needs to learn from me in order to bumble his way through this oil-soaked, consumer-oriented, mythology-based civilization that somehow arose out of the desert sands.

And maybe there's another lesson as well. Our mythologies are like religions. You may think that your money is the only way to manage an economic system, just as you may think that your god is the only god, but someone else might think that their money and their god are different – and right. But, to step outside ourselves and view our own cultural biases, it doesn't hurt to sit on a hot rock, share an orange with someone from a different upbringing and culture and view the world through their eyes. And don't forget to leave the peels in plain sight for the baboons, because we share the planet with them as well.

On the way home, as we walk back across the rock slab, Jawas suddenly veers right and heads eastward, clearly not in the direction of the cyad grove.

"Hey, where are we going?"

Jawas points toward a low-lying ridge that caps the eastern edge of the summit plateau. "Do you see the finger?" he asks.

I scan the ridge. "Oh yes, I see what you're saying. Funny; I didn't notice it beforehand, but now that you mention it, I do see a distinct finger-shaped rock over there."

Jawas stops, turns and makes direct eye contact: "Know this rock." He holds up his own finger and bends it slightly to mimic the shape of the rock. "We go at the rock."

My mind becomes full of questions.

We follow the arc of the pointing rock as if it were a red exit sign in a subway station, until we reach a small thorn thicket. Jawas parts the branches, carefully not to break any, like opening a rickety gate that his grandfather built, and beckons me to follow. And there, in a fold in the rocks, we enter the coolness of a natural cave.

I look around. If this were a family gathering place, or a sanctuary for spiritual gatherings, I would expect that the area in front of the cave would be well-trampled, like the campground in the cyad grove. Inside the cave, there might be some altar-like focal point. But I see no evidence of peaceful congregation.

I smile, "Nice place."

Jawas smiles back, "No peoples know we are on this place now."

I return Jawas's smile. Is this another tourist attraction? Or an important piece of information that could save my life if the shit hits the fan? Am I creating a paranoid story in my head about an imagined danger? Am I puffing up my own ego to create a self-ag-grandized image of myself as a heroic journalist, chronicling....? What am I chronicling now? What is real? And what is this airy-nothing edifice of wayward neural transmissions? I want to sit down and ask Jawas, "C'mon now, good buddy. What is going on around here?" But I don't think I'll get a satisfying answer, so I don't ask. Instead, I turn a switch in my brain to route the image of that finger-shaped rock from short-term memory to another file cabinet called long-term memory. Important image to remember. Click, click. There. Done. Saved both on my hard drive and in the cloud. I've got lots of giga-bytes of storage left in my mysterious lump of grey matter, and I can always delete this information later if I don't need it.

We rest a few minutes, sip some water and return through the peaceful, ancient cyads, across the plateau and back down past the elephant climbing wall, to camp.

CHAPTER 9

A LION, AN ELEPHANT, AND A LEOPARD

Tina thinks that I might feel disappointed because I haven't seen a lion yet. She explains that with the drought, the lions, like many of the Samburu herders, have retreated farther into the remote mountains. I don't know how disappointed I am, actually, even though we're discussing my feelings and I guess I should know how I feel. Of course, I wanted to see the lion that day with Dipa, and I have thought about hitching up one of those recalcitrant camels and following ancient trails to mysterious valleys. But I am here, at the Motel at the End of the World, and the camels are grazing peacefully near the corral, and the journey is what it is, and the moment is what it is, and all those clichés. Anyway, on my behalf, Tina suggests we visit the nearby Samburu National Reserve, one of many game parks in Kenya. And I am thankful for that opportunity.

The Samburu National Reserve is a 165 km² sanctuary for a wide variety of African animals who are struggling to stay alive as farmland encroaches, poachers kill and drought devastates the landscape. As a comparison, Banff National Park in Canada is 6600 km², 40 times larger, and Manhattan Island logs in at 59 km², around one-third the size. As we say in Montana slang, the Samburu National Reserve is bigger than a breadbox and smaller than a D10 Cat. The entrance fee is c$93 per person per day, and if you want mints on the pillow and wildlife viewing from the veranda of a palatial suite, you can stay at the Elephant Bedroom Camp for c$843 per night (breakfast included). There is a word in Russian, *puteshevstinek*, for a dirtbag traveller who, in the old days before mass media, was fed and sheltered along the way in exchange for telling stories, entertaining and carrying the news. The heyday of the *puteshevstinek*, or the wandering minstrel who will sing *The Iliad* for you in exchange for dinner, is in the past. Today, the mantra is "Passport and credit card, please." On the positive side, as we all join hands on the Ragged Edge of the Anthropocene, rich people are keeping the African wildlife alive, and at least a piddling fraction of the tourist dollars end up in the hands of Samburu motel help. So that's the way the world works these days.

Dipa picks us up in the morning in his battered Land Rover. Tina sits in the front seat, and Ian piles in the back with me. I take my camera, binos and water bottle, but no *rungu* or stick. No one sends me back to my tent for these last two items, because we all understand that today's expedition is qualitatively different from anything I have done so far in Africa. When we reach the park gate, Dipa speaks to the bored, sleepy guard, who waives our entry fee.

The website tells me that the Samburu National Reserve is home to lions, leopards, giraffes, zebras, elephants and a host of other mammals, as well as 450 species of birds. But the species with the highest population density and the greatest ecological impact per individual is – you guessed it – humans. I'm not a trained wildlife biologist, and don't know the scientific techniques for counting individuals that move quickly, intermingle, spread out and mix again. But any time I look across the savannah plain, I might see a herd of zebras or a family of elephants, but I will assuredly see the dust clouds of many Land Rovers, Toyota Land Cruisers and Nissan suvs zooming about at high rates of speed relative to the normal pace of African wildlife. I might be tempted to conclude that there is some overriding organization to it all, like the co-operative behaviour of forager ants, but it seems to be more chaotic than that.

Dipa, who is a trained and skilful tracker, and has stayed alive and built stature within his tribe by virtue of athletic ability, Indigenous wisdom and 21st-century statesmanship, knows that in the game park, if you want to see a lion, you don't look for the soft impression

FROM TOP   Sunrise in Samburu; on my first day at the Motel at the End of the World, Ian soft talks me into paying him $20 for a camel ride.

When I arrive in Samburu, it hasn't rained in three years.

FROM TOP   One of the homes in the village near the Motel at the End of the World; the interior of a Samburu home.

FROM TOP Tina Ramme, my host in Samburu; after a lion eats one of the cows,
The Boy herds the remaining animals to the safety of the village corral, or *boma*.

FROM TOP It's normal, in Samburu, for young boys to herd valuable cattle on the savannah, exposed to the full complement of dangerous African predators; Dipa, the regional headman.

FROM TOP   When we reach the carcass of the lion-kill cow, Dipa sits down, wipes the lion slobber off a portion of the hindquarter, cuts himself a healthy slice and calmly eats the meat; when he finishes his lunch, Dipa pulls out his cellphone and conducts some tribal business.

Jawas, my constant hiking companion.

FROM TOP   I never see a lion in the wild, but we see several from the safety of the Land Rover, on our visit to the Samburu National Reserve; a leopard in the Samburu National Reserve.

FROM TOP　Tina takes wildlife photos at the Samburu National Reserve; frequently, the camel I call "Lightning Bolt" is content to go for a leisurely stroll. But every now and then he misbehaves and then his handlers treat him with great cruelty. So, eventually, he runs away.

FROM TOP After we realize Lightning Bolt is running away in earnest, Jawas tells me to stop following the tracks. Then he calls around on his cellphone until he reaches someone who has seen him; I'm afraid that Lightning Bolt may have disappeared into the broad savannah, and we will never find him. Instead, he joins another camel herd at this nearby village.

FROM TOP   I speak no Samburu, so I often don't know what is going on, but I take notice when Dipa is clearly giving detailed instructions to armed men with serious expressions; boys are always fascinated by weaponry.

With a casual demeanour, a young man heads off into the savannah with his spear,
a few sticks and a small bag of lunch.

After Dipa explains that I will be one of the best men at the wedding, he sends me to the village to get a pair of sandals made for the occasion. This woman cuts off a piece of hide and then passes it over to the shoemaker.

As the wedding approaches, warrior/herders from deep in the savannah appear in and around camp.

FROM TOP   Herding goats, like herding cattle, is fraught with danger. One day a pack of wild dogs attacks the goatherd; one of the warrior/herders and I retrieve and butcher a goat that is mortally wounded by the wild dogs.

Sometimes I wonder why I am just about the only person around here who isn't well armed.

FROM TOP   The day of the wedding, all the women dress in their most elaborate finery; as part of the wedding festivities, the women join together in song.

FROM TOP   Tina joins the chorus of Samburu women; women build a house for the newlyweds. Here they peel bark from sticks that will be used as framing for the walls.

FROM TOP   Next, the women place sticks vertically into the ground, and bind them together with the horizontal sticks they have prepared; as evening approaches, and the wedding day draws to a close, the young men and women join in a vigorous line dance.

FROM TOP   Tina asks me to join this group of warrior/herders, ostensibly to track a lion; we cross a set of recent lion tracks. But after examining the tracks, the warrior/herder leads us in a different direction.

We are clearly searching the savannah for something, but I fear this "something" is human enemies, not lions.

FROM TOP   I stare at the well-worn stock, the curved clip of bullets and the
trigger polished by use, then peer into the bushes for signs of imminent danger;
suddenly, armed men are scattered throughout the savannah, yet everyone seems
relaxed, casual almost.

One of the warrior/herders climbs a rock for one last scan of the savannah but finds nothing alarming.

FROM TOP   Deep in my heart, I realize that if we encounter trouble, these men will lay down their lives for me. Without mutual language, I don't know how to thank them; Samburu at sunset.

of padded feet in the sand, or a flock of vultures patiently riding thermals, waiting for an opportunity to scavenge a recent kill. You look for a dense concentration of stationary vehicles, because people congregate around an apex predator, because a photo of a lion or a leopard is worth more 'Likes' and 'Comments' on Facebook than an image of a zebra or a gazelle. We kick up a huge dust cloud churning over the dry, pulverized surface of a crude road, jockey for position, and sure enough, come close to a large male lion, mane shimmering in the sun, half napping, squinty eyes staring back calmly at the phalanx of cameras clicking and whirring away.

I compare the lion to one of the passengers on a subway train at rush hour. He sees me in the crowd, but he sees so many people, all day long, every day, that he becomes immune to seeing. I am there, but I am an inconsequential component of an anonymous crowd, neither friend, foe nor food.

I create an imaginary narrative in which the lion is saying, "Ho hum. This is my job. I lie in the sun, digest my last meal, stare at the cameras, and don't run away or eat someone, and all those people-animals wave their plastic representations of imaginary money around at the hotels and entrance gate and the locals give me this park, where there is plenty to eat, a river flowing through it even in the midst of this terrible drought, and for the most part, no poachers roaming about to shoot me. Not a bad day's work, really."

I watch the tourists, on vacation from their cities and jobs, standing in their roofless safari wagons, experiencing Nature in this wonderful game park, in a way that perhaps they have never and will never experience again. But, through a series of sequential steps, over a few generations, the primordial African wilderness has been gradually replaced by something else, and I feel walled in by the Anthropocene.

To understand this game park, as it exists today, let's go back to Day 1 here in Kenya, when I was driving north in Anthony's car. I described a kid by the roadside, trying to sell a live chicken, which was flapping its wings in fear and panic. This is straight-up capitalism. Set a price and you get what you see: squawk, feathers and all. But this game park is carefully calculated to delude us into buying a mythological representation of wilderness, something that cannot possibly exist, unless we rewrite the English language, or the rules of logic, or our cultural baselines.

Any journey into true wilderness involves at least three essential components: vulnerability, discomfort and solitude. Life slows down; it takes time. Self-reliance is a prerequisite to survival. And survival is not guaranteed. Every time I venture into the Far North, I repeat, as a mantra, an imaginary conversation I once had with a white wolf: "Welcome to the Far North. You are guaranteed to be cold, hungry, strung-out, exhausted, and come home with frostbite scars on your face. You might die out here. Welcome. It's good to see you." But the managers of the game park have an economic incentive to create a visual experience without the physical components of hunger, exhaustion and so forth, and certainly without killing any of their clients. Vulnerability, discomfort and solitude do not fit into the creed of the hotelier. As a corollary, they discourage self-reliance because it is safer to trust trained professional guides. Thus, they create an artificial replica of the experience they are advertising – something that does not and cannot possibly exist. A mythology. If someone promises you a wilderness experience complete with flush toilets and catered room service, beware. That person is a carnival barker. If someone promises you a wilderness hotel, remember: a hotel is a place where the owner hopes there will be a lot of people gathered together in a crowded dining room – the more the merrier. Following this logic, a hotel that provides wilderness solitude cannot possibly exist. The moment someone revs up the bulldozer to dig the footings, the rules of engagement have changed.

Yes, the game park is precious because it preserves a unique and irreplaceable community of plants and animals and provides immense joy for a lot of people. If we look at it from a hierarchal human perspective, the game park becomes a vital cultural heritage for all the *Homo sapiens* on the planet. From the perspective of the plants, animals, rocks and rivers, a few of them are lucky enough to survive the holocaust. Either way, if you take down the fences, send the tourists home, burn the hotels to the ground and eliminate the anti-poaching patrols, then cities, towns and farmlands will swoop into this space virtually instantaneously, as if sucked into a vortex by a vacuum. Therefore, we should be thankful for what we have, not bellyaching about what we have lost.

Perhaps I am a hopeless romantic, unwilling to accept the reality of the Anthropocene, but I fear that as soon as we accept a diminished definition of wilderness, we ratchet down our conservation efforts to match the new definition. It's like when a little global warming melts some arctic ice, which reduces the albedo, which creates more heat, which melts more ice.... And then, in either example, it doesn't take too many years or too many generations before we have forgotten the baseline, and eventually, before there is virtually nothing left. And, along the way, we lose something vital within ourselves.

Thus, after all the millions of copies of *Walden* and *Silent Spring* have been sold and read, we still need to sit down and reacquaint ourselves with the essence of a healthy, sustainable, compassionate, symbiotic relationship between fragile two-legged humans and all the other living and non-living entities out there.

Since I am contemplating this relationship as I stand in the Land Rover taking pictures, I feel the need to emphasize that anyone who journeys into wilderness, or some semblance of wilderness, on a mission to look at something and to return home with a photograph, is missing nine-tenths of the experience. It's like the fable of five blind people, each touching a portion of an elephant and trying to describe the whole animal. The blind person who grasps the elephant's tail says, "Oh, an elephant is like a long, skinny, furry snake." And so forth. Oh yes, we all marvel at pretty landscapes and snap images of lions when given the opportunity. We all "ooh and ah" at towering mountains or colourful parrots flying through the foliage. But the problem is that if our mission is primarily to see something, then anything that gets in the way of this seeing becomes an inconvenient aside, as in: "Oh darn. Phooey. Oh well. I guess I will have to tough it out and endure this cold, heat, thirst, or whatever if I want to see what I came here to see." Which is totally missing the point. We come here for a total mind-body-spirit experience. We come here to turn off that analytical, busy, ever-active part of our brain that has become so handy in so many urban ways, but which creates a barrier between us and the rest of the planet. We come here to feel this place in our pores, our skin, our heart, through sweat or frostbite, through hunger and fatigue, to seek unity, to revitalize our animal inheritance. If the wind comes up and blows dust around, that is a wondrous desert windstorm to enjoy, not a bummer because it leads to blurry photos of the lion.

I know I'm inviting criticism. I totally understand that tens of thousands of people sign up for the "Five-Star Wilderness Five-Day

Safari," watch the vanishing fauna of the great savannahs and return home feeling wonderfully energized. On average, about 1,000 tourists visit the Serengeti Park in Tanzania *every day*. Without this massive influx of tourist dollars, there would be no means to keep impoverished poachers, ranchers and farmers from annihilating the wildebeest, zebra and lions. The great herds and their predators would disappear, just as lions disappeared in medieval Greece. As Carl Safina writes: "Several tourist vans appear from nearby lodges, jostling for clear views of Wendy's family. [Wendy is an elephant matriarch.] *Snap snap snap* go the cameras. The vapid snapping is the only thing competing economically with killing the elephants. Bless the tourists."[77] As a confirmation of Safina's words, when the Covid pandemic reduced tourism to essentially zero in the summer of 2020, and the cash stream from the game parks dried up like the creeks had dried up during the drought, people throughout East Africa who had worked as cooks, motel maids and guides reverted to raising cattle again. But with pasture limited, they encroached upon the protected grasslands, poaching intensified and the wildlife suffered drastically.[78]

So, game parks are a win-win situation for the tourists, the locals and the animals. Perfect. Wonderful. Stupendous. I speak from the bottom of my heart.

Several years ago, I was fortunate to have coffee with Dr. Paul Ehrlich, the biologist who wrote the groundbreaking book, *The Population Bomb*, published in 1968. The previous day, he had given a talk in which he argued that the current world human population (at that time) of seven billion was unsustainable,[79] and that humans would have to cut back to two or three billion if we expected to stick around on this planet for the foreseeable future. As we sat across a table, I asked the obvious question, "How can we realistically and peacefully decrease our population by more than half?"

....

77 Carl Safina, *Beyond Words: What Animals Think and Feel* (New York: Henry Holt, 2015), p. 130.

78 Max Bearak, "Corona Virus Is Crushing Tourism and Cutting off a Lifeline for Wildlife," *The Washington Post*, July 17, 2020, https://www.washingtonpost.com/graphics/2020/world/coronavirus-africa-tourism-wildlife/.

79 That was a few years ago; the population as I write this is over 7.5 billion.

His answer was that we needed "A Consciousness Revolution."

I suggest that one way to initiate this Consciousness Revolution is to journey to a place on the edge of the abyss, where you will be too cold, too hot, too tired or too scared, so you become friends with the wind. You might die along the way. But that is a small matter. Welcome. It's good to see you.

You argue that this statement is idealistic mumbo-jumbo. No one that I know of lives in a cave and eats roots and berries. We all fall for the Luxury Trap and eventually come home to warm houses and drive in air-conditioned cars, even members of the North Face extreme team. It's the ultimate paradox of our times. But that's okay. Perhaps you can journey into wilderness only every now and then, or perhaps you live in a city and the greenest environment available is the city park. Fine. My suggestion is that however and whenever you make the journey, immerse yourself as a whole-body experience. Breathe deeply. Look, listen. Feel. The abyss is everywhere. Step off the precipice and there is always a Consciousness Revolution at the other end of what we thought was unknowable.

And don't forget that I am offering you a pathway prejudiced by my own bias. There are many, perhaps easier ways to initiate the same transformation: music, meditation, many ways. If I were an oboe player, I could write a book called *Zen and the Art of Oboe Playing*. But I am a wilderness traveller so that is what I write about.

In *The Once and Future World: Nature As It Was, As It Is, As It Could Be*, J.B. MacKinnon argues that every time we lose a bit of wilderness, or comprehension of wilderness, we reset our baseline, forget what was in the past. And then the baseline of our mind shifts. "We have forgotten what nature can be and adapted to a diminished world of our own making." And, I would add, we have forgotten the joy and pain of the persistence hunt. Of living inside a body capable of the persistence hunt. When someone misrepresents wilderness for profit, and we learn to expect mints on the pillow as part of our wilderness experience, then it becomes that much more difficult to fathom or implement Dr. Ehrlich's Consciousness Revolution. Our profligate compulsion to experience what we are so earnestly trying to save will destroy what we think we are saving. It sounds draconian, but as a society, we need to listen to Joseph Campbell, who argues that we need to die before we can be reborn.

It should be clear by now to anyone who is alive and aware today that there are too many humans in the world and nearly every one of us who lives in the developed world owns, or wants, too much stuff and burns too much fuel. As our conversation continued, Dr. Ehrlich explained that you can't use logic to convince people to procreate less and want less. It must come from inside and be a joyous journey, not a guilt-driven obligation. I suggest that wilderness is one window that can open a vision to live simply, open our awareness and find joy in the NOW.

The great Inuit shaman Igjugarjuk famously taught, "All true wisdom is only to be learned far from the dwellings of men, out in the great solitudes; and is only to be attained through suffering. Privation and suffering are the only things that can open the mind of man to those things that are hidden from others."[80] True wilderness is a great teacher if we open our hearts and minds and create space for the wisdom to enter.

In 1972–73, shortly after the publication of *The Population Bomb*, and partly in response to Dr. Ehrlich's alarm, the Norwegian philosopher Arne Næss introduced the discipline of Deep Ecology. The premise is that the living environment, as a whole, has inalienable rights, and it is a fundamental injustice against the natural order when people set themselves haughtily, artificially and dangerously on top of some imaginary, mythological hierarchy that shoves Nature into the shadows. Instead, every lion, cyad tree, mosquito and everything else is sacred and therefore has a basic moral (and legal) right to live and flourish, independent of how handy or economically beneficial it is for human use. Deep Ecology wasn't a new discovery or awakening at all, but a critical rediscovery of the Aboriginal relationship with the Earth that guided and implemented our survival for millions of years.

Our grail is wholeness, unity. It's not easy. If all we can do is preserve a fraction of wilderness, that's so much better than nothing. If all we can do is preserve a fraction of our own primordial humanity and wisdom, that's better than nothing. As I explained in the last chapter, the Koryak shaman Moolynaut grew up in a skin tent, while I grew up going to Park Avenue school. I remember my first day in that school.

----

80 Knud Rasmussen, *Across Arctic America: Narrative of the Fifth Thule Expedition* (Fairbanks: University of Alaska Press [Classic Reprint Series], 1999), p. 81.

We all lined up, shortest to tallest, and marched down a hallway built of parallel rows of concrete blocks that to my young eyes stretched to a focal point of infinity. At 6 years old, I didn't have the words to express the fear that my childhood of growing up in the woods was over, forever, and that the rest of my life would be an orderly passage within a climate-controlled symmetrical hallway lined with concrete blocks. I didn't have the words, but I stepped out of line, sat down on the grey linoleum floor and started to cry. As I sat at my desk throughout that year, and the following years, being careful to pretend that I was attentive even if I was daydreaming, learning the three Rs, I lost some of my primordial inheritance. I can never become Moolynaut or Jawas. No modern Siberian Koryak, who went to Russian schools, have been able to assimilate the shamanic power of Moolynaut. That's okay. What's left is wondrous and joyful. We all live in the Anthropocene, a geological epoch of significant, ubiquitous and universal human impact on planetary geology and ecosystems. That isn't going to change anytime soon. But each one of us can take positive steps to preserve our own sanity, if nothing else.

Back to the moment: A few dozen people are standing on the seats of their roofless safari wagons furiously snapping photos of the lion. Tina, Dipa and Ian look at me expectantly. I don't want to appear jaded or ungrateful, so I dutifully take out my camera. I only have the telephoto lens because Raven broke the wide angle. I aim the camera and the tiny motor goes *whirr*. The lion morphs into clear focus and the ecosystem surrounding it disappears. I block out the sensation that it is hot outside, or that zebras are grazing on the distant plain, or that there are other people around me. My world has become two-dimensional, and I can adjust the apparent distance between me and the lion by rotating the zoom collar. The lion is isolated – unreal – certainly not dangerous. I am isolated in the diminished perspective of my viewfinder. I snap off a few frames. Looking back at the images on my computer screen, they're ho-hum photos compared to what I could pull up in 0.23 seconds on Google, royalty-free. But they are all in focus, and after I saturate the washed-out midday colours in Photoshop, they're not too bad.

The lion hasn't moved since we arrived and there are only so many ways to compose a photo of a sleeping animal, so I put down my camera. Lions hang out in the game park and eat zebras but don't eat the tourists and mostly don't get shot. But it's a deal with the devil because when lions become a tourist attraction, all the people, myself included – guilty as charged – fly over here in airplanes that burn a godawful amount of fuel, which spews carbon dioxide into the air, which melts the arctic ice cap, which screws up the climate big time, causing this drought that threatens the survival of the lion. So, the lion is lying in the sun in relative security at the expense of its children's security. Just as you and I are doing. You might argue that the lion at least has no ability to control the outcome, whereas people do have control. Yeah, but I'm not so sure that I have appreciably more ability to alter the course of world history than the lion does. But I do get to worry about our distant future more than the lion does. Because I'm a conscious storytelling human with a think-too-much-know-it-all brain.

I take a deep breath. Oh boy. Way too much thinking. So I watch the lion sleep here on the Ragged Edge of the Anthropocene. Shut it down, Jon; slow it down. The lion isn't talking to me, but it is. The rocks aren't talking to me, but they are. The desert sky isn't talking to me, but it is. Isn't that better now?

Calmer now, and with more clarity, I lift my binos and focus on the lion's serene face. Steadying my arms, I look directly into its eyes, highlighted by black markings pointing toward its blunt nose, like a movie star with too much mascara. At other times and places, I have talked with animals from a different species. When Patches, our neighbour's cat who occasionally visits us, jumps on my lap, I look into her one good eye, because she lost the other in a fight, I suppose, when she was a feral animal living outside in the Montana forest, before she found a people-house to live in. Patches looks back at me and we both know that despite her continued inclinations toward wildness, we are neighbours, friends and family.

But that level of communication isn't happening today. That's okay, lion, I don't need to intrude on your space any more than I am doing already. But, even if the conversation is one-sided, I concentrate on turning off the analytical me, the storytelling animal, the writer of books, and focus in on the quiet majesty of this lion, of all lions, and of Gaia herself.

It's time for lunch, so we drive to the park headquarters, with immaculately manicured lawns and gravelled walkways. The black people in the Land Rover, Dipa and Ian, disappear into the staff quarters and Tina and I head to the restaurant. Wait a minute. I thought Dipa and Ian were our buddies. Tribe. Didn't Dipa and I track the out-of-game-park lion together and become blood brothers in shared danger? Isn't Dipa the tribal headman?

The restaurant is immaculately clean, with flowers on the table and small candleholders for the evening meal. I wash my hands in a 'whites-only' bathroom. A long buffet table is heavy with a variety of vegetables, meats, fish and fresh fruit. Food, sustenance, in a glorious overflowing cornucopia, unavailable to 95 per cent of the humans on this planet. Black people in white chef uniforms are serving a line of white tourists. Lunch is $20 for all you can eat. I've been sitting in a car all day and I'm not that hungry, but I really should treat Tina, and although it's not my style, I can afford $40 for lunch. But Tina talks to the maître d', who loves Tina for all she has done for the villagers, so we are allowed one small plate, which is plenty, for free. The food is quite good, but I don't feel comfortable here and want to finish my meal and get on with the day.

After lunch, we drive to the banks of the languid Ewaso Ng'iro River to watch elephants. It's seriously hot and they are sensible enough to take their afternoon mud baths – rolling, squirting themselves with their trunks, frolicking, having a good time, being a family. Dipa tells me that there are crocodiles in the river, but they don't mess with the elephants. After half an hour, the elephants start climbing back up toward dry ground. The babies slip in the gooey muck and struggle climbing the banks, so adults nudge them gently with their trunks until the young regain their footing. Tina tells me of a baby elephant who was orphaned by poachers near camp and rescued by a team of wildlife biologists. At first it wouldn't eat, but eventually it imprinted on one of the human handlers and under his care and affection began to regain its health. When they introduced the poor orphan to a captive urban herd in Nairobi, the adults surrounded the distraught baby and wrapped it with their trunks, hugging it repeatedly.

It crosses my mind that in the United States, the Republicans have adopted the elephant as the symbol of their party. At the same time, they work assiduously to cut the safety nets for the disadvantaged, inventing elaborate mythologies to convince themselves that compassion is a bad thing. Unfortunately, the elephants can't sue the Republican Party for defamation of character. But we can watch the elephants and learn from them.

Once again: when in Rome, do as the Romans. I shoot some still photos, switch the camera to video, and film a mamma and baby as they walk slowly but purposefully directly toward the Land Rover. I keep them in focus, gradually shifting the camera as they approach. First there are two elephants in the frame of the viewfinder, then one, then part of an elephant, then just the elephant's head, until I have a flash realization: "I am concentrating on the abstraction within the camera, but in the Real World, out there on the savannah, this elephant must be close. Furthermore, an elephant is big, and I am just a weak, fragile collection of bones and protoplasm. I wonder if there is a problem here?" I lower the camera, and there she is, about ten metres away. She's not charging or waving her ears or showing any overt signs of hostility or aggression. She doesn't reach out her trunk and embrace me, either. We stare at each other. For whatever reason, of all the people on the imaginary subway train of this game park, she decided to walk up to the four of us in this vehicle. I look her in the eye. I can't hazard a guess at what she's thinking, or worse yet, try to put her thoughts into human language. But she is curious enough, or interested enough, to go out of her way, in the midst of a busy day of eating, mud bathing and child care, to walk over to the Land Rover and check us out.

Some years before, while I was kayaking along the coast of Kamchatka, a grey whale approached, surfaced and rolled over onto its side to float gently alongside and stare at me, less than a paddle stroke away. As with the elephant, we made close eye contact. Another time, off the coast of Ellesmere, a polar bear gently poked a hole in the door to our tent to see what was inside. Off Cape Horn, dolphins swam by to join me surfing, breaking waves in a deep channel. Once, in the woods behind my house, a wolf sat down in the trail I was hiking on, blocking my path. I sat down and we looked at each other for 15 minutes. And what was that raven doing or saying to me when it swooped low past my face to steal my camera? Maybe, earlier in the day, the lion was talking to me as well, but I was just not open and attentive enough to reciprocate.

There are doors connecting us to nature's creatures if we're patient and observant enough. I feel certain that there are more doors than

Jon Turk

we are patient and aware enough to see or open. Moolynaut tells me that Kutcha, the Siberian Raven, flew to The Woman Who Lives on the Highest Mountain on my behalf, to ask her to heal my damaged pelvis. And I was healed. And if trees communicate with one another and nurture each other in some chemical way, do they talk with us as well? There are no answers, and it's too easy to get all tangled up in the definitions of our words, which aren't effective in communicating these ideas because our language is limited by our perceptions of the world beyond language. No matter. No need for entanglement here. Today an elephant paid me a visit from one sentient creature to another along a lazy river in a parched landscape within a game park. And that visit opened doors of wonder to the natural world.

But why do I need the spectacular animals, the lion and the elephant, to hold open the doors? Why aren't all the autos lining up to photograph the zebras? Or the ants? Aren't they wondrous as well? I think of the bare, whitened spar on the top of my favourite ski run. It's a long climb to get there, and every time I reach the spot I feel as if I am returning to visit an old friend. If a dead tree can become a dear friend, then barriers break down and doors open everywhere.

That evening, when the game park expedition is over, as I'm walking to dinner, David meets me on the path and asks me what animals I saw in the park today. I run down the list.

"Did you see a giraffe?" he asks.

"No. No giraffes."

David responds seriously, "In Kenya, we learn not to worry because you didn't see a giraffe today."

Good advice.

After dinner, in the middle of the night, as if the day weren't full enough, a leopard visits me at my tent camp. Previously, Tina had warned me that she lived in the neighbourhood and that leopards, like most felines, define and defend a territory. While human territories are delineated by survey stakes and government fiat, animal territories are established and enforced by ancient custom, protocol and sometimes violence. In this case, my tent site on the hillside lies just a smidge on the human side of the boundary between the human's camp and the leopard's hard-won hunting ground.

After I've gone to bed and am sleeping soundly, the leopard crosses the border, walks stealthily to the door of my tent, a flimsy canvas barrier with fabric flaps held together with intertwined sticks, takes a deep breath and growls. It isn't a lion's bellicose roar, but more like a cross between a fierce guttural grunt and a pig snorting. Deeply penetrating. I had never heard a leopard growl before, but I know what it is as soon as the sound disrupts my sleep. I grab my *rungu*, spring out of bed and crouch, as ready for action as I can be. She circles the tent slowly, counterclockwise, and then jumps up on the large rock beside the tent, to stand directly above me. I can feel the power of that leap, the crouched legs, the explosive extension, the soft accurate landing on the narrow tip of the rock. Then, when her tactical advantage is solidified, when we both know that any moment she can leap through the ceiling and land directly on top of me, a furry muscular bundle of teeth and claws, she growls again, louder and more ferocious than before.

I step to the side, hopefully to give myself an extra millisecond should she come flying through the ceiling like a Rambo-esque ninja assailant. Once again, I am faced with the question, should I project dominance, assuming the attitude, "You are Bad-Ass, but I am more Bad-Ass"? Hence, should I growl, yell and scream, tossing human hostility into the night? No. A thousand times: no. If the leopard had wanted to kill me in a direct confrontation, for food or out of territorial prerogative, I'd be dead already. She is talking to me, communicating, as good neighbours do, speaking on her own behalf and on behalf of herself and all the leopards, as well as the lions, elephants, polar bears and Jurassic cyad trees:

"I know you're here and I know you're a white man. Most white men come and then leave after a day or two, but you've been staying around for a while. So, if you're going to hang out here, I just want you to be sure to understand that I was here first. This is my territory. Don't you know that we are in the middle of a three-year drought? Your food comes to you in trucks. Mine doesn't. Hunting is hard and I need every bit of territory I have. Please, please, I implore you, I threaten you: Respect my space. Don't push me into the abyss. Don't push all of us into the abyss. I'm talking to you. Listen up."

My fear, which arose so precipitously at the first growl in the night, begins to subside. My body no longer needs to pump adrenaline into the bloodstream, and the hormones that are already in the system begin to dissipate. My breathing slows, the tension in the muscles relaxes. This leopard is not hunting me, and she is not out-of-control angry. She is simply trying to communicate to the best of her ability, asking for a little humility on my part, so she can emerge from this confrontation with her integrity, her homeland and her survival intact.

I reply softly, "It's okay. Thank you. You are well spoken. I didn't come from faraway Montana to steal your land. Yes, I am on the edge of your territory, but I won't push further. And I will go home soon enough."

She jumps off the rock with a barely perceptible, muffled thud, circles the tent, growling the whole time, and then jumps on the rock again, for emphasis, with an even more dramatic grunt-growl-snort. And then a third time.

"Thank you, leopard. I will cherish this moment. I will go home soon enough. And I will tell the world that you spoke to me."

She slips silently into the thicket, moving unseen and unheard through the tangled brambles and thorns.

CHAPTER 10

LOST CAMEL

Dipa shows up at breakfast the following morning and asks me to help him unload the Land Rover: two 50 lb. bags of sugar, a large burlap sack of chai and several cases of boxed, ultra-pasteurized, ultra-homogenized milk, which seems an odd item for dairy farmers to purchase.

"What's all this stuff for?"

"The wedding," he said with a perplexed look as if I'm expected to know about the wedding. "The wedding is tomorrow."

No, I don't know about the wedding, partly, I suppose, because I am hard of hearing, partly because people are speaking Samburu much of the time, and assuredly because no one told me directly. Fine, we are planning a wedding, which, as in all cultures throughout time, will be a joyful gathering of the tribes and a ceremony to celebrate the hoped-for continuance of *Homo sapiens* DNA.

Dipa reaches into the folds of his clothing and pulls out a fist-sized bundle of something tied up inside a black plastic bag.

"Because you are a warrior now. You will come to the wedding as a warrior."

This is also news to me. When did I become a warrior? And what did I do to deserve this honour?

Dipa unties the knot securing the bag with the drama of my mother opening a mystery present on my birthday. With all the anticipation of a 4-year-old, I peer inside to see a handful of powdered red ochre dye.

Red ochre has been used as a ceremonial coloration for at least 200,000 years. The earliest works of symbolic art found in the Blombos Cave were cut into red ochre rock. Many of the European cave paintings, including the 35,000-year-old bison panel we discussed in Chapter 5, were painted with red ochre. The use of ochre throughout Paleolithic Europe was so intense and ubiquitous that this mineral dye lies 15–20 centimetres thick on the floors of many caves.

Dipa smiles broadly and the gap in his teeth stands out. He raises a pinch of the dye between his fingers. "We put it in your hair and paint your face, so you can participate in the ceremony."

I smile back – honoured and excited that someone is going to paint red lines on my face and dye my hair, but also mystified. Then I wonder if my contribution to the ceremony might become more intense than I bargained for. Is this going to be a wedding where we all dance, sing and get a little drunk? Or will this be more similar to the Sun Dance of the Aboriginal tribes of the North American plains, where you must pierce your skin and rip the flesh off your chest in a day of fasting and self-mutilation?

Traditionally, ceremony has so many functions: to bring a tribe together, to pray, to initiate, and to rev people into a frenzy and rally them into battle. Ceremony is a dramatic enactment of myth, and like all myth, it can evoke cohesion or separation, peace or war, holy matrimony or murder, joy or suffering, religious ecstasy or initiation. The ancient gatherings in the serpent cave 70,000 years ago helped lift *Homo sapiens* from the brink of extinction. Hitler's rallies were also a form of ceremony. Yin and yang. Ecstasy and horror.

I am a warrior now, whatever that means, and I puff up my ego with an inflated self-image. I have been chosen. Therefore, I must prove myself worthy. If they pierce me with needles, I will endure the pain without flinching. I fall hook, line and sinker for the rise in my own status and promise of tribal acceptance. Thus, I join the untold millions of warriors before me. If they wave a flag, which is merely a mythological representation of an imagined order created in people's minds, and play a raucous marching tune on the bugle – will I really charge into battle?

Dipa drives off and I hang around the dining area until Ian and Jawas show up and ask me to come down and help them train the camels. Whew; this is so much more straightforward. The pressure from my swelling brain subsides and my emotions settle down as if a great danger has passed. All kinds of useless hormones and equally useless hormone-controlled thoughts dissipate. My ego relaxes. Life has returned to normal.

We walk down the hill, cross the dry wash and follow the road to the corral. An old herder, whom I've met casually before, greets us with a smile. He manages a flock of 30 goats, who stay alive by eating the last vestiges of virtually non-existent vegetation, and the small herd of five camels, who forage mainly on whatever spiny tree leaves they can reach. Tina has told me that she bought the camels so the motel can offer rides for the tourists, as Ian did early in my stay, and the local staff can earn a bit of ready cash.

Our task of the morning is to train the camels to kneel, accept a passenger, and then stand up and go for a short walk. The camels are reluctant students. They are offered no reward when they perform as expected, but someone is sure to pinch their lips or twist an ear if they fail to obey promptly. The camels resist, get punished, bawl and cry. The men smack the poor animals with thorn branches. Finally, we load a crude pack saddle onto one of the camels. The saddle is made of sticks tied together inexpertly with string. The ends of the sticks jab into the camel's flanks. Ian instructs me to climb aboard, which I do – with hesitation. Prodded, poked and pulled, the camel takes a few steps, then stops, bawling and howling pitifully, sounding alarmingly like a human baby.

Ian pinches the camel's lower lip; the old herder whacks it with a stick.

"Whoa, whoa. I'm not riding this camel under these conditions."

"Okay, then, c'mon down. You can take the lead rope and pull it."

Ian orders the camel to kneel. Perhaps because it knows that I will dismount if it obeys, the camel does as instructed. I jump off and walk toward its head. I reach my hand out to pet it, and it jerks its head away, reflexively. I reach my hand out again, ever so slowly this time, as the frightened animal gauges me cautiously. I scratch it under the chin gently. The camel cocks its head and looks at me. I stare back and notice a prominent lightning-shaped scar under its left eye.

"Okay, buddy," I reply softly. "We're going for a walk now."

I tug on the lead rope. The animal resists. I turn back and cluck softly. The camel cocks its head again and then starts up slowly, like a freight train beginning to roll. Soon the lead rope slackens as it falls into a rhythm behind me.

That evening, as I am eating dinner with Tina, across a small table with a white tablecloth, by a cheery fire, Dipa drops by to tell us that the wedding will not take place tomorrow, after all. There is some confusion about the phases of the moon.

Well, it's more complicated than that.

For a wedding to occur, the phases of the moon must coincide with numerological considerations based on the Samburu calendar. Dipa shakes his head woefully. That alignment has not occurred, he says with mournful finality.

Well, it's more complicated than that.

For a wedding to occur, the bride and groom must sacrifice a bull, with the vow that the marriage will endure until the bull returns to life. But, due to the drought, the groom has hired herders to drive the cattle deep into the mountains to find grass and water. And he doesn't know exactly where his herd is at the moment. There are many possible locations, all far apart from one another. And even if he could find them, it would be unrealistic to either separate the bull from the herd or to bring the entire herd back to the village, because there is no water. But, unfortunately, if we delay until the Red Moon, then the delay will necessarily extend for another month, which would be inconvenient because the bride and groom are anxious to get married.

Tina reminds Dipa that she has arranged for contractors to drill a well and hopefully find water at the camp, so that the remaining cows won't die of thirst and the tourists can flush their toilets. The drillers are from Nairobi and charge a per diem fee just to be here. They plan to work six days a week, but break on Sunday, because they are Christians and Sunday is the Lord's Day. Because Tina, and potentially Dipa, should be around to oversee the drilling operation, it would be economically convenient if the moon, the numerology and the cows all aligned to have the wedding on Sunday.

We are at an impasse created by a complex, interwoven set of realities and mythologies. Watering the cows so they don't die of thirst is a reality. Moving the cows so they can find forage during a drought is a reality. Working or resting on Sunday is a mythology. Getting married when the moon cycle coincides with numerological considerations of the Samburu calendar is also a mythology. Depending on your anthropological view of things, marriage may or may not be a mythology, but sex and procreation lie in the reality camp.

We, as humans, whether we live in Toronto or Samburu, certainly manage to make our lives complicated. That is reality.

Just for fun, I suggest the following exercise. Starting with what you eat for breakfast, break your day into mythologies and realities: why you bother to go to work, what you buy in the store, why you argue or make love with your spouse, why you worry about why you didn't see a giraffe today. Don't stress over this too much or, worse yet, turn this task into its own mythology. But if we are striving toward Dr. Ehrlich's Consciousness Revolution, we need a strong and unbiased bullshit meter.

It's an important exercise, because, as we shall see in the next chapter, when the shit hits the fan and when we are dealing with consequences much more severe than one's own ego, imagined beliefs, tribal acceptance, or even a wedding, it can become literally a matter of life and death to separate truth from fiction.

After dinner, I return to my tent, place my *rungu* on the bedside table next to my cot, in case the leopard should return, close my eyes, and take stock of the day. I'm chastened and even a bit scared at my reaction to my warrior status and imagined participation in the ceremony I still know next to nothing about. Humans are preprogrammed to be attracted to ceremony – a dramatic enactment of tribal mythologies that endowed our ancestors with the strength and co-operative cohesion to survive. But, as a corollary, fictional narratives take precedence over truth. If members of my tribe can only be married, procreate and guarantee the survival of the tribe under certain specific and outrageous conditions, then our tribe stands apart from your tribe. It is inconvenient to follow the mythological conditions, to be sure, but at the same time they set us apart as a cohesive unit. We help each other – and as a result, we survive in a chaotic and often hostile world.

But this is dangerous ground because all ceremony is an imagined order. Anyone who creates a narrative and then shouts "Follow Me!" has the potential to cause trouble.

Even though there is no leopard and no danger, I reach out and grasp my *rungu,* slide my hand along the smooth, hard wood, lift it and feel its balance and swing weight. There is elegant simplicity in the NOW. We've all been present, sometimes, occasionally, or every once in a while. Maybe presence strikes us on the head while tracking the lion. Of course, your awareness heightens when there is a lion in the bushes. But presence is also there, if you open yourself to it, while watching a squirrel in the park, brushing your teeth, eating dinner, or lying in your bed holding your *rungu.* And it's a glorious place to be.

A few days later, a busload of Russian tourists show up. Dipa has hired women from the local village to dress in their finery and entertain. The women sing, then begin a simple dance by swaying with their vocal beat and shuffling their feet. The Russians drink vodka, and dance along with the women. Ian moves to the centre and claps his hands to attract attention. He shouts, "We will now all do the *adamu!*" Neither the Russians nor I know what the *adamu* is, so we stop to watch as Ian leaps into the air, launching off both feet simultaneously and landing on his toes, heels never touching the ground. Repeat. Each leap is higher than the previous one, body erect, hands by his side. He starts grunting. Then he stops to instruct. "We will do the *adamu* and grunt like lions." With no further explanation, and without any deeper knowledge of the cultural significance of the dance, the jolly, half-drunk Russians and I leap as high, erect and gracefully as we can, and grunt as ferociously as possible. We laugh at ourselves. The Samburu laugh at us, or with us; it doesn't matter.

Someone turns on European music. A middle-aged Russian woman fills my vodka glass and we dance together in the African night. She slips seamlessly out of my orbit and I dance with Ian, then a 6-year-old Samburu girl, followed by a burly Russian guy who wiggles his bulging stomach like a belly dancer.

If you strip away all the mythologies, stir in a busload of Russians on vacation, and add enough vodka, then ceremony becomes a spontaneous party, and everyone has a jolly good time without all the fuss and commotion.

Over the next few days, Tina spends most of her time elsewhere, getting cars fixed and managing management; it's unclear to me. I help the old goat herder pick up trash along the roadway and we find plastic everywhere. I assemble some new beds for the next round of tourists. I resolve not to lose my conditioning, so I won't be too far behind on my mountain bike when I get home, so I charge up the trail to the first ridge on Mt. Sabache-Ololokwe every chance I get. Jawas accompanies me frequently. At first, he finds this activity sort of weird, but soon he gets into it, and we push each other, pumping hard, sweating profusely, and gradually knocking off 15 minutes from our time. We ritually share an orange at the top. One day a group of British tourists show up to climb the mountain and camp in the cyad grove. They have no intention of carrying their own food and water up the steep trail, and the motel is short-staffed today, so I porter up a load. The Brits let me know that this is improper, but I ignore them. Then they let me know that they think I'm kind of a jerk for carrying the *rungu*, but I know that Jawas would correct me if I left it at home, so I shrug off the criticism. They thank me when I drop my load at the ridge crest, but they don't tip me.

Over the next few days, with Tina still away, my dinner simplifies to a staple of maize, sautéed carrots, cabbage and onion. The table with the white tablecloth disappears and no one bothers to light a cheery bonfire at mealtime. The staff serves me on the veranda closer to the kitchen, so they don't have to walk as far. Moses, Ian and David often hang about at mealtime, chatting, but Jawas only appears when it is time for our speed hikes up the mountain. Days pass.

One morning Jawas shows up at breakfast to tell me that someone forgot to close the gate securely and one of the camels escaped from the *boma* last night. I ask if it was the one with the lightning bolt scar beneath its left eye. Jawas looks at me with interest, and then nods.

"How do you know what camel run away?"

This is not time for a lecture on camel whispering, so I just smile and shrug, but I'm not at all surprised that Lightning Bolt wanted outta there.

Jawas asks if I will help him find the camel.

I grab my *rungu* and stick and we head out. Then I stop and tap Jawas on the shoulder. "Hold on a second. I'm going to bring my day pack and some water."

"The camel is close. You will not want this water."

I look off into the scrub desert and try to imagine what thoughts are flowing through the camel's head. Did this camel bust out of the *boma* for some casual midnight grazing? Or is it feeling so abused that this is The Great Escape?

I smile at Jawas. "I'm not walking into the desert without water."

We pick up the tracks at the *boma* gate, but I am immediately confused.

"Hey Jawas. It looks to me as if the camel is returning to the *boma*, not escaping."

Jawas is so confused by my rookie question that he doesn't even have the presence to say, "No, siree!"

But after struggling across our language and knowledge barriers for some minutes, I figure out what is happening. Camels belong to the same biological family as deer and elk, who leave characteristic tracks of cloven hooves. But whereas a deer or elk steps with its weight forward, so the fronts of the hooves dig deepest, camels have evolved with broad snowshoe feet and a gait designed to step down with the heel of the foot hitting prior to the toe, so they can stay afloat and move more efficiently on soft sand. As a result, to a Montana tracker like me, the camel appears to be walking backward.

With that lesson established, it's easy to follow Lightning Bolt out of the *boma*, across the dirt road that leads to the motel, and then eastward as it heads toward the A-2 Road and the broad central valley. This camel is travelling in an unerringly straight line, as if following a compass bearing. I measure the length of its stride against my own, so I will be aware if it changes its gait. When we reach the main valley, the camel turns north, toward the sparsely populated desert, and away from the higher concentration of villages and people around the town of Archers Post. I follow the tracks, feeling stupid that I didn't bring three litres of water rather than one and a half. Jawas hangs back and waves his arms, calling me. I turn around and we reconnoitre.

"The camel went that way," he tells me, pointing south.

I shake my head in denial and confusion. "But the tracks clearly go north."

"No, siree! The camel. He go that way."

"How do you know this?" I ask, expecting some Deep Earth tidbit of Aboriginal wisdom. Jawas lifts his cellphone out of the fold of his garments. "A woman call me. She is at the goats. She see the camel. Yes siree. He go that way."

We turn south, and after a kilometre or two I am pleasantly surprised to cross the camel's tracks again. Or *a* camel's tracks. In his classic, *Arabian Sands*, British explorer Wilfred Thesiger reports the Bedouins could identify up to a hundred individual camels by their unique tracks. In the murderous tribal world of the post-Second World War Middle East, if you crossed a camel track, it would be a matter of life or death to know whether you were close to friend or foe. Neither Jawas nor I are nearly that good. I guess there are not enough enemies, or too many cellphones, around here to induce us to sharpen our senses.

From the information of the phone call, we assume that Lightning Bolt veered north, then backtracked south and that we have picked up his tracks again. But we're not sure. Whatever animal we are now following, the prints are spaced farther apart than the tracks we were following this morning. Either this is a larger animal, or if it is indeed Lightning Bolt, as we both suspect, it is picking up speed, heading somewhere specific, striding out.

Jawas must be having the same thoughts because he announces, "The camel. Yes, siree! He is gone far."

If I am tracking elk in Montana and I see that the herd is moving fast and straight, I give up. I haven't forgotten what I said earlier about !Kung tribesmen running down an antelope on a persistence hunt, but there is no way I can catch a herd of fast-moving elk in steep mountainous terrain. I am old, Montana is a cold-weather environment, not a desert, so you can't count on the animal developing heatstroke, and I just don't have that speed and endurance. So, here in Samburu, if it were my call, we would turn back. The camel is lost. Gone. Darn.

But there is no way Jawas will turn back. This camel is too valuable. Jawas's pocketbook, pride and status as a warrior are on the line. Oh, right. And I am a warrior now, too.

This could be a long day.

I start whining. Not to Jawas. The situation is not that bad – yet. But to myself.

"Stupid camel. I'm 71 years old. What am I doing here? Why am I even in Africa anyway? What am I doing at this silly Motel at the End of the World? I should have brought more water. The sun is hot. Do I give a shit about this camel? No, not at all. Not one tiny little bit.

After all the beatings and abuse it endured, I'm rooting for Lightning Bolt to make a clean escape. Go, Lightning Bolt. Go."

And while I'm in a grumpy mood, let's talk about who's domesticating who. Did humans domesticate camels so they can carry loads around for us? Or did camels domesticate humans so we will care for them so they can reproduce and spread their DNA? It's one of those circular questions to ponder when you have nothing else to ponder because you are chasing a dumb camel around the desert. "Boy, oh boy. That camel sure has me wrapped around its little finger. And if I find it, then what? I get to bring it water and food."

Except for dogs and cats, most domestic animals have a grim life: caged, corralled and miserable. Some, like Lightning Bolt, are beaten, others are overworked, while others are stuffed with an unhealthy diet of grains and antibiotics, so we can eat them. But in terms of DNA dispersal, the Darwinian trick of making yourself useful or edible for humans has sure been a good survival strategy. Camels have domesticated humans. Given the reality of this situation, what's my role in this ancient DNA dance, out here in this desert with Jawas and not enough water?

I've made myself miserable by overthinking a situation or over-focusing on small discomforts – just like this – a million times. For example: I love ski touring. But every time I climb a mountain to ski back down, I slip into Mr. Whine-Fest for some of the time. "Poor me." And so forth. I love hiking, camping and mountain biking, but every time…. You get the idea.

I would like to think that I would have learned by now not to go there. I would like to believe that I am stronger than that. But I'm not.

Fortunately, I've been in this headspace enough times to know what to do. Give the complaining a little space. Don't complain about the fact that you are complaining. That gets you nowhere. Then, slow it down. Breathe evenly. Look around. I remind myself: if there had been a lion or a black mamba close by five minutes ago, when I was focused on being miserable, I would be dead by now. Awareness, Jon, awareness.

Look around at this ecosystem. I've been in deep deserts where there has been scant rainfall for millennia. The vegetation in those ecosystems is adapted to the expected lack of rainfall – sparsely spaced cactus with a few low-lying bushes here and there. But this ecosystem is a dense collection of trees and shrubs that is adapted to a semi-desert, seasonal monsoon weather cycle. If the monsoon stalls out and the rains don't come, everything suffers. Everything edible has been eaten, even the thin green cambium beneath the tough bark of some of the trees. And what hasn't been eaten has withered.

I stop whining long enough to look around. I look for lions and snakes. I look at rocks and dead trees. Then, without willing myself to do this, without even noticing at first, some force deep inside me silently switches the looking into a full body sensation of feeling. I feel the atmosphere as it embraces me, feel it suck the moisture out of my pores, feel how different it is from the spruce-scented atmosphere of summer in Montana or frigid crystalline atmosphere of a northern winter. I feel the sun and a slight wisp of wind that probably had been wafting through the scrub all morning but I hadn't noticed. I feel my footsteps in the sand. Would it be more efficient to step down on my toes, as an elk steps, or to land on my heels, as Lightning Bolt walks? Lightning Bolt evolved to travel far in this landscape, but he is a camel and I am two-legged, and my knees articulate differently. Many modern ultra-runners hit on the balls of their feet for more efficient travel and fewer injuries. I have far to go today and I must concentrate to make every footstep as efficient and pain-free as possible. "Think about the efficiency of your stride, Jon, and nothing else, as if your life depended on it."

And then something happens that transcends words. I can tell you what I see, feel, smell or hear. I can describe my footsteps. But I can't really explain how something inexplicable inside me goes out and another inexplicable thing takes its place. Is it my brain that is transferring the data? Or the brain-like neurons that are embedded in my heart? Or my skin, or blood? It doesn't matter. A whole complex assemblage of worries, thoughts, logic – an entire self-image of myself as Warrior Jon Turk who went to Park Avenue school and wrote this many books – gets shelved in some nook or cranny where it is, at least for the moment, blissfully inaccessible. Gone. Poof. And the physical landscape around me becomes ghostlike and enters, wraps around the spaces between my ribs, and overtakes the brain and heart neurons. I am no longer inconvenienced by the desert – because we are intertwined. If my mouth is dry and my arms feel as if their imaginary leaves are withered in the heat, that's just the way things are out here in this global warming-induced desiccation. I have broken through the barrier of thinking or passing analytical judgment on the state of the present. And – Presto – I am here, NOW, tracking this camel in the desert with Jawas. This awareness has no basis in imaginary creatures, or narrative, or stories in my head. For me, this is all the strength, all the power, all the cohesiveness I need.

I step carefully, resolutely, and the ground presses upward against my feet like an old friend's reassuring touch. I have no food, little water and no idea how many hours, or days, we expect to travel. But none of that is reason to worry, because worry is an anticipation of some possible future outcome, and the future is not my problem.

There is a saying I learned long ago: "When the Going Gets Tough – The Tough Get Going."

That might work sometimes and in some places. But not out here, today. I'm not going to get tougher than the desert-hardened camel we are tracking, or the equatorial sun that beats down, or the desert itself. It doesn't work that way. But if I open myself to what is around me, breathe it all in, become part of and not separate from it, accept my own vulnerability, then it's all okay – more than okay.

I've broken through this barrier from complaining to accepting a million times. But I've only needed to break the barrier because I was the culprit who built it in the first place. You'd think I'd have learned by now how to skip the bullshit and go straight to nirvana. But I haven't learned that trick. Others have found the passageway; that's their good fortune. For now, today, this morning, I can only laugh at my own frailty and foolishness. Perhaps I find humour and not despair in it all because, next time I make myself miserable for no good reason, I can remember that I have broken through the barriers before. Maybe I don't know how to blast the self-created barriers that stand between me and contentment to smithereens, and maybe I don't know how to climb over them, but if I'm patient with myself, I know how to tunnel through or find the door, what-ever metaphor you choose. I know that I can find this doorway any time I go into nature, allow myself some patience and perhaps offer up a pinch of suffering. And I know that the door will close again if I become inattentive, lazy or complacent. That's okay. I am in the desert now, with Jawas, following a camel, because it has domesticated me, and I need to take it back to the *boma* and feed it and bring it water.

Suddenly the track of another camel joins in from the east, then a second unexplained track appears, and a third. We come to a clearing, and it's obvious a small herd of camels were milling around out here, having a party. On the other side of the clearing tracks, spread out, coalesce, double back and spread out again, all trending generally south by southeast, wandering this way and that, churning the desert sand. Lightning Bolt has slipped into the crowd, and from our perspective, has disappeared. We sit on a log. It's noon, and while I have been sipping water parsimoniously, Jawas hasn't had anything to drink all morning. I carefully equalize what's left from my two water bottles and hand one to Jawas. He smiles, nods, accepts the water almost ceremoniously and takes a drink. Friendship is one of those emotions, like connectivity with an ecosystem, that fills you up inside, chases away the demons and becomes a whole-body experience.

Our various organs send signals to the brain, but the brain interprets them. Thus, eyes send electrochemical signals to the brain, but we "see" with our brain, not with our eyes. My stomach is empty, and my blood sugar is low, so it sends signals to the brain. The brain evaluates. Yes, these signals are an accurate clinical accounting of the State of the World in my body. But the brain has the final say in how that data will be interpreted. Since there is no food in my day pack, and there will be no food forthcoming anytime soon, on this day, my brain decides that low blood sugar should not be interpreted as a reminder to eat a sandwich. Instead, because my brain and I have come to a good frame of being, we interpret hunger as a joyful cathartic cleansing, a sensual awareness coupled with the sensual awareness of the landscape around us. The drought has desiccated the desert, the lack of a peanut butter sandwich has shrivelled my stomach; all empty, clean, stripped down to basics. Unity. I'm fully aware that the brain is fickle and could turn on me at any moment, but for now, we're all good.

Robert Sapolsky is a professor of neurology and neurological sciences at Stanford University who conducted his early research on baboons here in Kenya. He has spent a lifetime analyzing and elucidating the relationship between the internal biological processes

Jon Turk

we can't observe directly and the external emotions we feel and express. In his newest book, *Behave: The Biology of Humans at Our Best and Worst*, he states that "it actually makes no sense to distinguish between aspects of a behavior that are 'biological' and those that would be described, as, say, 'psychological' or 'cultural.' Utterly intertwined."[81] Sapolsky goes on to explain that "human behavior is indeed a mess, a subject involving brain chemistry, hormones, sensory cues, prenatal environment, early experience, genes, both biological and cultural evolution, and ecological pressures, among other things."[82]

I have just given you a description of the cleansing, soothing, simplifying I felt as Jawas and I wandered out into the desert to search for poor, maligned Lightning Bolt, who busted out of the *boma* and headed south. It should be obvious that these fundamental feelings are nearly universal, available to anyone 24/7, free of charge, without appointment, who will take the time to go for a walk in the park, woods, desert or mountains. We'll start with Sapolsky's brilliant work and ask, "What can we learn from basic biology to appreciate the emotional value of a thirsty walk across the desert wilderness?"

Dopamine is a chemical, both a neurotransmitter and a hormone, synthesized in numerous regions of the brain. The body releases dopamine when it experiences pleasure in the form of, say, sex or food. Teach a monkey that when she presses a lever ten times she gets a raisin and she will accomplish the task, eat the raisin and experience a flood of dopamine. Then a research scientist manipulates the situation so that next time, when she presses the lever ten times, she gets two raisins. Bingo. This is not just good, it's wonderful. Even more dopamine is released into her system. Now what happens if the third time, she's back to one raisin? Darn. Whereas just a few moments ago one raisin was sufficient reward to trigger a dopamine release, now one raisin is a disappointment and initiates a *decrease* in dopamine.

As another experiment: Give a monkey a slice of cucumber and the monkey will eat it happily. Dopamine release. Give a monkey a

....

81   Robert Sapolsky, *Behave: The Biology of Humans at Our Best and Worst*, Reprint ed. (New York: Penguin, 2018), p. 13.

82   Robert Sapolsky, *Behave: The Biology of Humans at Our Best and Worst*, Reprint ed. (New York: Penguin, 2018), p. 13.

choice between cucumber and a grape, and the monkey will choose the grape. Now, give one monkey in a room a slice of cucumber, and give a grape to the other. Watch out. The poor deprived monkey, who was previously happy with the cucumber, is bummed. Dopamine levels go down. Anger goes up.

These experiments prove that our reward centres are not absolute, but relative to our prior experience. Thus, Sapolsky argues, "If we were designed by engineers, as we consumed more, we'd desire less. But our frequent human tragedy is that the more we consume, the hungrier we get." Our modern society blasts us constantly with abundant powerful dopamine-releasing stimuli such as loud music, delicious food, drugs and alcohol. These "unnaturally strong explosions of synthetic experience, sensation, and pleasure evoke unnaturally strong degrees of habituation." As a result, simple pleasures that once were joyful become the one raisin instead of two, or the cucumber instead of the grape. We now become unhappy, or even angry, not by misfortune, but by insufficiently excessive fortune. "Soon we barely notice the fleeting whispers caused by leaves in autumn."[83]

Returning to my emotional about-face during my morning walk. In the beginning, even though I was in a beautiful place with a good friend, with no real cares in the world, I thought of myself as the poor deprived monkey who received one raisin instead of two or the cucumber instead of the grape. But then, after walking through the savannah for merely a few hours, the habituation of the synthetic pleasures of the civilized world mysteriously slipped away, and I became happy with what I had and where I was. It's hard to imagine that humans are that malleable and fickle, but all evidence points to the fact that we are.

Humans have spent 99 per cent of their tenure on Earth living in close association with Nature. Therefore we "feel" more whole, complete, grounded when in contact with Nature. Again, this "feeling" is impossible to describe, but it's quantifiable. Thousands of experiments have shown that people perform better and are happier when they are in contact with Nature. In this sense we're not necessarily talking about remote deserts, alpine glaciers or other hard-to-access

....

83   These last three quotes are all from Robert Sapolsky, *Behave: The Biology of Humans at Our Best and Worst*, Reprint ed. (New York: Penguin, 2018), p. 69.

Jon Turk

wilderness. If you separate hospitalized patients into three groups, one in a room with bare walls, one in a room with a photograph of a mountain landscape, and a final group with a window opening up to a park, those with the window heal faster than those with the photo, who heal faster than those with nothing. In other studies, elderly adults tend to live longer if they have access to a park; college students perform better on cognitive tests when they study next to a window looking onto natural settings; and children with ADHD perform better in social networking after extensive outdoor activities. When landscape architects plant trees in public housing projects, the number of aggressive and violent interpersonal conflicts decreases significantly.[84]

As Oliver Sacks wrote in "The Healing Power of Gardens":

> In 40 years of medical practice, I have found only two types of non-pharmaceutical "therapy" to be vitally important for patients with chronic neurological diseases: music and gardens.
>
> As a scientist, I cannot say exactly how nature exerts its calming and organizing effects on our brains, but I have seen in my patients the restorative and healing powers of nature and gardens, even for those who are deeply disabled neurologically.
>
> I have a number of patients with very advanced dementia or Alzheimer's disease, who may have very little sense of orientation to their surroundings. They have forgotten, or cannot access, how to tie their shoes or handle cooking implements. But put them in front of a flower bed with some seedlings, and they will know exactly what to do – I have never seen such a patient plant something upside down.[85]

----

84 All the examples in this paragraph are taken from Eric Brymer, Elizabeth Freeman and Miles Richardson, "The Well-being Impacts of Human-Nature Relationships," https://www.frontiersin.org/articles/10.3389/fpsyg.2019.01611/full#B7.

85 Oliver Sacks, "The Healing Power of Gardens," *The New York Times*, April 18, 2019, https://www.nytimes.com/2019/04/18/opinion/sunday/oliver-sacks-gardens.html?searchResultPosition=1.

Too often, we humans overthink ourselves. If most dogs hold their heads out of car windows when they go on a drive, we can safely say that there are innate attributes in doggy souls that cause dogs to 'like' to hang their heads out the window. People are similar. Time spent in Nature makes almost all people feel good. It makes us feel whole, in our brains, our minds and our bodies. It's as simple as that.

Back to the present. After resting and drinking, Jawas reasons that it will be foolish to try to follow the tracks, but that the camels will get thirsty, just as we are, and will head to the nearest village where people will give them water. We beeline in that direction. Soon the cellphone rings.

"Yup, we've got your camel." Four camels from another village also ran away. They joined up with Lightning Bolt and had a jolly fun day off, free from the rigours of domesticating people. But then they decided not to really run away, into the trackless savannah where they would have to find their own food and water, and watch out for lions, so they wandered on down to a village of stick houses and desperately poor people with desperately skinny goats with nothing to eat and no respite in sight. Someone from yet another village had come down to claim his lost camels and was herding them back northward along the A-2 Road, along with Lightning Bolt. Would we mind picking up our camel and taking him home?

With this information, we find the camels easily enough, plodding along the roadside followed by a small boy half carrying and half dragging a bag of groceries that is clearly too heavy for him to manage. I approach and, through sign language, indicate that I would be happy to help him carry the groceries. The boy looks at me in fright and attempts to flee, running as fast as his skinny little legs and barefoot feet will carry him.

"Of course. I'm a big strange white man. He thinks I'm trying to steal his groceries."

Jawas intercedes, calms the boy, and ties the bag onto a camel's halter. We head north. The knot slips, the bag falls and the camel steps on one corner, squishing some of the contents.

"That boy is quite small," I remark. "How old is he?"

Jawas tells me, "Five."

"He can't be five," I respond, incredulously. "The villagers wouldn't send a five-year-old out on the savannah, alone, with wild lions around, to retrieve four valuable camels."

"Would they?"

"Yes, siree! That boy has five," and Jawas holds up five fingers to be sure I understand.

When my kids were 5 years old, I was still worried that they might stuff rocks in their mouths and swallow them or fall while running with a pair of scissors and poke an eye out. Send them off alone in the wilderness, far from home in the desert sun, without even a *rungu*? Unthinkable. Now I feel truly chagrined that I fell into a fit of self-whining earlier in the day. But the past is over and it's still a long thirsty walk back to the Motel at the End of the World.

CHAPTER 11

MYTHOLOGIES WE LOVE
AND KILL FOR

A few days later, I walk down to breakfast and notice a new person in camp: a tall, burly guy with a slight pot belly, a broad face and large lips pursed tightly together. He is wearing the traditional Samburu red skirt and beaded necklace, but in addition he is adorned with criss-crossed strings of beads across his chest, a delicate gold chain that runs under his chin and over his ears, and black armbands wrapped tightly around ample biceps, like an inner city gangsta. And, oh yes, before I forget; he is carrying a battle-worn AK-47 and a bullet-studded cartridge belt. Clearly, this is a guy you would want on your side if you bumbled into a small war or insurrection. The friendly, innocuous night guard who regularly greets me in the mornings is nowhere to be seen. I nod and exchange pleasantries with this new warrior. He speaks no English, but we communicate through stance and facial expressions. I note that while he's fearsome, he has a sweet smile and an easygoing demeanour.

Tina shows up with news of trouble last night in the small nearby town of Archers Post. Dipa and the head engineer of the water drilling crew had gone in for a few beers. Someone pulled a knife on Dipa. Bad idea. The assailant was slower than a black mamba snake, who is slower than Dipa. Dipa disarmed the guy, pronto, grabbed the guy's arm and waved the knife in front of his face.

"You are a foolish man. I could kill you in two seconds. But today, you are also a lucky man. I will just take you to the police and they will put you in jail."

But that wasn't the end of it. Someone shot the engineer in the knee. Apparently, the gunman could easily have killed the engineer but elected to maim him instead. In a wealthy Western society, surgeons could repair or replace the knee, but here in Kenya, the man will be crippled for life.

A week ago, Tina had shown me an iPhone video of a massacre south of here, along the A-2 Road. But that was relatively far away, and I invented many reasons why this wasn't my problem. Perhaps it was related to the upcoming election, which didn't seem all that immediate here in Samburu. It involved a different tribe, with a whole different politics. And while I was rationalizing, I reasoned that there are dangers everywhere on Earth. There are muggings in New York City, and people die in car wrecks on the Montana highways.

I ask Tina if last night's trouble in Archers Post represents the sort of random acts of violence that can occur in any frontier town bar, or is indicative of a more serious regional issue that could threaten all of us here at the Motel at the End of the World. Is this related to the election? And if so, how? Or is something else going on?

"Well," Tina explains. "We're not sure, but the man who shot the engineer had an accomplice with him who may have been a policeman, so it could be a prelude of bigger trouble. In any case, no one was charged with the shooting."

Tina explains further that this assumption that the police were the perpetrators was not a paranoid, unsupported fear but a terrifying possibility based on past events. During the year between February 2009 and January 2010, police, using trucks and helicopter gunships, had attacked ten different Samburu villages in this immediate vicinity – about an average of one a month.

According to one victim: "I heard bullets, so I rushed out of my house. I was only about five metres outside when a bullet hit me in the arm, just below the elbow. My children were screaming. I saw the police kicking and beating them. Everyone was running and crying."[86]

....

86 Paula Palmer, "When the Police Are the Perpetrators," *Cultural Survival* 34, no. 1 (March 2010): 14ff.

Another woman had given birth to her fourth child a few hours before the raid. The older children were out tending the cows. When the attackers ordered her out of her hut, she was still sore, so was slow to rise. A policeman ordered her to hurry up and when she continued to move slowly, he shot her in the head, her blood spilling over her newborn.

In another eyewitness report, "Children, women and men were running and crying as uniformed police beat them with heavy sticks and rifle butts. Lopeyok Lenkupai picked up his two babies and started running toward the edge of the village, but police bullets hit him in the hip and the chest, and he fell to the ground.... A police helicopter swooped down and circled the village to keep the people from escaping. The police herded us like cows outside the village to an open field.... They told us to lie down, and then they stepped on us with their heavy boots, they kicked us and caned us. They beat the children and the ladies who were pregnant, the elders, everyone. They beat us all."[87]

As Tina told these stories, by a cheery fire, across the small table with the clean white tablecloth, after a fine meal that filled our bellies, she paused and asked if I would mind waiting a moment while she went back to her quarters and brought me a copy of the magazine *Cultural Survival*, which had documented these massacres.

When she returned, she asked, "Have you met Tiepe yet?"

I said I had – a pleasant, young, smiling kid who was home for vacation from his studies to become an engineer. He drove a battered Honda 90 and let me take it out for a spin one afternoon. Tina handed me the magazine. On the back page there was a copy of a letter Tiepe had written on three-holed school notebook paper. On the top right, in careful, neat printing, was the date, 23 January 2010. Followed by the salutation: "Dear President Obama,"

There were no more words, only a detailed drawing of the battle that had engulfed his village. On the top of the drawing, in the crude, cartoonish pen strokes of a 10-year-old boy, there were three helicopter gunships, hovering over a village. People from the village were lying down and police were shooting into the crowd.

87 Paula Palmer, "When the Police Are the Perpetrators," *Cultural Survival* 34, no. 1 (March 2010): 17

Little dots showed the trajectory of the bullets from the muzzle of one gun into a stick hut. On the bottom left, the police were shooting the village cows.

Tina's tale was too shocking and disturbing for me to make any sense out of it. I had no meaningful verbal response. What do you say? I had only been here a few short weeks, but I had made friends among these kind, gentle, strong and beautiful people. What kind of human being would shoot a nursing mother in the head, in her own home, hours after she had given birth? What kind of human being is that? How does one individual's brain justify such an atrocity? I had read about these sorts of massacres in the newspapers, but this was here, now. Perpetuated against people I knew. Every person I spoke to every day had hidden memories of these battles. Now, in real time, last night, not years ago, or in some distant place, someone had shot the driller and maimed him for life. My mind couldn't process this information on a philosophical and emotional level, so I didn't try to process it. Not immediately. I would have time for processing – later. Right now, I started with two simple and obvious questions, with important feedback for my own survival.

"First, what is going on? What are the motivations? Why is this happening?"

If I could understand the answer to the first question, then I might have a handle on answering a second, which was less theoretical, more selfish and immediate: "Am I, are we, in real danger, right now? Is it possible, remotely conceivable, that someone will come charging into the Motel at the End of the World in a tank, pickup truck or helicopter gunship and mow us all down: Tina, Dipa, Jawas and me? Today, tomorrow, or the next day?"

Tina doesn't have any solid information on the motivations behind what happened in Archers Post last night, but she suggests I read the article in *Cultural Survival* to establish some background about the atrocities that had occurred seven years previously. In the meantime, she will make some phone calls, text her contacts in Nairobi and get answers back to me ASAP.

I return to my still peaceful tent pavilion on the top of the hill, look over the scrub savannah, watch the monkeys, glance up at the ridge to Sabache-Ololokwe, which has become my friend now, and read the magazine article Tina has given me.

According to journalist Paula Palmer, the 2009 and 2010 government-sanctioned murders, rapes and robberies were due to a complex overlapping set of evolving conditions. She writes, "Through the centuries, the Samburu and their pastoralist neighbors have occasionally raided each other's cattle to replenish their stocks after droughts and to exert dominance over prized water sources and territory.... But in the months leading up to the February 2009 police attacks, cattle raiding among the Samburu and their rival tribes had intensified in both frequency and violence, mainly due to the increasing availability of guns in the region."[88]

The first reason offered by the government for the brutal police raids was to recover stolen cattle, return them to their rightful owners and punish the thieves. But that argument doesn't hold up, not one tiny little bit. You don't need to shoot nursing mothers in the head, or rape other women, in an effort to prosecute a bunch of rustlers. In other instances, the police had shot entire herds, or stolen (redistributed) lawfully owned cattle without any semblance of trial or judication. One Samburu elder, a retired sergeant in the Kenyan army, told Paula, "I have never stolen any cattle. I retired from the army and have always been a 100-percent government person. I bought my cattle with my pension when I retired. But the police took all 170 of my cattle. After 32 years of government service, I feel bitter."[89]

Scratch that argument. The next argument, or explanation, is, in my mind, even more obtuse, circular and downright ridiculous than the first. The entire Horn of Africa is frequently a lawless place. Somali ocean pirates were boarding ships and kidnapping crews at the time. Less well-known road pirates were making parts of northern Kenya so unsafe that a Catholic bishop threatened to remove all the church's mission staff, including teachers, health professionals and aid workers, unless the government could provide better security. And at the same time, al-Shabab fanatical Muslim terrorists were on the rampage. In addition to an uncounted number of small atrocities, al-Shabab squads and suicide bombers had attacked nightclubs

---

88 Paula Palmer, "When the Police Are the Perpetrators," *Cultural Survival* 34, no. 1 (March 2010): 18.

89 Paula Palmer, "When the Police Are the Perpetrators," *Cultural Survival* 34, no. 1 (March 2010): 19.

and hotels in Kenya's larger cities, murdered politicians and, in 1998, killed 213 people in a bombing of the US Embassy in Nairobi. So the Kenyan government decided that they needed to impose law and order in the sparsely populated deserts where the Samburu live. So they created a myth that they needed to reduce the number of fire-arms in the region, so they initiated a series of pogroms to murder, rape, burn villages, terrorize children and kill people's cattle.

Can you wrap your head around that as a logical, coherent argument for a series of government-sponsored police massacres against innocent people who were arming to defend themselves against al-Shabab?

I can't.

I wish that the leopard would return to provide some animal com-munication and sanity to this situation.

The engineer was a working guy who had come up here to help with the water situation. I can guarantee you that he wasn't part of a political conspiracy. But someone shot him yesterday. I came here to track lions and to connect with myself by disconnecting from the barrage of digital information that bombards me in daily life back home. I can guarantee you that I'm not part of a political conspir-acy to threaten the dominant power structure of Kenya. Should I be concerned that someone might shoot me? Right now, I desperately want more information. Camp life during the past few days has been so peaceful. Yet human violence from afar is like an avalanche in the mountains: everything is fine – until it isn't. And then you've lost your window of opportunity to seek shelter, take precautions and make measured, logical decisions.

The following morning, the burly guard with the AK greets me with a friendly, casual hello. Moses brings me two fried eggs, two bland slices of white toast with margarine, and a glass of ultra-pas-teurized, slightly bitter orange juice from a box. Business as usual. I walk back up the hill toward my tent, along the trail that is so familiar by now. The self-domesticated gnu that hangs around camp comes up to me like an old friend or a puppy eager for a scratch on the head. A couple of vervet monkeys scamper along the top rail of the fence made of bent and twisted branches and thin logs. I enjoy the morning coolness while it lasts, because the up-canyon breeze presages yet another hot equatorial day. I reach the stone veranda in front of my tent, sit in my almost-comfortable camp chair, take a moment to look out over the vista of scrub and savannah, pick up a book and read more of Harari's *Sapiens*.

He writes that everything that happens is natural. If it wasn't natural, it wouldn't happen. It's not natural for apples to fall from the ground upward onto the tree, men to get pregnant or cheetahs to run faster than the speed of light – so these things never happen. On the other hand: some people are nice. Some people shoot unarmed women in the head. Hitler thought it was a good idea to start a world war and murder six million Jews in the concentration camps – just because he could. The ancient Babylonian monarch Hammurabi codified laws proclaiming that some people were superior to others and were worth more and held greater rights in the eyes of the law. And so forth. All these things are natural because they happen – or have happened. Here, at the Motel at the End of the World, beneath the sacred mountain patrolled by the leopard, where elephants climb upward on their knees and elbows to seek refuge, I was looking at humanity directly in the face, as one is always looking at humanity directly in the face.

The next morning, Jawas moves me into the maze-like thicket, as I wrote in the opening teaser in Chapter 1. Part of the reason for my move could be that a busload of German tourists was scheduled to arrive soon. Whereas the Russian tourists had stayed in the campground near the goat and camel corrals, the Germans were booked to stay in the more expensive motel accommodations, which were wall tents with verandas and bathrooms. Thus, they needed my tent-camp for paying guests. Yes, no problem. But why didn't they move me to the established tourist camp, where the Russians had camped? Why into the thicket? What were those fresh machete scars all about? Did someone really build that maze just yesterday or the day before? At the time, and even to this day, I have no idea how close we were to an actual Wild West shoot-em-up.

That night, as I stand with my back against the tree to protect myself against the leopard who may or may not be in the neighbourhood, I don't know how realistic or paranoid it is for me to be afraid of an attack from human assailants who may or may not be in the neighbourhood. I do know that I am afraid, but that nothing happens.

The night passes and the sun rises again.

After all this time with no full-package paying guests, the imminent arrival of the Germans is a big deal. Apparently, those tourists harbour no fear. Or not enough fear to jump on an airplane and head home. Do they know more or less than I know? The full staff congregates. Tomorrow, the plumber is coming to fix the toilets. Meanwhile, we have chores to do. Cash money is about to start rolling in.

The next evening at dinner Tina tells me that she's received a text from a Kenyan general warning her that as the election approaches and domestic violence threatens in the streets and barrios of Nairobi, the government has pulled its troops out of the sparsely inhabited northern desert to respond to potential urban problems. According to the general's report, the prime minister has procured and is deploying huge boat-like armoured personnel carriers with multiple machine gun stations to quell any potential election violence. Meanwhile, since the military presence has diminished along the border, bands of Somali road pirates and al-Shabab rebels have slipped south from Somalia and are sneaking across the desert toward Samburu.

After a pause, to let all that soak in, Tina suggests a few practical guidelines. If government troops should move in to massacre a village, I should separate myself from the Samburu and play the lost and clueless white man tourist. Government troops would be unlikely to provoke an international incident by mowing down a white-haired, elderly American out to spend money in the country. But, on the other hand, if a rogue band of Somali road pirates or al-Shabab should attack, my best bet would be to stick tight with the most competent and well-armed Samburu I can find. These guys are tough and battle-savvy. They know the terrain and, while they are defenceless against helicopter gunships and armoured personnel carriers, they can more than hold their own against armed intruders with a level of weaponry similar to theirs.

"Why would al-Shabab attack us? I asked. "Why not a luxury hotel with a bunch of rich foreign tourists to kidnap?"

"Well, it's not always about money," Tina answered. "A few weeks ago, al-Shabab did, in fact, attack a local native village."

"Really? I guess I wish you would have told me that."

Tina shrugs.

Later, after I got home to Montana, just to confirm the verity of Tina's concern, I did a little research and found the following account in *The New York Times*:

July 07, 2017: al-Shabab extremists from neighboring Somalia beheaded nine civilians in an attack on a village in Kenya's southeast early Saturday, officials said, adding to growing concerns the Islamic militant group has taken up a bloody new strategy.... This East Africa country has seen an increase in attacks claimed by al-Shabab in recent weeks, ... presenting a huge problem for Kenya's security agencies ahead of the Aug. 8 presidential election.... On election day, security agencies will be strained while attempting to stop any possible violence and al-Shabab could take advantage, he said.[90]

The conversation with Tina continued: "Oh, and one more thing. A question. You live in Montana, don't you?"

The question seemed out of place, in a way, but maybe not, so I looked at her carefully, and responded guardedly, "Yes."

"By any chance, do you ever hunt deer or elk?"

Again, a guarded, "Yes."

"So. Are you a fairly good shot?"

"Tina," I asked, although I already knew the answer. "Where is this conversation going?"

"Well, if trouble should overtake us, you see, we have more guns here than you have seen. If trouble comes, can we count on you to help out?"

I shake my head slowly. "This is a wonderful place. I've made dear friends. I can help fixing toilets, making beds or searching for a lost camel. But this is not my war. I have no idea who is who or what this war is about. If trouble comes, I hope to be far away before it shows up. Tina, I don't want to be here. I don't want to be in a situation where I have to shoot someone. I want to go home."

"I thought you might say that, so I called Anthony, the driver who took you here. He told me that the road is too dangerous right now to drive on, so he will not come and get you until the situation cools down. Your best bet is to hang here for a few days. I think we're okay right here, right now. We're relatively out of the way and we're well

90 "Al-Shabab Beheads 9 People in Kenyan Village," *The New York Times*, July 8, 2017, https://www.nytimes.com/2017/07/08/world/africa/al-shabab-kenya.html.

armed, not like seven years ago when we were caught by surprise. We just need a little time to allow the situation to evolve and hopefully stabilize."

"Okay. So be it."

We talk about other things, to ease the tension, and then I bid goodnight and start down the path toward my camp in the thicket.

"Hold it, Jon. It's too dangerous for you to walk back to your camp alone, in the dark. I'll call Jawas and ask him to escort you."

Tina disappears into the kitchen and returns with Jawas, who is unarmed – not even carrying his *rungu*. I love Jawas, and trust that he would do what he could, but if real danger is lurking, and if someone is going to guide me home, where is the big guy with the assault rifle?

Jawas and I walk down the trail, in silence, across the wash, and stop to watch the moon rise over the ridge that we have climbed so many times.

"Jon. This moon, he is large one more time this night. Jon. Do you like walking in the moon?"

"Yes, Jawas, I do."

"Jon. Do you have a moon where you live? On your village at Montana?"

"Yes, we do, Jawas. It's the same moon that you have. It shines in both places."

"Yes, siree. That is good you have a moon on your village at Montana. And it is good that it is the same moon we have."

Jawas drops me off and leaves me alone. I lie down in my tent, but my mind is too busy spinning to allow me to sleep.

— — ⁄ —

This isn't the first time that someone has asked me to join a war. Back in midsummer 1968, just after the Tet offensive rolled full steam through South Vietnam, I was herded onto a bus with a bunch of other potential recruits and we drove down the highway to the armed forces induction centre in Denver, to see if we were mentally and physically fit enough to murder or be murdered in Vietnam. Almost immediately, I got in trouble for refusing to sign an affidavit swearing that I had never had subversive thoughts, been in contact with people who had subversive thoughts or read any literature written by anyone who had subversive thoughts. I told the information officer, "I'm sorry, Sir. I have lots of subversive thoughts. Every day. I go to the University in Boulder, Colorado, and hang out in the fountain area. Everyone there has subversive thoughts, by your definition." But he was unimpressed with my logic and proceeded to lecture me on the evil of my ways and lifestyle. And then he threatened to send me directly to the front lines where I would have a high probability of getting shot. I didn't know it then, but that conversation was the genesis for this book. As the information officer droned on and on, it was abundantly clear, as if I hadn't known it already, that his argument, and the Vietnam War itself, was a response to an elaborate mythology, and that I was being asked, or ordered, to join a mass movement, a mob, a herd, and to kill people, and possibly to get killed myself, following a narrative that someone had made up out of thin air, for some reason that I couldn't possibly understand.

After a few hours of aggressive questioning and angry denouncements, we determined, not surprisingly, that neither of us was about to change our views, and there was nothing either of us could do about that, so the information officer sent me on to my physical exam. Like any good university student, I had prepared myself for the exam. Even before a doctor told me to pull down my pants and bend over so he could shove his finger up my butt, I handed the presiding officer ironclad documentation to procure a medical deferment, because I had faked medical papers. All that happened a half-century ago. Now, here in Samburu, war had snuck in the back door and caught up with me in a more tangible and immediate way. There were no medical deferments available. And I couldn't get out of this war by arguing the meaning of 'subversive' or by complaining, "Gimmie a break. I came here to track lions." The disquieting thought was that if I were inadvertently engulfed in a bloody firefight, yes, I would grab a gun and shoot to kill, to save my own skin. But I didn't want to be in that situation – not one tiny little bit.

So I tried to evaluate the actual risk I faced, but found it impossible to construct a coherent, logical explanation, or series of explanations, to place a probability onto the threats and rumours that were available to me. First, as explained above, there were

Jon Turk

three potential factions, the central government, al-Shabab and the Somali road pirates, each with their own tactics and weaponry, and each with their own set of grievances, needs, rationalizations and beliefs.

Nothing made sense then, and even in hindsight, nothing makes sense now. Tina told me that the government was trying to run the Samburu off their Aboriginal land because they had discovered oil there. But I never saw any evidence of drilling operations or heard talk of active drilling. Even later, when I got home, an internet search didn't indicate that there is a whole lot of oil in northeastern Kenya. And you can drill for oil without shooting nursing mothers in the head. It's been done in other places. Like Texas. The killing for oil argument might be real or it might be fuzzy. There certainly have been lots of times throughout the world, for many centuries, where Aboriginal people have been murdered to pave the way for resource extraction. But there have also been lots of times where resource extraction has taken place without genocide. And the fact that there isn't that much oil in Samburu throws weight against the argument that this is a resource war.

A *Washington Post* article, posted online on December 30, 2019, talks about a Chinese military base northeast of Samburu in the nation of Djibouti, as part of China's 'string of pearls' military expansion throughout the world.[91] Maybe the A-2 Road and the government atrocities in Samburu were an early prelude to this military expansion. But that argument doesn't hold up all that well to scrutiny either. The Samburu weren't raiding truck convoys on the A-2 Road, and in the absence of armed insurrection, you don't have to commit atrocities to build a road, even if it is on or through someone's sovereign territory. The government intrusion doesn't make sense to me, unless it is another horrid, inexcusable case of blind tribal racist hatred. Which is what I believe it is.

Now, what about the threat from the Somali road pirates and al-Shabab fanatical Muslim extremists? There are reasons why

91   "In strategic Djibouti, a microcosm of China's growing foothold in Africa," *The Washington Post*, December 30, 2019, https://www.washingtonpost.com/world/ africa/in-strategic-djibouti-a-microcosm-of-chinas-growing-foothold-in- africa/2019/12/29/a6e664ea-beab-11e9-a8b0-7ed8a0d5dc5d_story.html.

Somalia has collapsed into anarchy, while other countries, Namibia, for example, are relatively peaceful. In a similar manner there are reasons why al-Shabab extremists have the specific grievances and tactics that they have. But this is not a political book, so I will forgo a detailed analysis of an attack in a remote region of Kenya that didn't actually occur, but which might have occurred, or had been threatened to occur. I am interested in the broad reasons why people behave the way they do, not necessarily the specifics of this turmoil in this forgotten corner of the world.

We've already established that world wars, small wars and regional insurrections are all based on tribalism, mythologies, hierarchies, imagined orders, memes and so on. The rich consolidate power, ego and imaginary money (to buy non-imaginary stuff), while the peasants shoot, get shot and hack each other up with machetes.

So. Where do we go from here?

I promised that I wouldn't provide handy-dandy checklists on how to save the world. And I plan to keep that promise. But I think that if we spend a little time understanding the modern biological and social science that explores our propensity to "rally 'round the flag, boys," we might have an opportunity to step outside our own dangerously big brains, to look at ourselves from a fresh perspective and to witness our own foolishness. I don't know if any of us can save the world, but if I can understand what motivates me to act, and then laugh at myself, and if you can laugh at yourself, then at least we've made some progress.

Referencing my current predicament, or any predicament with a propensity or reality for violence, let's look at human behaviour more closely. First, it's important to separate the motives and emotions of leaders who order people into war from the foot soldiers who pull the triggers or pull down their pants to force themselves upon some terrified and defenceless woman. As Tolstoy stated in *War and Peace*, it's easy to understand why one madman, in this case Napoleon, would want to attack Russia. There is always one madman out there with a lust for power, fame, acclamation and riches. But why did nearly a million infantrymen follow him, with the certainty that their lives would be disrupted and that they would endure hardship, and the high probability that they would be maimed, killed or frozen – all for little or no reward?

Most history books concentrate on macroeconomic effects and the minds of the leaders, but I am more interested in the minds of the followers.

And that's where storytelling, mythology, comes in. After people abandoned their hunter-gatherer past and congregated into cities, with large numbers of inhabitants, the leaders of those cities, and later countries, quickly learned that people are spellbound by myth. And whereas in small tribes, myth created the cohesion needed to defend the tribe against the real and present danger of neighbouring tribes, in the city states, leaders hijacked myth to invent dangers and manipulate the defence response to justify atrocious behaviour directed outward. But as human societies became ever larger and more complex, warfare was not merely focused on the neighbouring tribe who might threaten to steal my food supply or waterhole. Instead, these new myths became justification for far-flung conquests over abstract ideas such as religion or national honour or for subjugating political enemies within a nation. It's deeply wired in our DNA; it's been going on essentially forever; and it remains a tragic presence today.

Given what we know so far, the techniques used by political or religious leaders to generate mass movements, mass hysteria and mass murder are terrifyingly simple.

First, create a tribe. Many people in modern society are cut adrift and lonely. You get a job in a distant city where you have no friends, family or support group. Maybe you are married or even have a few cute little kids. It doesn't matter: one person, or a small family in an apartment with IKEA furniture and an internet connection, is not a tribe. As Sebastian Junger points out, people in a middle-class or upper-middle-class suburb can survive physically without a tribe.[92] You don't need to co-operate with your neighbours; all of your group needs are taken care of, automatically. Police and fire departments maintain order and safety, city work crews repair the streets and the sanitation department picks up the garbage. Most of the time nothing dangerous happens, and when something dangerous does happen, someone else manages the problem. No sacrifice or courage

---

92 Sebastian Junger, *Tribe: On Homecoming and Belonging*, Reprint ed. (New York: Grand Central, 2020).

is needed. But the downside of all this wondrous security is that non-tribal existence is lonely. This feeling is linked to fundamental evolutionary survival. In tribal societies, anyone who is banished from the tribe cannot feed, clothe or defend himself, and that banishment becomes a death sentence. And people retain a subliminal fear of losing their tribe, even in modern urban environments. Stress from loneliness is exacerbated when other external forms of stress are also present, such as economic hardship or death of a loved one. In any of these circumstances, most people need a tribe. If an individual doesn't have one, it becomes a natural instinct to create a tribe, or find one. There are countless tribes to create or choose from. My backcountry skiing buddies form a de facto tribe of shared fun, activity and danger. A pottery guild, choir or reading club are other examples. But we also have the option to join one or more political or religious tribes, a mass movement, whether created 5,000 years ago or yesterday.

All political or religious tribes are built around a combination of stories and symbols — imagined orders. Previously, I explained that when creating a unifying tribal myth, fiction always trumps truth, and the more outrageous the fiction the better, because if my tribe believes that ravens were born out of clamshells, and your tribe thinks that is hogwash, my shared tribal belief conveys a bonding identity that draws my tribe together. A holy writ cannot be understood. It must be believed in. Think hard now, let's come up with a fiction that will get people riled up, angry, eager to follow a leader across the steppe to attack Russia or some such nonsense. Hmm. Let's try this one, just because it is current. How about: "Climate change is a hoax." Or: "Evolutionary theory is a hoax, perpetuated by some tribe that lives across the river and that we choose to dislike anyway, for other reasons." Well, that's okay, I guess, but a little humdrum. So, I go to the QAnon website to find something fun. How about the totally imaginary exposé known as Frazzledrip that purports to reveal a video showing Hillary Clinton and her buddies attacking and mutilating a young girl and drinking her blood?[93] Here's another. When I was hanging out in the Arizona desert, an old loner guy carefully explained that Covid vaccines are a mechanism Bill Gates

---

93 https://www.nytimes.com/2021/02/05/opinion/qanon-hillary-clinton. html?action=click&module=Opinion&pgtype=Homepage.

is using to implant zombie chips into all the unsuspecting suckers who allow themselves to be vaccinated. According to this conspiracy theory, once enough people are inoculated with these chips, all Bill has to do is pull a master switch, and presto, everyone turns into a zombie who motors around mindlessly fulfilling his fondest and most nefarious dreams and desires. Think those fictions will work? You bet they will; because they have worked – are working. Any story will work if you craft it right and deliver it frequently and forcefully enough. Large groups of people love to believe stories together, stories that join us into a tribe, so we can all sway to the beat of a hypnotic trance. Or brandish our assault rifles together in a mob.

History has shown, repeatedly, that the details of the myth are unimportant. Once people are seeking a mass movement, they can alter their political philosophy in a heartbeat. The Nazis recruited from the Communists. You can replace one mass movement mythology with another much more easily than you can replace mythology with reason.

As Harvard's Jill Lepore puts it, authoritarian leaders "replace history with tried-and-true fictions – false tales of national decline at the hands of invented threats, melded to fictitious stories of renewed national greatness, engineered by the leader himself, who is both author of the fiction and its mythic hero."[94]

Then it always helps to attach symbols to the stories. A symbol is nothing more than an imagined representation of an imagined order. Flags work great. The flag, itself, is a piece of cloth, colourful and jaunty, waving in the breeze, but it reminds us of a story that we are members of such-and-such a nation or tribe, which is nothing more than an agreement of some sort, about arbitrary lines drawn on a map, and defended by soldiers who march to the flag – a circular reasoning if there ever was one. In 21st-century USA, we have just proven conclusively that red baseball caps are excellent tribal symbols. And those who came before red baseball caps proved conclusively that if you make up a good enough story about it, a wooden cross or a replica wooden cross cast in silver or gold can suffice. Or

94 Jill Lepore, "A New Americanism: Why a Nation Needs a National Story,"
    Foreign Affairs, March/April 2019, https://www.foreignaffairs.com/articles/
    united-states/2019-02-05/new-americanism-nationalism-jill-lepore.

a yarmulke. Or a turban. The sky and your imagination are the only limiting factors here.

In one experiment to illustrate the effects of tribal symbols on human behaviour, a scientist embedded in a crowd at an English football match pretends to slip and injure his ankle. Does anyone help him? Well, that depends on what colour shirt he is wearing. You guessed it. If he is wearing the home team's sweatshirt, people rush to his aid. But if he is wearing either a neutral shirt or, worse yet, the shirt of the opposing team, well, good luck, buddy.[95] As Sapolsky argues in *Behave*, "No brain operates in a vacuum.... The wealth of information streaming into the brain influences the likelihood of pro- or antisocial acts.... Pertinent information ranges from something as simple and unidimensional as shirt color to things as complex and subtle as cues about ideology [a red baseball cap (my addition)]. Information is subliminal.... Just before we decide upon some of our most consequential acts, we are less rational and autonomous decision makers than we like to think."[96] To put this in plain words, how did wearing a mask to protect myself, my friends and my neighbours from contracting Covid come to be regarded as a symbol of allegiance to a leader and a specific political philosophy?

Stories and symbols are fine, but there is one more critical factor to add to the mix: fear. To understand fear, it is helpful to understand the biology of an important hormone – oxytocin. Google oxytocin and at first glance you will learn that "it's sometimes known as the 'cuddle hormone' or the 'love hormone,' because it is released when people snuggle up or bond socially." But the story is more complicated than that. When scientists first started studying oxytocin, they learned that it stimulated uterine contraction during labour and milk letdown afterward. Because the first studies showed that oxytocin was associated with childbirth and child rearing, scientists then injected oxytocin into a virgin rat, and learned that the hormone caused her to groom and lick another mother's pups. On the other hand, if the researchers chemically blocked the action of oxytocin in

---

95 Robert Sapolsky, *Behave: The Biology of Humans at Our Best and Worst*, Reprint ed. (New York: Penguin, 2018), p. 90.

96 Robert Sapolsky, *Behave: The Biology of Humans at Our Best and Worst*, Reprint ed. (New York: Penguin, 2018), p. 94.

a new mother, she abandoned her own children. In addition, when a female rat gave birth, the oxytocin levels increased in *a nearby male rat* who was watching.[97]

Researchers began broadening their scope and learned that these hormones regulate behaviour not just between mother or father and child, but between adult members of a family or tribe. In one interesting study, couples were asked to discuss a conflict. When the researcher sprayed oxytocin up their noses, they reduced the level of stress hormones in their bloodstream and started communicating more positively. Other studies showed that people rate strangers' faces as more trustworthy when their oxytocin levels are elevated. Under the influence of artificial doses of the hormone, people are more trusting in economic games and are more charitable and altruistic. According to Sapolsky, "So, oxytocin elicits prosocial behavior and oxytocin is released when we experience prosocial behavior.... In other words, a warm and fuzzy feedback loop."[98]

Ah, but now the dark side. While oxytocin promotes loving, caring, maternal behaviour from adult to child, it also promotes protective behaviour in the face of intruders, potential intruders or imagined intruders. Over a large range of experiments, scientists have shown that oxytocin enhances prosocial behaviour directed toward trusted people in your family and tribe, but more aggressive behaviour toward potentially dangerous strangers from outside the tribe. It's a love drug, but also an attack drug. It's a ME and US, buddy-buddy drug and at the same time an US vs. THEM, violent attack drug, the mother mouse attacking the cat.

And that's the beauty and tragedy of mammalian, and especially human, behaviour. People are wonderful. They come together in times of need, race into burning buildings to extract a child, an elder, or someone's pet cat, and give to charities. They care for children with severe congenital disabilities and elders who no longer have the strength to reciprocate. But loyalty is frequently limited to interactions within the tribe, or the perceived tribe, or imagined tribe.

....

97 Robert Sapolsky, *Behave: The Biology of Humans at Our Best and Worst*, Reprint ed. (New York: Penguin, 2018), p. 104.

98 Robert Sapolsky, *Behave: The Biology of Humans at Our Best and Worst*, Reprint ed. (New York: Penguin, 2018), p. 107.

People have a long history, from the beginning of our tenure on Earth to the present, of being terrible, horrible and violent toward members of other tribes.

The human brain and endocrine system didn't evolve to be a shining example of the most wondrous concoction of protoplasm, bone, DNA, mitochondria, blood and guts on the planet. No. Every organism, from bacteria to slime worms to *Homo sapiens*, evolved its own unique niche of characteristics, with survival as the only criteria. The only critical question is: Does that adaptation work to ensure the continuation of that line of DNA down through the generations? If the DNA hangs in there, the adaptation is good. If the organism dies and/or fails to produce viable offspring, out the door with that evolutionary experiment. So one important function of the human brain is to respond quickly, efficiently, and violently if need be, to immediate threats to its survival. The brain perceives a situation. Because we have marvelously big brains, we can tell ourselves a story about that situation. Then the brain knows that it needs to act quickly; it understands that careful analysis of the situation takes up precious time, so it will overlook, discount and dismiss additional data to preserve the story it believes is correct. As a result, all a leader has to do is create an imagined threat, tell us a story about that threat, and all too often many people will dismiss the obvious fact, right in front of their eyes, that it is not okay to shoot a mother in the head immediately after she has given birth, or at any other time, for that matter.

If you are an evil madman, like Napoleon or Hitler, whether you understand the science or not, the path to dominance is clear. Invent mythologies, symbols and memes to create an imagined tribe. Remember, truth is not merely unnecessary, it is an annoying hindrance. The more outrageous the lie or assemblage of lies, the better, because we know that those guys over there are inferior because they won't believe it. We are better than they are. We are special. We are unified. And above all, use the cudgel of real or imagined fear to stir your tribe into a hormone-based frenzy.

Outrageous mythologies are so effective that time and time again, when told a good story, normal human beings, who love their parents and children, and maybe even go to church, have repeatedly swooned into hypnotic trances to kill their neighbours while voting for, supporting, fighting for and – yes – dying for good storytellers who all too often steal all the money, diminish personal freedom and deliver poor health care, unreliable public infrastructure and so forth.

Hitler was open about his channelling of fear and hatred, and unapologetic: "it is essential to have a tangible enemy, not merely an abstract one."[99] Or, another Hitlerism: "people more readily fall victims to the big lie than the small lie" because, while they might fib in their daily lives about small things, "it would never come into their heads to fabricate colossal untruths."[100] And (my addition), big lies make better stories; they are more useful in creating tribal identity, separating US from THEM. Thus, political differences, which might have been legitimate originally, "become a war between good and evil that demands unconditional support for the leader of the tribe. If you talk against your own camp you betray it and get expelled from the tribe."[101]

Nazi henchman Hermann Göring expressed similar thoughts: "The people can always be brought to the bidding of the leaders. That is easy. All you have to do is tell them they are being attacked and denounce the pacifists for lack of patriotism and exposing the country to danger. It works the same way in any country."[102]

Eric Hoffer (1902–1983) was a self-educated, philosopher/writer who worked in restaurants, as a migrant fieldworker, and as a gold prospector. After Pearl Harbor, he became a stevedore on the San Francisco docks. In 1951, he published a book, *The True Believer: Thoughts on the Nature of Mass Movements*.[103] It became a bestseller

99 Eric Hoffer, *The True Believer: Thoughts on the Nature of Mass Movements*, Reprint ed. (New York: Harper Perennial Modern Classics, 2019), p. 91.

100 Andrew Higgins, "The Art of the Lie? The Bigger the Better," *The New York Times*, January 10, 2021, https://www.nytimes.com/2021/01/10/world/europe/trump-truth-lies-power.html.

101 Andrew Higgins, "The Art of the Lie? The Bigger the Better," *The New York Times*, January 10, 2021, https://www.nytimes.com/2021/01/10/world/europe/trump-truth-lies-power.html.

102 Jeffrey Sachs, "Trump Is Taking US Down the Path to Tyranny," *CNN*, July 24, 2018, 2018/07/23/opinions/trump-is-taking-us-down-the-path-to-tyranny-sachs/index.html.

103 Eric Hoffer, *The True Believer: Thoughts on the Nature of Mass Movements*, Reprint ed. (New York: Harper Perennial Modern Classics, 2019).

after President Dwight Eisenhower cited the book in a press conference as an important warning about blindly following a leader, any leader, including himself. Hoffer answers the question proposed by Tolstoy in *War and Peace*. Why did nearly a million soldiers follow Napoleon's orders to march into Russia? Because Napoleon convinced them that they were part of a wondrous tribe, defending the Greatness of France against the evil enemy Russians. According to Hoffer, for a person to be prepared for this level of self-sacrifice he must be stripped of individual identity and completely assimilated into a collective body.

"Who are you?"

"I am Jon."

"No good, let's try that again. Who are you?"

I am a [fill in the blank here] (member of Napoleon's liberating army, a Canadian, a Trumpy, an al-Shabab). Now the imagined order of the imagined tribe becomes the unifying factor and your entire identity. No free choice, no independent judgment, no internal morality. Liberating in a way; "I no longer have to think, just follow."

This blind acceptance of the leader was codified in the Bible when God commanded Abraham to sacrifice his firstborn son. So, Abraham took his son into the wilderness and pulled out his knife. But then God appeared out of the whirlwind and said, "Hold up. I was kidding. It was just a test. You passed the test. Now sacrifice a lamb instead." And in Sunday school we learned that Abraham was righteous.

Hoffer argues that mass movements germinate within an environment of fundamental discontent. People who are truly downtrodden, on the thin edge of survival, are so engaged in their next meal that they generally don't have the time or energy to follow mass movements. It is people who have some stuff, but who perceive that they don't have enough stuff, who are ripe for following mass movements. Happy people aren't willing to die to make themselves happier. But unhappy people have murdered, raped and committed ersatz suicide by marching into the cannons – over and over again – to seek a resolution to their perceived misery.

Hoffer writes, "People with a sense of fulfillment think it a good world and would like to conserve it as it is, while the frustrated favor radical change." And then he continues, "The tendency to look for all causes outside ourselves persists even when it is clear that our state of being" is the cause of our discontent.[104] By obvious extrapolation – as profound and simple as it is – the most important tool for the individual who does not want to fall under the hypnotic spell of the despot is to be content in the first place.

— — —

After Jawas walks me home to my thicket in the moonlight that night, I lie on my leaky air mattress, haphazardly half covered by the musty old sleeping bag, which I barely need because the nights are so warm. Once again, I have the time and space to take stock of my situation. I still haven't seen any violence yet, and maybe it will pass like a dark summer thunderhead that never materializes as rain and hail. But maybe that is wishful thinking. I have precious little data to form an intelligent opinion.

The absurdity and tragedy of it all becomes apparent when I realize that if someone is destined to shoot me, kidnap me or cut off my head, my assailant will be a person who doesn't know me, and couldn't possibly hold any personal grudge against me. All that intensely personal violence, redolent of countless other acts of senseless violence over the millennia, will be perpetuated in the retelling of some mythology in someone's head. Symbols. Imagined orders. The comings and goings of electrochemical circuits in our marvelously complex and often murderous brains. If, in an imaginary experiment, you could speak to an al-Shabab fanatical religious militant just before he swung the sword to cut off my head, and if you asked if he truly believed in the story that motivated his actions, he would say, "Yes, of course. It is not a story. It is reality. Truth."

But the tragedy of it all is that beneath all the stories, all people, even the crazy sociopaths, have the hormonal foundation for compassion. It's the oxytocin mechanism.

Many years ago, I was kayaking across the North Pacific Rim, from Japan to Alaska, with my dear friend Franz Helfenstein. We landed, cold and hungry, on a lonely island in the Kuril chain,

....

104 Eric Hoffer, *The True Believer: Thoughts on the Nature of Mass Movements*, Reprint ed. (New York: Harper Perennial Modern Classics, 2019), p. 6.

between northern Japan and the southern tip of the Kamchatka Peninsula. There was a small Russian military base on the island, and the bored soldiers, who had seen no other people for months, came pouring out of their barracks with guns and police dogs. They surrounded us, demanding to know whether the two of us, in our feeble plastic kayaks, were the advance team for an American assault on the soft underbelly of the great Russian nation, determined to march on Moscow, nine time zones away. I looked into the eyes of the officer in charge. He had a story in his head that Americans were the enemy. But I guessed that when he was an infant, his mother had sung him lullabies and bounced him on her knee, teaching him to love his fellow humans. Which set of realities or imagined realities was stronger, and which would win out in this situation?

I had a hunch that his anger at me, personally, was superficial, so I held out my hand, "Zdravstvuyte. Ty kak?" "Hello, how are you?"

He held a pistol in his right hand. In order to shake my hand and return my greeting, he would have to holster the firearm. He had to choose between alternate interpretations of reality or between the story in his head and the visual reality that Franz and I were two cold, bedraggled adventurers, and were not threatening him or planning to march across the Siberian tundra to launch a surprise single-handed attack on Moscow. He hesitated, holstered the pistol and reached out his hand.

"Zdravstvuyte. Ty kak?"

Before long we were all sitting around a cheery fire. One soldier pulled a bottle of vodka out of his boot. Another ran back to the barracks to trade his assault rifle in for a guitar.

In a similar vein, in December 1914, in the midst of the bitter battles of the First World War, French, British and German troops declared unofficial Christmas ceasefires. They met on the bloody soil of No Man's Land to exchange gifts, souvenirs and prisoners. They sang carols and played spirited games of soccer. And then when Christmas was over, they retreated to their trenches and resumed the slaughter.

Or, as a third example, many of the infantry soldiers in the American Civil War never fired their rifles. They could justify putting on a uniform, marching into battle, running into enemy cannons, being maimed, perhaps dying, but they could not, deep in their hearts, kill other Americans.

The stories in our head are not absolute. They are stories. They may be deeply embedded through a combination of upbringing, genetics and past experiences, but these stories are fundamentally installed and promoted by leaders with their own backgrounds and motivations. We can and do overcome our stories.

All this theory didn't change the realities that right now, at this moment, beyond the thicket, danger lurks. But danger had been lurking for days now and nothing tangible had happened. Time has a dulling effect, and my brain seems incapable of maintaining the fear level at high alert.

I am becoming fond of my little hideaway camp in the thicket. When I was a boy, playing endless hours in the woodlots adjacent to my home, there was a thicket of thorny wild rose down by the dam and my good pal Spiker Feen and I would go down there and crawl around for no good reason whatsoever. And now my African thicket here in Samburu is, illogically, taking on the same play-fort character. I joke to myself that I should put up a sign to mark my territory:

Boyze Fort

Groan ups Stay Owt

But I am a grownup now, so the imaginary sign is merely a joke to myself to ease the tension. I turn on my headlamp and decide to write down some thoughts in my journal on how to avoid the trap of becoming a *True Believer* in mass movements, and by extension, how to participate in life as a peaceful, positive human being.

I prop my journal up on my knees, take out my pen and write:

"First rule on how to participate in life as a peaceful, positive human being."

And then I stop and ask myself, "Now what is the first rule?"

You know how it happens sometimes, more as a surprise than a conscious thought, words wiggling through the maze formed by the folds in your brain, bumping into blind alleyways, then opening doorways, in a hurry to finally escape, yet dribbling out one at a time.

"Be Happy. Don't Worry."

No, I don't think that's right.

"Don't Worry. Be Happy."

Yes, I think that's the way the song goes.

Then the words that have been sequestered in a dusty corner for 25 years all join in the proper order, burst through the barriers, and the song sings itself.

> Here is a little song I wrote
> You might want to sing it note for note
> Don't worry. Be happy.
> In every life we have some trouble
> When you worry you make it double
> Don't worry, be happy...[105]

Then I'm doomed to sing those words and whistle that tune on auto-replay for the next three days.

But before being held hostage to the song, I write in my journal,

From the beginning of time, some people have been unhappy, and others have tried to teach the elements of happiness. Today, the happiness thing is a multibillion-dollar business with books, gurus, workshops, podcasts, marriage counsellors, cowboy poets, psychiatrists and on and on.

Be happy with what you own, because owning is not the point.

Don't worry about who you are, because who you are is an annoying abstraction, a figment of your imagination, a story, a mythology, an imagined order.

Have enough confidence in yourself so you don't become what others tell you to become.

The only fundamental concept you need to know is, as Eckhart Tolle frames it, The Power of NOW.

Or as Buddha taught: Pain is inevitable in every person's life, but the pursuit of happiness is the root of all suffering.

....

105 "Don't Worry, Be Happy" is sometimes confused with another song with similar lyrics by Bob Marley, but it was originally written and recorded by Bobby McFerrin in 1988, seven years after Marley's death.

It's so simple that it reads like a worn-out cliché that doesn't need to be repeated, again. And again. And again. But it's so often and tragically ignored that I'll say it anyway: If you're happy internally, if you're confident in yourself, then you won't have to join a mass movement and follow a leader who promises that he can make you happy, if only you will hate someone else.

The second guideline to avoiding falling hook, line and sinker for the next catchy and convenient mass movement that comes your way, and instead participating in life as a peaceful, positive human being is: Believe in data. Believe in science. Believe what your eyes and ears tell you. All politicians, clergy, teachers and writers (that includes me) stretch the truth a little now and again. But beware the teller of outrageous myths or the serial liar. If someone tells you that the sun rises in the east, yeah, that's a good start. But if someone tells you that the King of the Underworld is battling with – whatever – and this battle causes the sun to rise: Beware. There are nefarious reasons to spin that tale, to manipulate your thoughts, control your mind and prepare you to do something the storyteller wants you to do, and that you really shouldn't be doing.

Believing in truth shouldn't be too difficult to conceptualize, but throughout history it has been difficult to actualize. I repeat for the umpteenth time: Tribalism, ceremony and mythology brought Paleolithic tribes together and endowed us with the power to survive. But tribalism, ceremony and mythology are all two-edged swords that can strike outward or inward, depending on fine subtleties. Humans are a gregarious, friendly, herd-oriented, tribal species. But there are lots of ways to surround yourselves with a close, loving, caring circle of friends without putting on your red MAGA baseball cap and screaming your head off when a despot rallies the troops to disbelieve in evolution or climate change – or to hate someone based on the colour of their skin, or something like that.

My final suggestion is to be wary of fear. Fear is like salt. You need salt to stay alive, but too much salt is unhealthy. Similarly, if you have no fear, you'll die early; if you have too much you'll also die early. Fear can be a positive, tactile and life-saving response to an immediate problem that you have direct control over. There is a lion in the bushes. I can improve my probability of survival if I run away. But fear can also be an abstract response to a remote problem that I don't have control over, or that I have little control over, or that doesn't exist anyway. Then fear morphs into worry, anger or hatred.

Any time any leader beats the fear drum too loudly, you must understand his or her motives: to convince or cajole you to believe or behave in a specified way. As I quoted Hitler a few pages ago, "It is essential to have [fear] a tangible enemy, not merely an abstract one." And Göring: "All you have to do is tell them they are being attacked."

I find that the first kind of fear, the tactile and immediate kind, is wondrous and uplifting. You see a lion in the bushes. Fear. With fear comes uber-awareness. You live in the NOW. Eyes, ears, nose, muscles on full alert. Body tingling with aliveness. It's not the consequence – death – that you think about. Thinking about death, sometime in the future, even a few seconds or minutes in the future, removes you from the action. True, immediate, tactile fear prepares you for the NOW, puts you in the NOW. Robert Sapolsky wrote a whole book on this subject, *Why Zebras Don't Get Ulcers*. A zebra sees a lion in the bushes, and like a person, goes into alert/action mode. Adrenaline and cortisol pour into the system. The zebra runs away, resulting in one of two outcomes. Either the zebra escapes or it gets eaten. If the zebra gets eaten, end of story. But if the zebra escapes, the release of fear hormones – adrenaline and cortisol – shuts down very quickly. Bingo. Lion is gone, fear is gone. Relax. The immediate danger is over so I can eat grass in peace and quiet (even though the long-term threat persists).

Humans are different. If a person escapes the lion, he or she tends to analyze the situation and project into the future. "Hmmm, that lion almost caught me. I barely got away. There are more lions in the savannah. Maybe I will not be so lucky next time." Therefore, the person continues to be afraid after the danger is gone. This analytical fear can have its advantages if I build a bramble fence around my hut, for example. But it can also cause chronic worry and stress that are damaging to health.

Beware of chronic fear, especially when a despot or a self-proclaimed leader warns you of an attack that is not tangible and immediate and commands action based on this mythology.

Humans are not necessarily helpless captives to a Paleolithic tribal past. We have wondrously complex cerebral cortexes that have the ability to generate cultural change that is millennia faster than genetic change. We don't have to replay the Second World War, or any other war, great or small, if we don't want to. We don't have to hate our neighbours for any reason whatsoever. Despite all the horrible and inexcusable hatred, aggression and racism that are evident in today's world, violent deaths have decreased in the 21st century, compared with earlier times. In ancient agricultural societies, human-to-human violence accounted for 15 per cent of all deaths. During the 20th century that number dropped to 5 per cent, and so far in the 21st century war and crime are responsible for only 1 per cent of global mortality.

We're gaining on it. Patterns can and do change. And I believe, or at least hope, that if we can understand, identify and discuss the Mythologies We Love and Kill For, clear away the smoke screens, listen to the countless voices guiding us into mindfulness, we, as a species, can continue to modify our behaviour to create a more peaceful and joyous world. There's a lot going for us. We don't have to blow it.

> One way or another
> One way or another
> This darkness got to give[106]

---

106 The Grateful Dead, "New Speedway Boogie," on the *Workingman's Dead* album. Written by Jerry Garcia and Robert Hunter.

CHAPTER 12

TO FLUSH A TOILET

When I launched into my career as a writer, half a century ago, I never imagined that I would someday write a chapter called "To Flush a Toilet." But here we are.

A few days ago, Tina told me that the German tour group that was about to arrive was composed of student ecotourists. They had been helping scientists evaluate the effectiveness of either attractants to lure malaria mosquitoes into traps or repellants to disperse them away from areas of high human habitation. With the research project complete, they were finishing their stay in Kenya with a cultural tour in Samburu.

At about the same time, a middle-aged woman named Kate, from Colorado, drives in, parks her rental car down at the goat and camel corral, and walks up to camp. She's lean, fit and tanned, travelling alone across a dangerous landscape. I'm starved for conversation and we have a lot in common. She is a backcountry skier, a mountain bike rider and a global traveller. We fall into an easy dialogue about ski locations and bike trails in British Columbia. But she didn't come here to chit-chat with me. She's a tour operator on a scouting mission to see if the Motel at the End of the World would be suitable for her clients.

We meet with Tina and take a tour of the premises. The toilet issue comes up. It has been front and centre on our minds anyway, because of the imminent arrival of the first guests to book a 'full meal deal' stay here in the weeks since I have arrived. We all agree that toilets that don't flush become yucky, especially in a tropical climate. But then I bring up the (apparently) annoying argument that we are in the midst of a drought, cows are dying of thirst and people could be next. Is it morally justifiable to drive the truck to some faraway place, fill it with expensive, somewhat purified water, drive it up the A-2 road and across the dry wash, and pump the water into the tank on top of the hill, so it can flow down, so we can all shit in it, only to flush it into the ground immediately after we are done? Perhaps we should use the current crisis to explore other options.

"Like what?" Kate asks.

"Well, how about composting toilets?"

Kate and Tina look at me with the slightly exasperated expression of people who must explain The Obvious to someone who is a bit daft.

"And where do you expect to buy composting toilets?"

That takes the momentum out of a more thorough argument I had been preparing. "I don't know," I answer, somewhat deflated. "Nairobi is a big city. There must be someone who sells composting toilets in Nairobi."

Tina shakes her head with finality. "Nope. No composting toilets available in Nairobi."

I don't have an internet connection to confirm or deny Tina's negative conclusion, but not wanting to give up that easily, I reply cheerfully, "We could make composting toilets. There are lots of sites on the internet that show you how. I've looked into it back home and they're not that hard to build. It would be a great project and would provide temporary employment for some of the local folks. And if there are no composting toilets for sale anywhere in Kenya, we could start a new micro-industry."

Kate explains patiently that we are not talking about manufacturing. We are talking about running a motel. And, if you are running a motel, any convenience that exists must work. If you have one light bulb in a room, it must work. If you have two light bulbs, both must work, even if you only need one. And by obvious extension: if you have toilets, they must work. So, either fix the toilets or pull them all out and totally remodel all the bathrooms, to expunge all evidence that toilets once existed here in the past. Which is a big job, which we obviously can't complete before the guests arrive. Which all adds up to: we must fix the toilets.

As I said, that was a few days ago. Then we had this scare over a potential small war or insurrection. But, judging from Tina's demeanour, the scare has vaporized as quickly as it appeared. But maybe not. The burly guy with the AK-47 hasn't vaporized as well. I deduce that we are enjoying a temporary ceasefire in a war that hasn't started yet. Or a war that may never start. Regardless, I have a small stash of solar-operated flashlights, and yesterday I gave the burly guy one as a present, for obvious reasons.

Tina calls the plumber, and he will arrive the day after tomorrow.

In the meantime, an exposed chunk of the main pipe drawing water from the tank on top of the hill springs a leak because it is old, brittle and weakened by too much UV radiation from the relentless equatorial sun. Tina asks me to fix it. "You can use a coin for a screwdriver, if you need one, and we might have a few wrenches. Someone raided the toolbox and stole most of the tools." Since there are no spare parts anyway, tools seem superfluous, and I give up before I even start. Soon, Tiepe comes to the rescue. He finds an almost hardened, almost used-up tube of Sparky Form-A-Gasket for sealing automotive manifolds and digs up some strips of old tire tube and rusty wire. He cuts out the segment of leaky pipe and asks me to help him pull the two functional ends of the now shortened pipe together. End-to-end butt joints are always tricky, but Tiepe is undeterred. I watch him as he bends over the project to carefully seal the new connection with the goop, tire tube and wire. He's a proud young kid from engineering school showing the old man that he is now a man. Wonderful. I think about the letter he wrote to President Obama and the drawing he made of the massacre many years ago, when he was still a boy. How can a person imagine the terror he experienced as the bullets were flying and his friends and relatives were being shot, kicked, caned and raped? How does he carry all that inside and still hold himself together? Because he must, I guess. I want to hug him. Or, sitting in this peaceful place by the water pipe in the scrub, I want to ask him about his feelings. But hugs, words and questions don't seem appropriate, so I watch him work, help when he needs me and compliment him effusively when the job is done and the water flows again.

Next, Tiepe tries, but fails, to build a toilet bowl float and flushing mechanism out of Sparky Form-A-Gasket, inner tube and wire. But we are still ahead of the game with the pipe being fixed – until the middle of the night, when the pipe breaks in a new place. Tiepe's splice held perfectly, but when he cut out the leaky section and then pulled the two ends together, he stressed the system, causing a new and more catastrophic failure farther down the line. A lot of precious water spilled out onto the ground as we slept. We shut off the main valve from the tank and thus cut off the water supply to the entire camp.

The next day the plumber shows up. He has a screwdriver, a rusted pair of pliers, a pipe wrench, a hacksaw blade and a roll of Teflon tape in a small cloth bag. He also has a truck full of new toilets: bowls, seats and reservoirs, the whole shebang. I pull Tina aside and explain that we don't need to replace the toilets in their entirety. The float mechanisms are broken, but all the ceramic parts are fine.

"But we have to be absolutely sure that the toilets will work when the tourists come, and the plumber said that we need to replace everything."

"He's cheating you by selling you toilets and labour you don't need. By analogy, if the fuel pump on your car breaks, you replace the fuel pump, not the entire engine."

My argument falls on deaf ears. Tourists are coming to spend money. The plumber said that we need new toilets. Let's get to work.

Tina instructs me to oversee his work, whatever that means. The plumber builds an ingenious flex joint out of a small chunk of plastic pipe and the ubiquitous tire tube, to absorb the tension and allow water to flow through the main pipe. Then we attack the toilet bowl problem. The bowl itself is cemented into the floor, but he replaces the entire reservoir, complete with its factory-installed float and flushing mechanism. It's wasteful and largely unnecessary, but "Hooray." It's mid-morning and now the pipe is fixed and the toilet in my unit flushes flawlessly.

Tina comes up and instructs the plumber to check every faucet and valve in every unit for leaks – and for me to oversee.

We inspect the shower faucet in my unit. Drip. Drip. Darn. He takes it apart. The washer is mangled. No surprise. He disappears. I wait. And wait. And wait. He shows up with one faucet washer in his pocket. Installs it. Good work. No leak. Then we move over one metre to the sink. Drip. Drip. Darn. We need a new washer. You guessed it. Groundhog Day. He disappears to find one more washer. I'm not making this up. No. This is really happening. I'm not really here in Kenya, at the Motel at the End of the World, in the Samburu stronghold, at Cochise's last stand, with murderous enemy assailants gathering in the desert, watching over a plumber's shoulder while he replaces shower and sink faucet washers – ONE AT A TIME – VERY SLOWLY.

It's noon. With the plumber off to some magic oasis where he finds faucet washers, I slip off to eat lunch. I'm upset. This whole plumbing scene, from beginning to end, is too painful for me. And what tradesman wants a watchdog peering over his shoulder every second of every working day? It's demeaning and insulting for both of us.

Way back in Boston, six months ago, in the plush conference room at the Harvard Travellers Club and in the spotlessly clean coffee shop in Cambridge, I didn't sign up for this. I desperately need to regroup, consolidate my emotions and calm down. I don't show up for my job as the plumber's watchdog in the afternoon. Instead, I try to escape out of camp, to climb Mt. Sabache-Ololokwe again. Just as I am slipping quietly into the bushes, I hear my name called. It's Tina, who has appeared out of her quarters at the critical moment. She won't allow me to leave camp on my own, because it's too dangerous.

"Tina. Look, sorry about this. I appreciate that you are concerned about my safety. But I really need to escape into wilderness right now. I'm a grown-up. I've faced danger many times in my life. Please let me make my own evaluation and decisions. In any case, if someone attacks camp, I'll be much safer on the mountain than down here in the line of fire."

Tina shakes her head. "You are a member of this community, not an independent individual. You've forgotten about lions and snakes that are always a danger on the land. And what if you should simply get lost? If something happens to you, it will reflect poorly on all of us. News will get out and it will be bad for business. These peoples' livelihoods are at stake. They have invested so much in this place and we can't risk it all for your selfish needs and desires."

I want to say something about how I signed up for this journey to track lions, not to help run a motel, but there is no use in arguing.

"Okay, Tina, but wait a minute."

I'm desperate to get out of camp, even in the oppressive heat of the early afternoon, so I ask if I can have permission to climb the mountain if Jawas will come along and protect me. We've travelled together so many times and Tina has trusted him to walk me home in the dark. Tina agrees, but Jawas is too busy with something and can't take the time. I find Jawas. We're friends in a way, and strangers in a way. He's poor and I'm rich, and we're from different tribes, but we tracked the lost camel and shared water in the desert together. I slip a US $10 bill into his hand and he suddenly becomes less busy. We cross the wash, pick up the familiar trail, and I feel emotionally embraced by the long thorns and scratchy scrub. Finally, I can relax, breathe deeply and feel the sweat streaming out of my pores, carrying my worries with it, as we push hard to gain the ridge in near-record time.

Dipa is waiting for me when we return. The wedding will be held tomorrow, and I need new shoes for the occasion. My made-in-China synthetic light hikers are not acceptable, so he sends me off to the closest village, near the A-2 Road, to be fitted with a pair of locally made sandals, crafted out of hide from a Samburu cow. He instructs me to get my new sandals this afternoon and be back down at the kitchen area at 5:30 the next morning to prepare for the ceremony.

He calls Tiepe on his cellphone to take me to the shoemaker's house. Tiepe shows up, I ride on the back of his Honda 90 to the village, and he stops in front of a stick hut/house lined and roofed with the usual mishmash of cardboard, cowhide and plastic sheeting. An older man, probably in his 60s, but it is hard to tell, comes out with a sheet of roughly tanned cowhide and a knife. He speaks no English but indicates that I should take off my shoes and step down on the hide. Then he pulls a piece of charred wood from the outdoor cooking fire, traces an outline of my foot and goes to work with the knife. It's a lazy afternoon in the village. Tiepe is giving the young, almost-naked, barefoot kids rides on his motorcycle. He accelerates, cranks the front wheel sharply and brakes suddenly, to put the machine into a skid. Then he accelerates again to spin the wheels and do doughnuts in the soft sand. The kids squeal in fright and simultaneously laugh in release of fright, when they discover that they aren't dead yet. No one thinks this is too dangerous. Remember: 5- and 10-year-old boys herding cows and camels in the savannah with lions in the bushes. A young mother lays a blanket down, nurses her baby and watches. A few other women join her, and they gossip and laugh. Tiepe tires with this game and charges off. The almost-naked, barefoot kids kick a bundle of plastic around as if it were a soccer ball. A teenager comes home with the goats, leans his spear against a tree and ducks into the hut.

My sandals are finished in an hour. They are painfully uncomfortable. The cowhide is poorly tanned and stiff. The thong that goes between my big toe and the next one over is so stiff it is almost sharp. I thank the shoemaker warmly, and limp toward camp until I am out of sight, then take the sandals off and put my light hikers back on.

It's dark the next morning when I meet Dipa at 5:30. We drive out to the A-2 road and about 20 minutes more to the village where the ceremony is to take place. This village is nearly identical to the others I have visited: half a dozen tiny stick houses, almost like doll houses or play forts, a *boma* for the cows and goats, and outside cooking fires where people can prepare meals, eat and socialize. I can tell immediately, by the look on people's faces and the tone of the conversation, that something is amiss. We get back in the Land Rover and Dipa explains that there is a problem with the bull. They need to sacrifice a bull to complete the marriage, but, you see, the bull ran away. Because of the drought, the groom had been grazing his cattle 60 kilometres away. Because the animals like to stick together, he drove the entire herd, including the sacrificial bull, back to the village. After walking such a distance, he was tired and needed a nap, so he hired some kids to watch the cattle, but they slacked off and the herd ran away. He thinks they returned to the remote pasture, but, even if his guess is correct, it's a 120-kilometre round trip on foot, in rough terrain, to retrieve the bull. The wedding needs to be postponed, again.

We return mid-morning and Dipa drops me off outside my thicket, down by the lower campground and the goat and camel corrals. I'm reading and idling my time, when I hear the throated rumble of a large, well-tuned, diesel engine. Watching the vehicle emerge from its dust cloud, I reflect that it is a cross between a bus and an armoured personnel carrier. True, there are no visible machine gun mounts, but it's significantly heavier and beefier than a normal bus, the windows are small and barred, and the luggage bays are triple sealed with heavy metal and multiple locks. I expect it to pull into the lower parking lot, but it keeps going.

"I guess the driver doesn't know the layout of the place, but surely he will stop when he comes to the lip of the dry wash. Surely, he isn't going to attempt to cross that steep gully in that thing, with loose soil on the slopes and deep sand in the bottom."

But I hear him downshift, followed by the squeak of brakes.

"Oh, no. He didn't even slow down to get out and look. Didn't he see that the climb out of the wash is less steep as you drive toward the main camp than it is on the way back out? Even if he makes it in, he'll never get that monster bus out of here."

I hear a laboured whine, the spin of tires, and then release.

"Whew, I guess he made it in, anyway."

I walk up to camp to check out the commotion.

By the time I get there, the 20 students are milling around while the driver and the local staff retrieve their baggage. All the students are freshly showered, freshly coiffed and have clean, pressed clothes. The smell of perfume and aftershave hangs in the air. The women are all dolled up with abundant and expensive-looking makeup. And their suitcases are humongous. With wheels, of course.

I walk up to the group and say, "Hi," to no one and everyone. A few heads turn in my direction, but the eyes inside those heads look through me as if I didn't exist. I try again with a "Welcome to our eco-camp. Did you have a nice trip in here?" One of the young men responds with the most minimal reply he can come up with, and then everyone ignores me again. Okay. Why should any of these kids want to interact with me? They're young, they have their own tribe, and they came to experience Samburu culture, not to interact with an old white-haired white guy, who is a bit scruffy under the best of circumstances, but even scruffier after these weeks in the bush. I retreat into the shadows, to be the fly on the wall.

The suitcase wheels sink into the soft desert sand. Of course. Students tug half-heartedly, and then look around, helplessly, like a bunch of 3-year-old children whose Bugs Bunny pull-toys have tipped over and stopped shouting in a scratchy mechanical voice, "What's Up, Doc." The burly guy shows up, and for the first time he is not carrying his AK-47. Did he misplace it? Lose it? Forget where he put it?

Did he just run out of his house, yelling over his shoulder, "Honey, I put my assault rifle down somewhere and I'm such a space case that I can't remember where I left it. Would you find it for me while I go down and help the tourists?"

I don't think so.

He throws one monster suitcase over his shoulder, grabs another by its handle, and charges up the hill with two of the kids struggling to keep up, even though they are carrying nothing.

This is what it has come to, here on the Ragged Edge of the Anthropocene.

When all the students have disappeared into their accommodations, a middle-aged man who is clearly the group leader approaches, introduces himself, and asks me who I am and what I am doing here. I tell him a shortened version of my story. Then I ask him what he knows about the small war and insurrection that is, or is not, raging around us.

He explains that, because this group is made up of high school students, he has government support, and with that, access to reports from German military intelligence. And yes, there is a problem. Tension flared up over election issues a few days ago, and his group was ready to pull the plug and fly home prematurely, but then the threats seemed to subside. His sources are confident that we are safe for the time being. They will stay here for a few days, as planned, and then skedaddle back to Europe. But, under guidance from the school board and the military, he has cancelled the next tour group that was originally scheduled to arrive in ten days.

"What are your plans?" he asks.

Part of me wants to hitch a ride with this group back to Nairobi, but I think about Tina's warning that if there is an attack from Somali road pirates or al-Shabab, I should stay clear of concentrations of European tourists. Anthony still won't drive the road. On the positive side, there's a locked strongbox next to the bus driver's seat that looks suspiciously the perfect size to hold an AK-47, so I strongly suspect that the driver is armed. Again, I have conflicting information and I wonder if I am being way too paranoid, but I can only go with my best guess and intuition. I decide to stick it out, for the time being, with my warrior-pals at the Motel at the End of the World. The German tourists are too alien, and the Samburu are my friends. I have new sandals and am expected to attend the wedding, whenever it happens.

— — —

In a section of *Sapiens* called "The Luxury Trap," Harari writes that around 12,000 to 10,000 years ago, "the rise of farming was a very gradual affair spread over centuries and millennia. A band of *Homo sapiens* gathering mushrooms and nuts and hunting deer and rabbit did not all of a sudden settle in a permanent village, ploughing fields, sowing wheat and carrying water from the river. The change proceeded by stages, each of which involved just a small alteration in daily life."[107]

At each stage in this development, people sought an easier, more secure life, free of hunger and want. Harari imagines that, at first, they camped near natural meadows with abundant grain. Later, they enlarged those meadows by burning scrub and forest in adjacent areas. Gradually, they learned to plant, water and plow. Temporary camps became permanent villages. As people became more settled and as food supply increased, women started having more babies, spaced closer together. They weaned children earlier and fed them on abundant, but nutrition-deficient, cooked cereal, rather than mother's milk with a rich, balanced complement of proteins and vitamins. There was more food but less nutrition, and more people who needed to be fed. Disease spread more rapidly in densely populated villages with inadequate sanitation. Adults worked harder. Lifespan and health declined dramatically.

Harari again:

> With time the 'wheat bargain' became more and more burdensome. Children died in droves, and adults ate bread by the sweat of their brows.... Paradoxically, a series of 'improvements', each of which was meant to make life easier, added up to a millstone around the necks of these farmers....
>
> One of history's few iron laws is that luxuries tend to become necessities and to spawn new obligations. Once people get used to a certain luxury, they take it for granted. Then they

107 Yuval Noah Harari, *Sapiens: A Brief History of Humankind* (New York: HarperCollins, 2015), p. 84.

begin to count on it. Finally, they reach a point where they can't live without it....[108]

Thus,

> Humanity's search for an easier life released immense forces of change that transformed the world in ways nobody envisioned or wanted.... A series of trivial decisions aimed mostly at filling a few stomachs and gaining a little security had the cumulative effect of forcing ancient foragers to spend their days carrying water buckets under a scorching sun.[109]

Let's jump now from the Middle East 10,000 years ago to the 21st century and start with a fable – a true story, but a fable, nevertheless.

I spent the most uncomfortable, dangerous night in my life with my dear partner, Franz Helfenstein. We were sailing northward in WindRider trimarans, on our journey to cross the North Pacific, from Japan to Alaska. The WindRiders are five metres long, about the same length as a sea kayak, and you sit in a cockpit, sealed off with a spray-skirt. You can't move around, go below for a cup of hot tea, or anything like that. One afternoon, we were washed out to sea in a storm and, unable to return to land, we spent the night battling for our lives amid huge waves and howling winds, in a cold, northern ocean. We had no protection from the elements other than our dry suits – no tent or sleeping bag – and needed to stay awake and vigilant so we wouldn't tip over and perish. Every few minutes, an especially steep wave would break over our heads, cascading across our body and robbing us of any heat accumulated by our exhausted muscles through shivering. We didn't speak about it at the time, because you never speak of these things in the heat of the action, but I wondered if we would survive the night.

I hope I never spend another night at sea, in a storm, in a cold ocean, in a sea kayak-like boat again. Let's think of my second most uncomfortable, dangerous night. That would be one of those numerous

---

108 Yuval Noah Harari, *Sapiens: A Brief History of Humankind* (New York: HarperCollins, 2015), p. 87.

109 Yuval Noah Harari, *Sapiens: A Brief History of Humankind* (New York: HarperCollins, 2015), p. 88.

times I have made an emergency bivouac on a rock wall, somewhere, again with a storm, again with no tent or sleeping bag. Pretty miserable, but without the additional worry that I might tip over and drown, and without the frigid waves splashing over my head, so a whole lot better than the night in the WindRider. Moving up the comfort ladder, I can recall many nights spent out in the elements, with no tent, but with a sleeping bag. Suddenly things are looking bright. If you add a tent to your meagre pile of possessions, you are 95 per cent on the way to luxury. Find a dirty, smelly, leaky shack on the Russian tundra with saggy bunks and the all-critical wood-burning stove, and you are 99 per cent on the way to luxury. And so on, until you take a giant leap to the most luxurious night I have ever spent. I can't single out this event with any exactitude. But, as I travel around giving presentations and keynotes, many kind and generous people have billeted me in their houses, some of which are quite elegant. From time to time, I have ended up in a mint-on-the-pillow hotel. Or should I say a mint-on-the-pillows hotel because there seems to be some rule of etiquette out there – which I have never understood – that says that two pillows are better than one and nine pillows are better than two, even though it would break anyone's neck to rest your head on nine pillows, so you have to stack them neatly on the floor, before you nod off to sleep – after you have eaten your mint, of course. The point I am trying to make is that it's incredibly inexpensive to make the first 99 per cent of this journey from abject misery, bordering on fear of death, to pretty darn opulent luxury in terms of basic survival. Cost rises astronomically from there on, until the last 1 per cent or 0.1 per cent is exorbitantly expensive. I call this scale of comfort, from the night in the kayak to a five-star hotel or a mansion, the Luxury Ladder.

But at each step along the way, as you gain comfort and security, you simultaneously lose a wondrous animal awareness. Returning to that night in the WindRider: I can still experience, in my mind's eye, those waves looming in inky blackness. Fighting through a wall of unimaginable fatigue, I feel the shape of each wave as it tilts the boat, and simultaneously tilts my pelvis, my epicentre, the focal point of my sexuality and physical balance. I have become the wave, we are inseparable. If the wave is steep enough, it breaks above me, curling into a thin row of white foam that dances into life as the luminescent algae dance, carouse and light up the darkness – external and internal. I will carry to my grave the image of those luminescent algae, lighting up my soul with me, as a warm internal glow.

As I climb up the Luxury Ladder, every time I add a minuscule layer of comfort, I subtract an even larger layer of wonder, of awareness, of connectivity with the Earth and myself. Where's the peak of the curve, the optimal balance? I don't know; it's an unanswerable question that depends on the time of year, the friends I'm with and the activities we are engaging in. A summer night with the stars aglow, with a warm sleeping bag, in the alpine tundra in the Montana mountains, cuddled close to my dear wife, Nina, is as close to nirvana as I can imagine. When the snow starts to fly in October, I prefer my house/cabin with a wood-burning stove and a cheery fire. And the mints on the nine-pillow top rung of the Luxury Ladder? Well, it's undeniably comfy. The roof doesn't leak. The toilets flush, of course. But, from the point of view of feeding your spirit, it's not a meaningful substitute for an alpine meadow in July, with wildflowers growing alongside a stream fed by summer snowmelt. It's not even a meaningful substitute for a frigid snowy ridge in January with the wind blowing your thoughts back into your head before they can form and escape into the cosmos, where they do no good anyway. No. Luxury is not a substitute for reality.

Here in the 21st century, the people living in a small Samburu village are subsisting close to the bottom of the Luxury Ladder, down there with the person in a kayak in a storm at sea. It may look romantic in the photos, with stick huts blending in with the natural scrub. And there would be benefits, living in close communication with the land, with your cows and goats breathing and chewing their cuds outside, surrounded by your loving, co-operative, tribe. There's no morning rush hour commute, no racing around to bring the kids to gymnastics and violin, no mortgages or other bills to pay, and no tax deadlines. But, like surviving a night in a storm in a WindRider, it would be undeniably harsh to survive in a Samburu village, on the edge of hunger all the time, worrying about too little or too much rain, with little or no medical attention, living in a hut too low to stand up in, with no electric lights to brighten the 12-hour equatorial nights, and no refrigerator to preserve food. So what rung on the Luxury Ladder optimizes human happiness? I can't tell you precisely; there are too many variables, and no one can draw an absolute line and say with certainty: "This is it."

But think of it this way. I was born in December 1945, four months and a day after the end of the Second World War. At that time, physicists had invented the atomic bomb, but there wasn't a single fully operational electronic computer in the world, and no television stations. (In my grandfather's time, Reuters News Service used passenger pigeons to transmit stock price changes from city to city.) Thus, the entire computer revolution, from its infancy to the iPhone, fits into my lifetime. Also, during my lifetime: the human population has tripled from 2.5 billion to 7.5 billion and global petroleum consumption has increased 18-fold.

Since we are talking about the Luxury Ladder, the per capita GDP (Gross Domestic Product) in the US, adjusted for inflation, increased by 79 per cent from 1980 to 2020. In 1980, I was 35 years old, and if I remember correctly, that wasn't exactly the Stone Age. I had everything I thought I needed: a car, a house, electric lights, a refrigerator, a few kayaks and two or three pairs of skis. After I looked up the GDP number, I asked myself, "Did I really increase every parameter of life by that much: how much living space I occupied, how many air conditioners, how many miles travelled in automobiles and airplanes, and on and on?" And then I got to thinking about all those people much less advantaged than me. Have they climbed the Luxury Ladder that much? Of course not. So I dug a little deeper, and learned, as if I hadn't known it already, that the bottom half of earners in the United States have seen their annual spending power increase by 20 per cent, while the top 0.01 per cent of earners have seen their wealth and consumption increase by a whopping 420 per cent.[110] *New York Times* columnists David Leonhardt and Yaryna Serkez write, "In effect, each household in the bottom 90 per cent is sending a check for $12,000 to every household in the top 1 per cent, year after year after year."[111] I don't know how angry we should get about this, but I

....

110 David Leonhardt and Yaryna Serkez, "America Will Struggle After Coronavirus. These Charts Show Why," *The New York Times*, April 10, 2020, https://www.nytimes.com/interactive/2020/04/10/opinion/coronavirus-us-economy-inequality.html.

111 David Leonhardt and Yaryna Serkez, "America Will Struggle After Coronavirus. These Charts Show Why," *The New York Times*, April 10, 2020, https://www.nytimes.com/interactive/2020/04/10/opinion/coronavirus-us-economy-inequality.html.

suspect we are not angry enough. Yes, I have plenty and I don't need or want to climb the Luxury Ladder any higher to live a rewarding and satisfying life. But we've talked about that already. I'm one of the lucky ones. In developed countries, the Luxury Ladder is so tall that you only need to climb a few rungs to lead a pretty darn opulent life. But what about the Samburu and all the other people in countries both rich and poor who simply can't climb even those few rungs, who don't have enough to eat, and so forth? But what about Mother Earth, who is crying because the rich have climbed too far and high? And what about the fact that the sustainability of civilization as we know it is on the line? Plastic bags and jet fuel are both manufactured from petroleum crude. So how many plastic bags do I have to patiently recycle or conserve to compensate for one rich person's journey on a private jet to Paris, for lunch? Or how about this one? Every year, the US military consumes more than 100 million barrels of oil. I would have to patiently recycle or conserve approximately 30,000 plastic bags to compensate for one second's paranoid military defence of the world's richest country. Well, perhaps that's too nihilist a way to look at the picture. There are other reasons to recycle plastic bags – to reduce the plastification of the oceans, for example. But, if you want to know the truth, I feel discouraged sometimes.

Harari's concept of a Luxury Trap is true enough, but it is predicated on how much wealth you are able to accumulate, hoard or steal, which depends on a lot of factors, including (but not exclusively) how much wealth your parents and grandparents were able to accumulate, hoard or steal and also how good a storyteller you happen to be.

It doesn't take a sophisticated calculation to show that this rate of growth, and perhaps capitalism itself, isn't sustainable in the long run. If the global population were to triple every 75 years, then in about 500 years there would be 46 trillion people, three-quarters of a million humans living on every square mile of land, including Antarctica and the Arctic tundra. Or, if global petroleum consumption were to increase as fast as it has during my lifetime, then in about 6½ lifetimes, people would be burning as much petroleum every year as there is water in all the Earth's oceans. You argue that I'm pushing the numbers game too far into fantasyland. Fine. In a recent article in the *New Yorker*, John Cassidy starts with the approximation that global growth of GDP will slow to 2 per cent annually. But even if this happens, the US economy will double in size by 2055, and a century from now it will be almost eight times its current size. And "you can readily summon up scenarios in which, by the end of the next century, global G.D.P. has risen fiftyfold, or even a hundred-fold."[112] Can the Earth possibly support essentially unlimited human economic growth? In the same article just quoted, Cassidy reports that all the current presidential candidates "insist that it is. Given the right policy measures and continued technological progress, we can enjoy perpetual growth and prosperity while reducing carbon emissions and our consumption of natural resources."[113] Oh me, oh my. If you were about to board an airplane, and a team of competent engineers reported that the wings were about to fall off that plane, while the airline company executive engineer told you with equal conviction that the plane was safe, would you board the airplane? The fable is obvious. Most scientists, and, in my mind, pure common sense, conclude that unlimited growth is impossible on a finite planet. Politicians disagree. Are you happy to jump on board the airplane?

The problem with that fable is that in real life, you *are* on that airplane, whether you like it or not. But you are one person in a crowded planet of 7.5 billion people. If you move to the forest and eat roots and berries, your behaviour doesn't change Harari's fundamental argument that almost everyone else in the world will fall for the Luxury Trap, if given the opportunity. Whenever possible, most human beings keep going to the imaginary hardware store to buy an ever-taller, ever-higher and ever-shakier Luxury Ladder. It's an addiction. As we continue to climb, most of us in developed countries are well past the point where we continue to improve the overall quality of our lives, counting the pluses and minuses. How can I support that statement? First, start with the obvious: no one really needs nine pillows to improve their quality of life – do they? But ignoring extreme opulence, the per capita GDP in the United States is growing – slowly, but growing – even for the people on

....

112 John Cassidy, "Steady State: Challenging the Wisdom of Economic Growth," *The New Yorker*, February 10, 2020, p. 24.

113 John Cassidy, "Steady State: Challenging the Wisdom of Economic Growth," *The New Yorker*, February 10, 2020, p. 26.

the lower economic rungs. Most people have more than my family had when I was born, and an even larger percentage of people have more than my parents or grandparents had when they were born. Yet, on average, people are becoming less happy. How do we know that? One critical indicator is 'deaths of despair,' which are rapidly increasing. People kill themselves with increasing frequency: rapidly by suicide, a little more slowly with opioid addiction, and even more gradually through alcoholism and overeating. Today, across the world, more people die from suicide than from war and crime combined. In addition, mortality through obesity and self-induced diabetes is epidemic. As Harari writes in *Homo Deus*, "Sugar is now more dangerous than gunpowder."[114]

Tragically, the inequality, the Luxury Trap and the Luxury Ladder are playing out before me, right here in the desert sands, at the Motel at the End of the World, with our busload of student ecotourists. They came here to help scientists develop strategies to combat malaria, and to experience a cultural connectivity with the Samburu. But in their innate need, or expectation, to shit in a bowl of trucked-in, purified water, during a terrible drought, they lost all emotional connectivity with the objects of their quest. They were physically here, but they had tweaked their expectations into an imagined reality that was no longer what they came to see. And we don't even have to ask what was in those suitcases that were so heavy that the kids couldn't walk to their accommodations without the burly guy coming to the rescue. The term "ecotourist" is not compatible with "I want." Where are the young kids, travelling light and fancy free, with a day pack and a miniscule budget, hitchhiking and riding local buses? They're still out there somewhere, I'm sure of it, but they aren't here, at this place, at this time.

—   —   —

Harari set the genesis of the Luxury Trap back at the onset of the Agricultural Revolution 12,000–10,000 years ago. But if we carry the Luxury Trap forward into the 21st century, we run into a new set

114. Yuval Noah Harari, *Homo Deus: A Brief History of Tomorrow*, Reprint ed. (New York: Harper Perennial, 2018), p. 21.

of conditions. Whereas the earliest hunter-gatherers who first sowed seeds presumably were responding to their own logic, today there are a lot of people out there who are working hard to convince us to embrace the Luxury Trap, so we follow another person's logic, not our own. In this sense, buying too much stuff, or demanding too many luxuries, is closely parallel to marching into battle. Why did nearly a million soldiers follow Napoleon into Russia? Why do a billion or seven billion people think they will smell better and are therefore more socially (sexually) attractive if they smear themselves with some scent – either perfume, aftershave or underarm deodorant? Same question. In one scenario the soldiers are following a skilful, storytelling, hypnotic political despot. In the other scenario the student ecotourists are following skilful, storytelling, hypnotic corporate advertising executives. Same game. Join the Pepsi Generation. Join a wondrous, imaginary, mythological tribe where everyone is 'Light and Lively.'

In a recent article in a financial news website, I read a revealing summary of corporate strategy: "Some companies sell computers, some sell services, some sell dishwashers. The one thing that every company sells is its story."[115]

In Chapter 5, I explain how the brain acts as an expectation machine. To link the brain's propensity to depend on expectation with the current discussion about the Luxury Trap, consider the following experiment. In 1999, Harvard psychologists Chris Chabris and Daniel Simons gathered six people on a basketball court, three in white T-shirts and three in black. With video cameras rolling, they were given two basketballs and asked to move randomly, while passing the balls quickly, white to white and black to black. After ten seconds of frenzied activity, a woman dressed in a gorilla suit calmly strode into the scene. She stopped in the middle of the action, beat her chest in a crude and comical enactment of gorilla behaviour, and slowly ambled out of the picture, spending nine seconds on screen. Chris and Dan assembled audiences and instructed them to watch the video and count how many times the players in white shirts

....

115 Paul Vigna, "This Week's Winners and Losers in the Stock Market," *Wall Street Journal*, May 15, 2020, https://www.fidelity.com/insights/markets-economy/wall-street-reality.

passed the ball. After the viewers wrote down the number of passes, they were asked, "And oh, by the way, did you see anything unusual in the video?" Incredibly, half of the experimental observers counted the passes but simply did not see or did not recall seeing the woman in the gorilla suit. I encourage you to put this book down and watch the video (http://www.theinvisiblegorilla.com/gorilla_experiment.html); it's worth a good laugh.

The authors write: "This experiment reveals two things: that we are missing a lot of what goes on around us, and that we have no idea that we are missing so much."[116]

This experiment makes sense in terms of the expectation machine mechanism. Our brain is trained to tune out information it thinks it doesn't need at the moment, even such obvious information as a woman walking onto the basketball court dressed in a gorilla suit.

To survive in this world, everyone must simultaneously tune out and tune in. Tune out extraneous information when it gets in the way of performing necessary tasks and tune in when that information is vital. That's why we have big brains: to sort through all the confusion, look, listen and observe, when it is in our interest, and also to ignore all kinds of data, including bullshit fed to us by people who have a personal agenda to promote if we believe in their bullshit.

If you have a group of people with similar medical problems, and you give everyone a pill, an often surprisingly large percentage of them will get better even if that pill contains no medicine in it whatsoever. This is called the placebo effect. Stub your toe and it hurts. Take a placebo, a sugar pill, and your brain's expectation mechanism can be so powerful that it will release natural opioids into the blood stream that are as effective as if you had taken an external opioid. Peer pressure can also be a placebo, or the opposite, a nocebo, which is an expectation that you will feel worse. If you line up a group of schoolchildren to get a shot, and the first five don't react to the pain, the sixth will most probably receive the shot stoically. But if the first five cry, the sixth will probably cry as well.

As Erik Vance writes in *Suggestible You*, "There is a wave of bottom-up information coming from the external world, through your senses, up into your brain. There is a wave of information coming

---

116 http://www.theinvisiblegorilla.com/gorilla_experiment.html.

from the cortex that consists of your evaluations, your beliefs, and your expectations. Consciousness is these two waves hitting each other. It's a collision."[117] That is how placebos, nocebos and hypnosis work.

That is how advertising works.

That's why we constantly and consistently fail to see the woman in the gorilla suit.

That is why so many of us are so desperately climbing the Luxury Ladder. We're all expectation machines, we're all susceptible and we're all guilty. Someone jumps on an airplane, burns a godawful amount of jet fuel, spills a godawful amount of carbon dioxide into the air and makes a godawful contribution to global warming to fly to Kenya and visit the Samburu and to see a lion. And that person comes back and tells a good story about that journey, complete, perhaps, with a slide show and a glass of fine wine. (Oh my gosh, that's me.) And you are fooled into thinking that the traveller must have had a better time than you did, because you only stayed home and went hiking in your backyard. You work overtime and max out your credit card so you can go to Kenya. AMO. Afraid of Missing Out.

The pursuit of happiness is the root of all unhappiness.

And:

The pursuit of happiness is killing the planet.

The Luxury Trap is another example of a story, or a series of stories, that others tell us and then we repeat to ourselves. Perhaps, every now and then, the teller of these stories has our best interests in mind, but way more often the teller is simply trying to sell us unnecessary stuff that we have to work hard to acquire and which is catastrophically bad for Mother Earth. We all know intellectually that we are being duped, even as we continue to follow. It seems as if it shouldn't be all that difficult to step back and ask if such-and-such a thing or journey really makes us happy, or if it is just a placebo that makes us imagine that we're happy. But if a medical placebo can induce a body to release natural opioids into the bloodstream that reduce pain, maybe Luxury Trap placebos make us addicted to

------

117 Erik Vance, *Suggestible You: The Curious Science of Your Brain's Ability to Deceive, Transform, and Heal.* (Washington, DC: National Geographic Press, 2016), p. 133.

a distorted concept that we equate with happiness. But how much does such-and-such a luxury cost in unhappiness in the other column of the Excel spreadsheet? Humans sure know how to turn simplicity into complexity within the marvelous and mysterious folds of our think-too-much-know-it-all brains.

In one experiment, a researcher assembles ten people in a room. One of those is a real subject who doesn't know what the experiment is about, and the other nine people are actors who are pretending to be subjects. The researcher holds up four fingers. "How many fingers am I holding up?" He asks. First person, one of the actors, responds, "Three." Second person, another actor: "Three." The experimental subject looks around at this new tribe of random people in a room. To avoid social miscue, being banished from the tribe, the experimental subject answers, "Three." Not always, but frequently enough.

All animals, not just humans, need to categorize to stay alive. It's helpful to recognize – very quickly – that lions and lion-like animals are dangerous. Or that a flash of movement in the bushes, too quick to identify, may be a lion, which is dangerous. But categorization is a close cousin to storytelling. This is associated with that, and there is a narrative that connects the two. The problem is that there is a negative side to storytelling-based categorization. If there is a toilet in your room, your brain will tell you a warm, fuzzy, expectation story of the joy of sitting down on a comfortable throne and shitting in a bowl of clean water, in a desert, in a drought. And if the flush toilet doesn't work, or if your friends visited a motel somewhere else with a flush toilet and you were stuck in a lousy motel with a composting toilet, you get bummed.

I have a dear friend in China. He was a young student during the Cultural Revolution that extended from 1966 to 1976. One day he told me, through many tears, that even though his father, whom he loved dearly, was imprisoned and tortured for imaginary crimes against the State, he was drawn into the social whirlwind of the moment, joined the Red Guards, and became a propaganda specialist for Mao. Imprisoning people like his father. The hypnotic power of the Red Guards was so strong that one day he was walking down the street with a group of comrades and saw his father, shackled in chains, working on the roadway with other prisoners. My friend looked away and pretended that he didn't see or recognize his father. When the Cultural Revolution was over, my friend slid seamlessly into a lucrative job as an advertising executive for a large bank. Political propaganda and advertising use exactly the same techniques: create an imaginary tribe, tell untruths, and people in your tribe will do what you tell them to do, persecute whomever you tell them to persecute, or buy what you tell them to buy, so they will feel superior to those people over there across the river who believe that the sun rises in the east.

——— —— ——

Back to the moment. After the ecotourists disappear into their newly flush toilet-equipped accommodations, Tiepe stops by and asks if I would like to hop on the back of his machine and head down valley for a ride. I don't have anything else to do, so off we go. The old Honda 90, overloaded with me on the back, barely makes it out of the wash on the far side, but it reluctantly pulls through. We zoom down the road until we reach the village where we were yesterday. Some of the almost-naked, barefoot kids come running out and Tiepe feels the need to grandstand, so he attempts a doughnut with me on the back. I'm caught by surprise and don't throw my weight into the turn, as I should have, so we go down, sprawled in the sand, upturned wheels spinning. Tiepe looks over at me with obvious concern, but when I jump up, laughing, the tension eases immediately. "But maybe you could do doughnuts alone on the bike?" he suggests. Because this is my tribe now, and because I used to ride motorcycles and now mountain bikes, and I love the feel of a two-wheeled vehicle under me, and because this is the most fun game in town today, I gesture to one of the almost-naked, barefoot kids, and he jumps on the back and presses his sweaty little chest tightly against me. I kick the engine to life, and his breathing revs up in cadence with the engine. I goose the throttle with the bike still in neutral. Whrrrr. Whrrr. Black smoke pours out the exhaust. Good audio and visual. He digs his fingers into my upper abdomen and grabs my floating ribs in a death-hold. I figure if we go down, he's going to hang onto those ribs, and this could hurt. What the hell. I kick it into gear and hit the throttle. The rear tire spins, the kid squeals, and we accelerate. Brake hard, crank the handlebars over, hit the throttle again and we execute a perfect doughnut in the desert sand.

By late afternoon, we haven't had lunch and are hungry. Tiepe reasons that with all the extra mouths to feed, there must be leftovers in the kitchen, so we zoom back to the main camp. Moses is washing dishes, obviously upset. He's the steady kid, always there, always eager to lend a helping hand, always quiet, but smiling. When I ask him, "What's wrong?" he bursts into tears. One of the teenagers requested a grilled chicken breast sandwich (white meat only) with lettuce and mayo on whole wheat toast for lunch and then yelled at Moses angrily when this was not available.

All the work we did to fix the flush toilets hasn't made those kids happy. The successful implementation of the Luxury Trap hasn't made them happy. Now one of them thinks he will be happy only if he has a grilled chicken sandwich, on whole wheat toast, white meat only. If this were a novel and I invented a scenario where a tourist came here to photograph a black man who dressed up in a red skirt and wore a beaded necklace, and then insulted him to tears because he couldn't conjure up this chicken sandwich out of the acacia and dust, you'd accuse me of stretching the fable beyond the limits of credibility. But this is not a novel and every word I write is true.

The scary thing is that these ecotourists don't even think about their surroundings long enough to imagine that their flush toilets are a luxury. They never stop long enough, or look around long enough, or have enough empathy with the exotic culture they have come to experience to even conceptualize every step in the long effort and supply chain behind their luxurious, wasteful, ecosystem-destroying – and totally unnecessary – flush toilets.

One of the perks at the Motel at the End of the World is that the village women dress up in their finery and do their traditional song and dance routine. When they show up, I recognize the young woman who was nursing her baby when the shoemaker was cutting out my sandals. I wave and smile and she waves back. She is standing shoulder to shoulder with the two women who were gossiping and laughing with her yesterday. The students take lots of photos, and clap politely, but they don't get up and dance, and no one pulls a vodka bottle out of his or her boot, as the jolly Russians did.

As I said earlier, it's a grave mistake to romanticize the poverty

Jon Turk

and deprivation of the modern Samburu. No one would choose to live in real fear of physical attack, to spend equatorial nights without electricity, or to grow up without quality medical attention or a balanced diet. But all that notwithstanding, the Samburu laugh and joke frequently, they live in a real tribe, not an imagined one, they help one another and co-operate more deeply than we can imagine. The Luxury Trap giveth and taketh away.

The next day, the German student ecotourists climb back in their bus to go home. And, you guessed it: The bus gets stuck in the wash on the way out. Really stuck. And, you guessed it, none of the students help dig it out. Tiepe jumps on his motorcycle and rallies men from the village who walk up and sweat in the hot sun all afternoon and most of the next morning, digging and building ramps out of logs and brush. I don't ask and no one tells me whether they're paid extra for that. But they get the bus out in time, so the students catch their plane back home.

Life returns to normal at the Motel at the End of the World.

CHAPTER 13

THE WARRIORS

Over the next few days, young men I haven't seen before appear in
and around camp. They are the same age as the motel staff – David,
Moses, Ian and Jawas – but they have shaved their heads, painted
their scalps with red ochre dye and wear elaborate headdresses.
Although every headdress is different, many have a row of pointy
white plastic spikes, like the armoured back fins of a stegosaurus, but
each is unique with its own personal assemblage of feathers, bits of
mirror, push pins and dangles. One man's headdress is adorned with
bright plastic roses, another with a small toy bird, nested in the feathers, appearing to sing out to the world. Although all the Samburu
men, motel staff and warriors alike, wear beaded necklaces, the
beadwork on these men is considerably more lavish in size, colour
and artistry. Each bead is only a millimetre in diameter, but there are
many beads, covering large portions of a man's chest, the product of
hours and hours of painstakingly carefully detail. A few of the men
carry AK-47s strung across their backs, as if an assault rifle were an
article of clothing, or a casual infusion of 21st-century technology,
like a wristwatch. Others carry the long traditional spears of the
Samburu and Maasai. The points are hammered out of whatever
pieces of steel the owner could find, and each has its own characteristic design, reminding me of knapped flint rather than anything one
might buy in a Western-style armament store. To add to the effect,

these shirtless men are young, lean, lithe and strong. These are the herder-warriors who live far out in the bush, and who have walked long distances back to civilization for the wedding.

Every human on Earth, from Toronto to Samburu, from the most fortunate to the most unfortunate, has some control over deciding how much he or she attempts to climb the Luxury Ladder. The motel staff Samburu I've been hanging out with these past weeks have elected to buy into Western capitalism by working in the tourism industry. I surmise that they have expectations, or hope, to live in a small house somewhere, rather than a stick hut, with electricity, or at least a solar panel or two, and access to medical attention. Other Samburu, whom I haven't met, have moved into Nairobi to become even more integrated with Western capitalism. On the other hand, these men with the stegosaurus headdresses live in the bush, in the old way, in small tribal groups, subsisting on milk and blood drawn from the carefully cut veins of their cattle.

In my own life, I have made a conscious decision to forgo many of the more opulent amenities of North American city life, to live more simply in the expansive Montana forest. But it's an unfair comparison, because North America is so outlandishly wealthy that even though I have stepped several rungs down the Luxury Ladder from what is possible, I'm still so far above the wealth of nearly all Samburu, and nearly all people throughout the world, that it's downright embarrassing. Yet I hold in my heart a romantic reverence for anyone who chooses wilderness over stuff, simplicity over complexity, true tribalism over the manufactured tribalism of advertisements and political rallies. I am drawn to these herder-warriors from the Deep Wild of the African savannah. I want to talk with them, travel with them and learn from them. But we have no common language, and I am just a tourist from afar. I am seeking a deep visceral feeling, not a set of verbal answers, and I have no intention of hiring Ian or Moses to be my interpreter, grabbing my notebook or, worse yet, a microphone, and asking a bunch of inane questions. It doesn't work that way. The questions themselves, combined with the structure of asking them, would create an environment that would confuse any answers these men might provide. Given all these frustrating limitations, my only option is to bide my time. We will engage in some meaningful way, or we won't, and I have no choice but to accept whatever outcome unfolds.

Tina charges off to get her car fixed and doesn't return for three days. The engine sounded fine before she left, and I don't quite understand why it takes that long to get a tune-up, or have a fuel pump installed, or a new starter motor, or whatever the mechanic can talk her into buying, but I'm long past trying to make any sense of this. It's a lazy day and I'm sitting in the main courtyard near the kitchen reading, writing in my journal and watching the sun pass overhead. Suddenly, a blond domestic dog comes streaking through camp, fast, low and purposeful, barking aggressively. I've seen this dog hanging around with the goats, always lazy and slow in the hot sun, always in the background, a thin, underfed cur with ribs standing out. It has acknowledged my existence, from time to time, with a casual nod in my direction, neither barking at me nor strolling over, tail wagging, seeking affection. But now this dog is moving quickly, with bared teeth, clearly chasing something. Within seconds, David comes running out of the kitchen wielding a spear. A spear? I've been in the kitchen many times and have never seen a spear. But like the AK-47s that appear and disappear back into hiding, I now realize that spears are always within easy reach. Jawas flashes by, throwing stones with the speed and accuracy of a trained baseball player. Off in the bushes, I catch a blur and a flash of fur that is not the blond dog. I rush over, following the action. The flash of fur resolves into an African wild dog, with huge ears and mottled colouring: black, tan and white. It's much bigger, broader in the chest and more muscular than the domestic dog, yet the small animal is chasing the large one, and the wild dog is fleeing, darting and dodging for its life. I hear humans shouting, followed by a primordial, non-human howl. Silence. By the time I catch up, in the laundry enclave, herded against a corral of thorns, backed against the concrete laundry sinks, in a pool of blood, is a dead African wild dog. I'm amazed that the Samburu dog and men could rally so quickly out of an otherwise sleepy afternoon to outrun and outmanoeuvre a wild dog, and to herd it into the laundry corral and kill it. The execution was fast, furious, coordinated and efficient.

The burly guy with the gold chain comes running up, too late to be part of the action. The three Samburu converse in excited voices and then David translates to tell me that a pack of wild dogs had attacked a goat herd in a village across the A-2 Road. The wild dogs killed several of the goats and wounded one badly. We will eat the wounded goat. Would I mind jumping on the back of the motorcycle with the burly guy, to help retrieve the wounded and now-doomed goat? I grab my *rungu* and off we go.

The tired shocks on the motorcycle bottom out with the combined weight of me and the burly guy. The soil in the wash is deeply rutted and disturbed from the churning tires of the Germans' bus, and all the digging that followed, so the motorcycle bogs down in the sandy bottom. Moses jogs over, from somewhere, appearing out of the ether. I notice that he is carrying an AK-47 now. He is such a sweet kid with such a warm laugh, working as motel maid, cook and occasional tour guide. Just a few days ago he was crying after being reprimanded by one of the German teenagers over the lack of a chicken sandwich. But I have just witnessed these young men in battle action. Now, with guns ever more present and obvious, it's reassuring to have them on my side, but scary to see how quick and lethal life can be around here. Moses pulls, I push, and the burly guy sits astride the bike, gooses the engine and pedals furiously with his feet. The Honda 90 is many tons lighter than the armoured bus, and with three of us working together, we quickly gain the flat road on the other side of the wash.

We reach the village and meet up with one of the forest dwellers with the stegosaurus headdresses. He's also a young kid, in his early 20s, short but stocky, and carrying an assault rifle. To offset his warrior attire and armament, he has a warm, friendly smile, revealing a cheery gap between his front teeth.

The wounded goat is lying on a pasture perched above rock outcrops close to the village. The warrior and I hike up together, in silence, scrambling over steep exposed rock. We reach the upper pasture and find the goat, which has been badly chewed by the wild dogs and is barely breathing. My companion slits its throat to put it out of its misery and we sit in the sand, catch our breaths and let it bleed out for a few minutes. Then he grabs one front and one hind leg on one side and motions me to do the same on the other. The goat is about as heavy as a small deer, not too much for two men to carry, but bulky enough, and awkward. The rock outcrop that we scrambled over on the way up seems steeper now, and if either of us slips, both will tumble down. We work together, carefully, bumping sweaty shoulder to sweaty shoulder and brushing against the goat frequently enough to smear blood over our legs and clothing. We reach flat terrain, scramble through the scrub and return, successful, to the village.

The burly guy is waiting for us with the motorcycle, and Moses shows up. The herder-warrior points to my *rungu*, points to the goat, now lying in the sand, points to blood stains on my legs, and smiles, showing off the gap in his teeth. Then he gives me a proud two thumbs up. The burly guy with the gold chain spontaneously grunts like a lion, and jumps up and down gently, executing a mild version of the lion dance. Moses holds his rifle above his head, pumps it up and down as if he were charging into battle, and joins in with the lion dance. The Samburu leap high, vaulting off their toes, bodies erect and rigid. Why not? I twirl my *rungu* in the air as if I were about to bash someone's head in, growl, and leap as high, straight and warlike as I can. The burly guy, who has been so serious, menacing and taciturn since I first saw him, explodes into a deep, cathartic – from the diaphragm – belly laugh. The laugh is contagious and soon we are all laughing so hard that we can't jump anymore.

I understand the limitations – that I am an old white man from afar – but I feel as if I am on Team Samburu now. Certainly third string, and probably just the water boy, but it doesn't matter. A few hundred years ago, Team Samburu got roughed up by colonialists and slave traders. More recently, they had a tough time with helicopter gunships, al-Shabab and Somali road pirates. But they're still here. And the team has made it into the Final Four. And this smiling, loving, thumbs-up silliness, this dancing and goofing around, is how it all began, here in this desert so many millennia ago, the tribal connectivity that gives us our unity and our power. Yes, all the adversaries over all the uncounted centuries have been Bad-Ass, but we are Bad-Ass as well.

Back at camp, Tina returns after a prolonged absence and the wedding is set to occur the next day. For real this time. Early in the morning, Dipa paints my head and face with red ochre dye and dresses me up in a Samburu cloak and necklace. I put on my new sandals and we drive down to the village. The groom is in his mid-30s and we join two additional best men: an older guy who may be the groom's father, and one of the young herder-warriors from the bush. With a crowd looking on, we line up in single file behind the groom, walk a few steps, kneel, rise, walk a few steps and kneel again.

I don't know the ritual myth behind this procession, and it makes no difference to me. It's ceremony, and if it tells the story of the birth of the raven out of the clamshell or the dance of the giraffe and the serpent, I find the underlying story unimportant. Stories are just one way to activate those mysterious folds and networks in our cerebral cortex, to give us reason and logic to behave in some manner or another. On the other hand, reality is wondrous, efficient and less easily corruptible. The reality, community and spontaneous ceremony of pushing a motorcycle out of the dry wash or dragging a dead goat down over rock slabs works just fine for me. I can feel the love and communal bonding of this tribe that has come together to honour the joining of one man and one woman. I am deeply honoured that these people have asked me to participate in this march.

We arrive at the groom's old house, duck low, and enter. The four of us crowd together and sit on the groom's bed, which is a sheet of rough-tanned cowhide lying on the sand. The house is so small that I don't have enough room to stretch my legs straight without bumping into one of the other men or risking scorching my new sandals in the embers of a small hearth, still warm from the morning's cooking fire. The house smells of smoke, cowhide and humans. All this man's worldly possessions fit into a green trunk, about the same size as the tourists' suitcases, resting in the corner.

I hear voices outside, something that sounds like a small sermon, and then singing. The groom motions for us to exit, so we crawl to the low doorway, and stand, blinking into the rising sun. The bride, whom I haven't seen before, is waiting in front of the doorway, straight-backed. She is a teenager, about half the groom's age. She is smiling, but behind the smile, she looks more scared than ebullient. And perhaps she should be. Marriage is an intense, enduring relationship between two otherwise independent human beings; perhaps we should all be scared, or at least sobered, by the responsibility. And for this young woman, marriage is also a dangerous proposition, for she will soon be pregnant, and then pregnant again and again, with all the dangers and responsibility of birth and child rearing in a land with little food or modern medical attention.

The bride, the groom, the other two best men and a few others walk solemnly into the bush. No one beckons me to follow, and most of the villagers resume their daily tasks as if nothing is happening, so I slip into the sidelines, lie down under the shade of a parched acacia tree, remove my painful sandals and take a nap. Tina finds me, brings some food and explains that the actual marriage ceremony occurs out of sight of most of the tribe. The groom kills the bull, sanctifying the union until the bull comes back to life. About mid-afternoon, after the sun has crossed its apex, the tribe gathers to build a new house for the now-married couple. One woman draws a square in the sand with a machete, about three metres by two metres, slightly larger than the groom's old house we had entered this morning. There will be two people now, and perhaps three in a little while, so they will need a little extra space. Another woman rings the perimeter with thorns, to repel any evil curses. Then women, and only women, pound vertical sticks in the sand around the perimeter. The sticks are all painted with red ochre and are spaced five or six centimetres apart. Next, the homebuilders lash horizontal sticks to the vertical with strips of bark. They add a domed roof of curved sticks, cover the roof with bits of tin and the usual mish-mash of plastic, grass thatch and cowhide. The walls are sided with cardboard, complete with the logos of furniture and bicycle manufacturers. The groom drags his green trunk over, then fetches the bride's trunk from her mother's house, and now all they need are a few stones to make a fire ring and a cowhide to sleep on, and they are done, finished. No mortgage hanging over their heads for the next 20 years.

The festivities ramp up as soon as the house is finished. The women start first, singing without musical accompaniment. They crowd close together, shoulder to shoulder, and sway in unison as a single organism. At certain points in the song, they throw out their chests, so their beaded necklaces bounce on their breasts. When they are finished, the warriors congregate behind the village, joined by young women in their teens and early 20s. The motel staff are not invited to join. There is clearly a separation, and those Samburu who have elected to enter the capitalist system have forfeited their right to participate in this ancestral ceremony. I wonder about their feelings, but again, that is not a question to ask. We all lose bits and pieces of our ancestral selves as we have marched resolutely from our

Stone Age ancestry into the 21st century. The Luxury Trap giveth and taketh away.

A huge, muscular, athletic man, head and shoulders taller than anyone else in the group, and decorated more lavishly than anyone, steps forward. Slowly, almost inaudibly, he starts grunting in a deep low growl. He springs into the air, lightly and tentatively, barely moving his quads, and bouncing on the balls of his feet, his heels never touching the ground. The ancient, primordial lion dance, the *adamu*, has begun. His grunts become louder, more guttural, and one by one, in a groundswell of song and emotion, the young men and women behind him emit a repetitive, lion-like growl and roar. The leader leaps higher than I can imagine a person can leap and remain rigid, exhibiting little outward evidence of exertion. Soon, everyone in this group is leaping and grunting, men and women alike. The ground seems to shake, and dust rises. A line forms and the vertical motion also becomes a forward motion. As they approach in a snake-like column, their coiled energy becomes palpable, and the sweat pours out of glistening skin, beading up on brows and bare chests. The grunting, without instrumental accompaniment, becomes musical; the male and female voices meld and harmonize as if driven by an invisible unity. The energy speaks of rising up, of perseverance, of connectivity with the Earth and its creatures, of tooth-and-claw survival on the savannah; it is tribal, communal, warlike and sexual all at the same time.

In Chapter 6, I explained that in traditional Samburu (and Maasai) society a male's life is divided into four stages: child, warrior, leader and elder. There is no category for teenager, that in-between time when a boy-man has the luxury to explore drinking, sex and almost lethal driving. The young warriors, the *morani*, live up to ten years together in a warrior's camp, an *emanyatta*, far from the home village.[118] These *morani* live under ascetic monastic conditions: celibate, distant and austere. There is no room out here for the whiner, for anger, recklessness or drug addiction. Everyone is honour-bound to contribute, care for the cattle, protect the tribal family back home and, perhaps even more important, to protect the culture – and to ask for nothing in return. When I try to imagine the mindset and lifestyle of a *moran*, I fear that any imagined stories or artificial metaphors will be insufficient

----

118 https://www.gadventures.com/blog/story-behind-maasai-jumping-dance/.

or, worse yet, inaccurate. So let's stick with a few observations from my time here. While still a child, even before becoming a *moran*, a 10-year-old boy, armed only with a club and a stick, faced the lion alone in the dense scrub, made critical life-and-death decisions and brought the precious herd of cattle back to the village. While still a child, even before becoming a *moran*, a 5-year-old boy, with no armament whatsoever, headed out into the savannah to find and retrieve his family's lost camels. And from that already formidable childhood foundation, when these boys grow up, they will be expected to become even more courageous, self-reliant and self-sacrificing.

Daylight slips away, and after the *adamu* is finished, I join Tina and Dipa in the Land Rover and we return to the Motel at the End of the World. Tina says goodnight and disappears into her lodging, Dipa drives off and I walk slowly back toward my thicket.

Jawas wasn't at the wedding and I haven't seen him all day, but he appears mysteriously and silently out of the night to walk me home, once again.

"Hey, Jawas. How are you doing? I haven't seen you all day."

He answers in a quiet, singsong voice, soft, like the night. "Yes, siree."

"I've been thinking about that wild dog that David killed yesterday. Will wild dogs attack humans?"

In a louder, more emphatic voice, he responds, "Yes, siree! And they do eat them people. Just the same they eat the goats."

"Really? And hyenas? Do they attack humans and eat them as well?"

"Yes, siree!"

We continue in silence.

Jawas adds, "And giraffes and elephants. They are danger. And lions. There is lions around, now."

I notice, with some alarm, his use of the word, "now," as if this were news that the situation has changed from what it was yesterday. And I wonder about giraffes. I've never heard about a giraffe attacking a lone white man walking home to his thicket in the night. But I don't bother to ask Jawas about that.

"Hey, Jawas," I ask. "You have no gun, no spear and no *rungu*. If a pack of hyenas, or a lion, or a giraffe (or a Somali road pirate) were to attack us, how would you protect me?"

"Yes, siree! When you walk at you camp at the night, you come at me. Every time. I walk home at you. Every time. Do not forget this."

The next morning, Tina reaffirms what Jawas told me last night, that a lion has been prowling in the area. Would I mind joining Dipa and three of the *morani* to patrol the camp perimeter and track the lion?

It's been a long time since anyone has mentioned lion tracking, and this is what I originally came to Kenya to do, so of course I agree. Dipa drives up in the Land Rover. One of the *morani* is the guy I helped retrieve the goat. He has an AK-47 slung over his shoulder.

"Hmm? Is he less in tune with lions than Dipa is? Or is this lion different? Or am I missing something here?"

In lieu of any mutual language, he smiles, pats me on the shoulder and gives me two thumbs up.

The five of us pack into the Land Rover and travel slowly over a rough track I haven't seen before that skirts the northern edge of our valley and then curves northward against the mountain. Eventually, the track ends in a wall of brush. The *morani* jump out and hack a path forward with machetes. Dipa acknowledges that this is slower than walking, but explains that he wants to show me something, and they will be building a road through here soon, so the work we are doing has a purpose.

We proceed for a quarter of a mile, abandon the vehicle at the edge of a low-slung ravine, scramble down into the gully and walk upstream until we reach an imposing, exposed stone cliff, about 75 metres high and 100 metres wide.

As I look up at the rock, Dipa explains, "I want you to see this place."

"Yes?"

"When the rains come, the rock collects the water, like the roof of a giant house. We will build a water tank here," he adds proudly. "We will store the rainwater and use it to grow tomatoes and other vegetables which we can eat. And maybe we will even sell some to pay for the water tank. This will make our lives better."

I nod, and respond, "Good idea, Dipa. That's a clever plan to use the cliff face to gather the water." I think of the baby tomato seedlings poking their tiny heads out of the soil. Who doesn't thrill at the sight of the first yellow tomato flowers, morphing into the green, round, marble-sized orbs, becoming larger, turning red, ripe and juicy until they are served over a bed of crisp lettuce?

While Dipa and I are talking, the young man I carried the goat with pushes through the thorns to the base of the cliff. He evaluates the rock, flips his assault rifle around until it is stable on his back, tests a lower handhold, kicks off the dust from his flip-flops, and starts to climb. I've been a rock climber in my younger days, and I watch his movement with a practised eye. The first three metres are a bit steep, but with a few strategic handholds and footholds. It's technical enough that most rock climbers would use ropes for protection, but easy enough so any professional mountaineer would free-solo it without a second thought. For those of my readers who are familiar with the terminology, I would rate it 5.7. Then the cliff slopes back, becoming less steep, reducing the grade to 5.5. This more gradual portion is the slab that will collect the rainwater. The second *moran* follows, and then the third.

The lead climber reaches a solid foothold, looks down, careful so his AK-47 doesn't slip off his shoulder, and motions me to join them.

"Is this a test? Or just boys inviting me to join in some old-fashioned fun?" I am reminded of doing doughnuts in the sand on Tiepe's motorcycle. Fun. The best game in town.

"What the hell, if those guys can climb this in flip-flops, I can climb it in my Chinese-made light hikers."

I approach the rock. Dipa calls me back. "It is too steep and dangerous for you."

I look at him and smile broadly. "Thank you, Dipa. But I'll be okay." And then I move onto the rock, feeling the smooth balance and kinetics of the sport. Dipa looks up, watches me for a few moments, and then approaches the rock and follows.

I move past the original steep part and scramble quickly up the lower-angle slab until the cliff steepens up again near the top. Two cracks split the face. The *morani* all follow the left-hand line, but the right-hand crack looks more secure to me. I move two steps right and reach the crack. I glance down. A fall here would be ever so nasty, probably lethal. And even if I were to survive, I am far from any medical attention, and even farther from competent medical attention. I got it. I've been in this zone before, not in this place, but in this zone. Danger. Care. Awareness. I slip my fingers into the crack,

Jon Turk

feeling the roughness of the granite and the bite of crystals into my knuckles. A joyful pain, because even though it hurts, it is a handhold I can trust with my life. Finding a sharp foothold, I move upward to gain a small ledge, where I pause, take out my camera and snap photos of these muscled rock-climbing warriors in their flip-flops, with their headdresses and assault rifle. I wonder if I could sell this photo to a North American climbing magazine.

Even farther right, Dipa has found a third route. We are at about the same elevation, separated by smooth rock slab. Dipa stops and we lock eyes. I smile, and he smiles back with the age-old, bonding smile of shared fun. Play. A universal, relaxing joy. All mammals play. We all reach the top at about the same time. The danger is over, so we shut off adrenalin production, but the residual hormone still races around in the blood. With nothing left to do, the adrenalin amps up joy, excitement, rapid-fire talk, laughter, two thumbs up with broad smiles.

We work our way down through the bushes to the base of the rock. As we return toward the Land Rover, Dipa's cellphone rings. He answers cheerily, then his face darkens and his voice grows serious. When we reach the vehicle, Dipa engages in a quiet conversation with the *morani*. Since I speak no Samburu, I wait patiently, watching people's body language. The young men listen, standing erect and stoic. Dipa instructs me to join them. He has some business to attend to back in town and will pick me up at dusk at the village where we watered the cows several weeks ago.

We set out north by northwest. My compadres move gracefully through the scrub. I walk as fast as I can, run a few steps, then walk again. After an hour, the warriors stop suddenly, peering at the ground. I catch up and follow their gaze to see soft, perfectly rounded pug marks outlined in the soft sand – fresh lion tracks.

My heart speeds up. After all this time at the Motel at the End of the World, all the frustration, the weeks of waiting, and the fear of external violence, here I am, finally, for the second time, on the African savannah, standing over the fresh footprints of a lion. The men talk earnestly among themselves, giving me time to speculate and wonder, for the umpteenth time, what we will do if, or when, we finally see the lion. Am I about to witness some deep interspecies communication the depth of which I can only imagine? I think about my conversation with the leopard some weeks ago. Can we replicate that exchange?

My friend from the goat retrieval adventure looks at me and points in the direction we had been walking before we crossed the tracks, at approximately right angles to the route the lion is travelling. And off we go.

As usual, I hurry to keep the pace.

Now, what just happened? This morning, Tina told me we would be tracking lions. But we just encountered fresh lion tracks and didn't follow them. There must be another explanation.

Perhaps these men have some insight into lion behaviour, and we are taking a shortcut to intercept the beast's presumed path a little farther down the trail. But, from everything I know about tracking and animal behaviour, that doesn't make sense. What alternate explanations can I come up with? Could we be just out for a walk, as people in developed countries go for a walk, for exercise and to enjoy the scenery? No. That doesn't make sense either.

As the afternoon shadows lengthen and we don't cross the tracks again, the first possibility seems less and less likely. The second never seemed plausible. I have never just "gone for a walk" with Aboriginal people living in close physical and emotional connectivity with the landscape. Our rock-climbing jaunt being the exception, life is generally too fragile and precarious out here, energy in the form of food calories too precious, so getting exercise for the sake of exercise, with no functional purpose, is not part of the local vocabulary.

Could it be that, after that phone call, Dipa had set us off on a mission that has nothing to do with lion tracking? Lion tracking was, after all, just an assumption on my part, a hope, a story Tina told me way back there in that coffee house in Cambridge and repeated this morning.

What could be more important than tracking a lion? What was that phone call about? Why did Dipa take off so suddenly? And why the gun this time? I look at the battle-worn stock, the trigger polished into a reflective metallic sheen by wear, like a railroad track, the curved clip of bullets, and the cartridge belt across the man's chest.

Then, I have an aha moment. "Oh shit. Maybe we're on a military patrol."

A week ago, Tina had asked if I was handy with a rifle. Yes, I'm handy enough, I guess, if I have to be. But I don't want to be. And anyway, that's an academic question because all I have now is my *rungu*. I faced a lion in the bush armed only with a *rungu* when I was with Dipa some weeks ago, but now that seems like child's play compared to facing al-Shabab or Somali road pirates.

We're travelling in flat, thick scrub – difficult country to navigate in. As I race along as fast as I can, I try my best to keep an eye out for thorns above me, thorns below my feet, snakes and whatever other dangers I can imagine. But more often than I choose to admit, I step on a thorn so long and rigid that it pokes right through my shoe and into my foot. It's way too painful to ignore, and I'm embarrassed to hold up the patrol, but I need to stop and pull it out.

These people we are looking for, or tracking or pursuing, either in reality or in my imagination – I cannot be confident that I can communicate with them as well as I communicated with the leopard. If they are what I think they are, or what they could be, they have been emotionally and psychologically damaged by encounters in their childhood, by encounters in their mothers' and fathers' child-hoods. Dealing with lions and leopards is easy compared to these. These people have complex stories in their heads.

"Okay," I remind myself. "We're not in acute danger, right here, right now, in this millisecond." But then, "Maybe we are in danger this millisecond because there could be an unseen sniper in the bushes. Can I fully expect to live for the next five seconds?" I try to focus on those next five seconds. As in *Zebras Don't Get Ulcers*, practise awareness, not fear. I stare deeply into the brush to see the complexity, the wonder and the beauty around me. Because if the argument about beauty I made earlier in this book is correct, then our human ancestors gained that razor-thin edge of survival through that warm, dopamine-fuzzy feeling of beauty, not the grating, adrenaline-jarring feeling of fear. And if I'm wrong, and all this talk of beauty is nothing more than a writer's mumbo-jumbo, I'd rather die with beauty in my heart than fear in my veins.

I trust that these *morani* have sharper senses than I have. I trust that they will lay down their lives for me if necessary. Love. Compassion. Honour. Emotions swirl. Calm yourself, Jon. It's counterproductive to flood the system with hormones that are not needed NOW. Or in the next five seconds. It's a beautiful afternoon in the scrub. The sun is lowering on the horizon and another day is passing. Watch out for thorns and snakes. Nothing else is important. How simple. How liberating.

The afternoon passes. When I tracked a real lion with Dipa, I harboured a deep visceral hope that we would connect with the lion and communicate with this king of beasts in whatever way I was capable of. But today I have no desire to engage in a firefight with murderous human assailants. If, in another time and place, I die in an avalanche or a storm at sea, well, that is Nature, impersonal, part of the everlasting flow. But human assailants have consciousness, they are listening to stories; presumably, they are exercising choice. But as Harari says, "If it happens, it's natural." So how is a human enemy different from an avalanche? Too much mumbo-jumbo from my think-too-much-know-it-all brain. I swing my *rungu* lightly, feeling its Paleolithic lethality, and its ludicrous futility in modern warfare. It wouldn't even stand up well against a well-sharpened machete. And I am an old man with a wooden club, potentially fighting strong, athletic, young men with assault rifles.

By keeping track of the sun, I understand that we are walking in a broad half-circle around the village where we watered the cows so many weeks ago. We encounter no people, no lions and no other tracks. It is almost dark by the time we reach the paved A-2 Road just north of the village, and finally stop to rest. I shoot a few more photos in the quiet light of dusk. One of my companions pantomimes that he would like to see the pictures. I hold the camera so he can see the screen and scroll through the recent frames. Gently, but firmly, he takes the camera. He looks me in the eye, smiles and one by one deletes every photo I've taken today.

I am surprised that he knows how to operate the camera. And alarmed that it is apparently important to have no documentation of our journey. No one in Samburu has ever shown concern or consternation at my photography. My marvelously complex brain, with its millions of folds and billions of neurons, does what it has been trained and evolved to do: create a plausible story from the meagre facts at hand. Fill in the dots, create an orderly sequence of cause and effect, and invent a narrative to explain my surroundings and the actions of the people around me. I can't verify this story with additional supporting evidence or a controlled experiment, as a scientist would and should do, but all I can say with certainty is that at that moment I believe this assumed logic of cause and effect.

Am I too paranoid to conclude that, should I be kidnapped, they want no evidence of this patrol to fall into anyone else's hands? Is this rock slab, the proposed water storage tank and vegetable garden, a secret? After all, a few weeks ago, someone shot the engineer who was designing the water tank closer to camp. As I have said before, I don't know, and I'll never know the truth. But I do know that right now, I am scared.

We walk south in the waning light until we reach the *boma* guarding the small village. Although I carried water with me, I haven't eaten all day, and I'm looking forward to the glass of warm milk and bowl of gruel that the villagers will offer me. About 50 metres from the *boma* gate, the three *morani* stop abruptly. Women and nearly naked, barefoot kids from the village come out to look. The two groups stand face to face, but apart. No one waves, calls out, says hello or gives anyone the two thumbs up. No one comes forth to offer food or drink. The *morani* stand straight, proud, silent and immutable.

When you are a warrior, you are a giver, not a taker, a contributor, not a liability. If my presumptions are correct, we just risked our lives to run an armed patrol to protect the village: the women, children, leaders, elders, cows and goats. But *morani* do not, and will not, take anything in return. Not even a warm glass of fresh goat milk. That glass of goat milk will come later, ten years from now, after they have permanently earned their place in society through their generosity, sacrifice, asceticism and courage.

I stand between the two groups, silent. I am a stranger, a foreigner, neither a *moran* nor a villager, a 21st-century creature of an unfathomable, distant, wealthy culture. I have been fortunate in my life to have stood naked in front of Moolynaut, to have hunkered down in the face of Siberian blizzards with Oleg, and now to have stood here with these men – and apart from them. I have been blessed to have learned from others, but my journey forward is my own.

In the distance, headlights pierce the soft night with their yellow glare, flaring upward into the treetops and then jolting into the bushes, as if they were blinking. It is Dipa's Land Rover bouncing over the rough track toward the village. He arrives, pokes his head out of the window, surveys the scene, and smiles – wordless.

I walk slowly toward the vehicle, stop, turn toward the three *morani* and watch their statuesque, expressionless forms in the artificial daylight of the Land Rover, with their bright headdresses, simultaneously jaunty and warlike. This is the last time in my life that I will experience a tribal, primordial display of this ancient consciousness.

Two trends converge toward this realization. First, I am getting older, and less able to travel in the hardscrabble manner required to reach the ragged edge of Western Civilization, where the old ways still hold sway. And second, the old ways are dying quickly. When I was in Siberia, my dear friend Lydia explained that she desperately wanted to preserve the ancient shamanic powers of the old woman Moolynaut and retain the wisdom of her people. But she could not make the journey. When Lydia was a little girl, the Russian conquerors tore her out of her family and culture, gave her a Russian name, forbid her to speak in the old language and forced her to sit at a desk and study reading, 'riting, and 'rithmetic. But in the process of training her brain to process Western Civilization, she irretrievably lost her ability to experience life in the Old Way. She told me that even though I had spent a lifetime seeking the deepest wilderness landscapes and seascapes in the world, even though I had kayaked across the North Pacific and skied remote ranges, I would never truly incorporate Moolynaut's Aboriginal consciousness into my own. Lydia went on to tell me that a few years ago, there were two great Koryak shamans of the Old Ways remaining in the world: Moolynaut and another woman in another village. When the other woman realized that her time on Earth was about to end, she tried to transfer her power to acolytes in the village but was unable to do so. Saddened, she walked out into the forest, embraced the biggest ancient tree she could find, and transferred all her power into the tree. The Power was so great that the tree exploded, simultaneously killing itself and the old woman.

This story is either true or a fable; it doesn't matter. The essence of the story is true; the ancient Power that sustained us for so many millennia is being lost in the onrush and easy convenience of technology. I look at the *morani* one last time and give them two thumbs up, but they continue to stare straight ahead as if I don't exist.

Back in the car, I consider asking Dipa a lot of questions about the day and the danger we face, but once again I decide not to verbalize this whole experience. Words won't change anything, and I take my cue from the statuesque *morani*.

— . — —

Today, and in the past few days, I have observed different, seemingly contradictory aspects of this abstract concept we call storytelling or mythology. Tracking is a pragmatic activity, essential to the survival of hunter-gatherer tribes throughout the world, that is based on our ability to imagine a narrative derived from the track before us. A footprint of a lion or an enemy assailant is a symbol, a representation of the lion or enemy, not the object itself. From this symbol we create a story. A lion was here. If the tracker is skilful, he or she can embellish the story with additional details: A lion was here recently – or a few days ago. The lion was walking – or running. Or, if we are tracking a person, we might know from past experience that the tread on the sandals or the stitching of the moccasins indicates that the person who walked here was a member of such-and-such a tribe. This type of storytelling is essential in the day-to-day pragmatic survival of the tribe. As I explained previously, storytelling shortcuts our reasoning process, creates a sequence of cause and effect based on past experience and cultural transmission of information, so we don't have to start from scratch and relearn, or rethink, every detail of life from the beginning, every time we encounter a situation. Storytelling helps us perform everyday tasks efficiently. If I see gazelle tracks spread out over a meadow, each animal moving in random directions, I know that the gazelles are feeding and moving slowly. If the tracks are lined up in single file, the herd is travelling somewhere. If I am a hunter, this story, this prediction, of gazelle behaviour becomes essential to my success in feeding myself, my family and my tribe.

This human desire to understand, to explain, to establish patterns related to cause and effect, eventually led to science, a great form of Power. Returning to the Klamath myth of volcanic eruptions from Chapter 5, Aboriginal people created the myth of the evil suitor and beautiful maiden to explain volcanic eruptions. But over the millennia, people refined the thought process and separated cause-and-effect reasoning from myth. Thus, science was born, and explanations were based on observation, experiment and conclusion. If you base your understanding of volcanic eruptions on the theory of plate tectonics, you can not only explain the eruption of one particular mountain, you can also predict the approximate location, frequency and explosiveness of volcanic eruptions throughout the world. And of course, science opened a new reality of technological ease, opulence and prosperity.

But there was another narrative going on this day in Samburu, more abstract. If *morani* voluntarily refuse to drink a warm glass of goat milk, they will find a different form of Power, harder to quantify than plate tectonic theory, because it involves the deepest mysteries of the human brain.

Recall that around 70,000 years ago, the human population declined to the point where our species was on the verge of extinction. And then suddenly, coinciding with the proliferation of the earliest mythology-based art, our species executed an evolutionary about-face, and our numbers started to grow, slowly at first, and then with exponential speed.

Homo sapiens didn't turn the tide on the survival game because we suddenly got stronger than a gorilla or faster than a gazelle, or grew sharper teeth and longer claws than a lion. Our anatomy stayed the same. Brute strength has never been our main calling card. And even today, when we have augmented the strength of our bodies with machines, when our bulldozers are stronger than a gorilla, our airplanes faster than a gazelle, and our weaponry so much more lethal than the teeth and claws of a lion, strength is still not our ticket to survival. As the blind man said in the post-apocalypse novel *Riddley Walker* (written in Riddley Speak), "I know all about strong 1 s I ben with the las lot it didn't help them nothing all ther strongness. You bes stay how ever you are don't look for no exter strongness."[119]

Homo sapiens didn't turn the tide on the survival game because we suddenly got smarter, either. By 70,000 years ago, our brains had already evolved to their current size, and regardless, the turnaround

---

119 Russell Hoban, *Riddley Walker*, Expanded ed. (Bloomington: University of Indiana Press, 1998), p. 81.

in our fortunes was so much quicker than any evolutionary change that the tipping point had to have been initiated by cultural adaptation, not biology.

Homo sapiens didn't turn the tide on the survival game because a renaissance in science and technology suddenly made our lives easier and more efficient. The archeological record shows unequivocally that art and technology arose hand in hand, more or less simultaneously. You cannot argue that improved hunting techniques came first, making life easier and giving us the free time to engage in art as a frivolous pursuit. No. The development of art, the establishment of myth, was an essential component of the rise of technology and science.

We turned the tide on the survival game because something triggered in our think-too-much-know-it-all brains down there in the serpent cave that endowed us, as individuals and tribes, with the Darwinian fitness to survive. Meaning: we were better adapted to grow, feed ourselves, evade enemies, procreate and raise our children to reproductive age so they could grow, feed themselves....

We're not going to be able to define this 'something' in a tidy manner, all tied up with red ribbon. But to broaden our perspective, it is essential to delve deeper into this 'something,' and to do that, we must explore shamanic tradition. Every hunter-gatherer culture, from the equatorial rainforests to the ice-bound Arctic, from as far back as we have an archeological record, to the tribal people encountered by Western anthropologists at the time of first contact, to the residual Aboriginal cultures of the 21st century, has embraced shamanic practices similar to those Paleolithic gatherings in the serpent cave.

Shamanism has no universal Great Book to codify dogma and practice. Shamanic traditions across the globe evolved independently, with no contact or exchange of ideas. Yet shamanism is remarkably similar from place to place, ecosystem to ecosystem, and tribe to tribe. The shamanic experience universally involves a journey to the Spirit World, or the Other World, as my Siberian friends called it. The spiritual leader, the shaman, is adept at travelling back and forth between the Real World and the Other World. Often the shaman will make this journey alone, to communicate with the higher beings and to beseech them to provide healing, bring rain or improve hunting fortunes. At other times, the shaman may advise or oversee a layperson's passage. Commonly, the spirit journey is initiated or facilitated by fasting, self-mutilation or other forms of self-induced pain and suffering. The shaman frequently experiences ritual death before the ascent, or the ceremony begins in a cavern, which is interpreted as a symbolic grave. And throughout the world, in every environment where psychotropic compounds are environmentally available, the shamanic journey was and is assisted by the hallucinogenic experience. In *Shamanic Voices: A Survey of Visionary Narratives*, Joan Halifax writes: "Shaman-hood implies something more than prescribed sacred action. It is an intimate, mystical encounter with the fields of life and death and the forces that fuse these realms."[120]

From all the evidence available, anthropologists are essentially certain that our Paleolithic ancestors took shamanic journeys similar to the rituals we observe today. They told stories about these journeys, which we call myth, and they created art to represent the stories. We are a storytelling species. The stories affected *Homo sapiens* in two different but related ways. They brought the tribes together to create cohesion and co-operation so essential to facing the travails and dangers of a harsh and dangerous existence. And they also changed the minds and behaviour of individuals to endow these individuals with a mental and emotional strength that augmented and amplified the physical strength of their arms, legs and teeth. The strength to survive.

We each have a mental attitude or approach to overcoming obstacles. This attitude or approach can enable us to complete our pragmatic tasks effectively and improve our odds of survival – somewhat independent of our physical strength. Thus, our physical strength draws from our spiritual or emotional strength.

I have a short personal anecdote to clarify what I mean.

In 2005, Erik Boomer and I undertook an ambitious and dangerous expedition to circumnavigate Ellesmere Island in the Canadian Arctic and Polar zone. We dragged kayaks across the sea ice northward along the western shore and then eastward across the northern coastline. In early July, we turned south, toward home. The northeast corner of Ellesmere is only 12 nautical miles from Greenland. The ice pack began to break up and start to move. A current drove the

120 Joan Halifax, *Shamanic Voices: A Survey of Visionary Narratives* (New York: Arkana [Penguin Group], 1979), p. 5.

ice southward into the bottleneck formed by the two land masses, creating tremendous pressure. It would be suicide to paddle into the churning, grinding ice, driven southward under the planetary forces of global currents and the spin of the Earth. But we had limited food, winter would arrive soon enough, and it would also be suicide to wait and starve or freeze to death.

A good friend and accomplished endurance athlete, Paul Attalla, texted us, "Be patient. Don't do anything stupid." We broke our bags apart, counted our food and then grimly packed everything up again. "Don't do anything stupid?" Fine. It would be stupid to paddle into the ice and get crushed and equally stupid to wait and starve.

Earlier, before I left home, Paul had told me that when you bump up against a seemingly insurmountable obstacle, you cannot overcome it through strength or willpower alone. You cannot talk yourself into pushing onward, tough it out, or rely on words or resolve. Instead you must find a way to enter into a blissful state that is beyond willpower, where you are just existing, waiting or charging forth, as conditions allow, in the flow, where the pain dissipates, where reality dissipates – but it doesn't. It just changes.

And if indeed there is a place beyond willpower, where pain stops, the glory is that this secret valley is guarded by pain itself, the gnarly old trickster troll under the bridge with a wry smile, a peaked rumpled green hat, dirty underwear and rotten teeth. So you must endure, or cross over, or worm your way through, or suffer through pain before you no longer need to endure anymore because the pain evaporates into something that we don't have a word for in the English language – perhaps because it is not a sufficiently significant part of our heritage. It is not bliss or contentment. That is way too foo-foo romantic. Maybe ecstasy comes close, if we seek its roots and not its modern connotations and the party drug that aligns with that mentality.[121]

There is an ineffable quality, or attitude, or acceptance, or approach – words again – that finds its source somewhere in the human brain and transcends the simple first-order command systems of "muscle do this," "leg do that," "arm throw the spear."

....

121 This section is borrowed and adapted from my previous book, *Crocodiles and Ice* (Fernie, BC: Oolichan Press, 2016), pp. 172–73.

This 'ineffable quality' has been communicated, and taught, through myth, ceremony and shamanic ritual, removing us from the ordinary world of direct observation and sensual contact into another realm of emotional, spiritual and physical awareness and functionality. We are a storytelling species. We have been seekers of this greater Power, or Power within our power, through music, dance, play, song, myth, art and a whole cornucopia of activities that, on the surface, seem frivolous, but in reality, have endowed Darwinian fitness on our species.

I journeyed to visit Moolynaut in Vyvenka six times over 15 years. The most important lesson from all these expeditions is that the survival of the tribe depends equally on the skill of the Hunter, the Pragmatist and the journeys of the Shaman, the spiritual leader. The Hunter lives by the stories in his head, by filling in the dots and anticipating the movement of the game he is following. He must remember the signs that remind him of narratives presaging an oncoming storm, or dangerously weak ice. These stories give him the tools to navigate a complex, dangerous and often confusing world. In Paleolithic times, a human couldn't find food on the tundra without these stories; and in modern times a human couldn't drive to work and hold a job as an insurance salesperson without these stories. But stories also cause Big Trouble when they fuel a person's ego or convince someone to worry about the past or the future. Because ego and worry steal the Power. And, as we have seen, stories can also cause Big Trouble when the storytelling art is hijacked by others to convince us to join a mass movement and to be angry, hateful and weak. As part of the balance, the yin and the yang, the great contradiction, the shaman leads us into the grave to bury our stories and fly with the Raven into the NOW. But then, contradiction upon contradiction, in an interlocking maze of contradictions, the journey into the Other World is a story, a representation of a Thing that is not reproducible or verifiable in any scientific, concrete manner.

We have stories coming and stories going. Stories that endow pragmatic efficiency. Stories that goad us into arguing with our spouses or marching to war. Stories that convince us it's okay to shoot a mother in the head just after she has given birth or to machine gun peaceful worshippers in a church or mosque. Stories that feed our ego. Stories that chase our ego into a dark corner of the brain where it can do no harm. Stories that break the fetters of our own inadequacies and release our deeper strengths. A whirlwind of conflicting, overlapping, contradictory stories, giving us power one day and then stealing that power the next day.

All I can say for certain is that when I took my own personal journey into the land of story, myth and power, I ended up finding peace, equanimity and strength on the Tundra, Mother Earth, Deep Wild. At one point in my long sequence of visits, Moolýnaut gave me the hallucinogenic mushroom to eat, to lead me to what she called the Other World, and what I might call this Power that I speak of. But I was incapable of following her through the dark labyrinth of her vision. Instead, I waited for a year until I was immersed in Deep Wilderness. Until I had travelled across the tundra on skis, pulling a sled, sleeping on the snow, facing ferocious blizzards and the return of spring sunshine, until my face was covered with frostbite scars and my stomach was hollow with hunger. Because my brain intuitively recognized that Wilderness is my greatest teacher. And then a great Raven came to pay me a visit. You can call this bird Kutcha the Spirit Messenger, or you can call it any old lawn and garden raven flying overhead seeking a food handout. It doesn't matter. Not one tiny little bit. Nature always surrounds us, providing wonder and solace if we only open our hearts to the wonder around us; if we only take time to talk with Raven: "And caw, caw, back to you, my friend with the outstretched wings balancing so gracefully on a thermal."

So that completes the Koryak triumvirate:

The Hunter, the Shaman and the Tundra.

The Pragmatist, the Spiritual Leader and the Planet.

I love my brain; I wouldn't so much as go to the mailbox without bringing it along. But it can be a downright pain in the neck sometimes. Over the course of my life, I have learned that whenever this balance becomes too confusing and I need to clear the cobwebs, I can always rely on Wilderness. Earth has no stories. It IS. It is in the NOW, all the time. No confusion. Oh, it will rain and get my new hairdo wet; it will freeze my toes; avalanche me down a mountainside; embrace me in an alpine meadow with fresh wildflowers – all those things. But it is the great Confusion Eliminator because it has no stories, good or bad, yin or yang. Infinite clarity. Infinite simplicity wrapped up in a package of wondrous and infinite complexity. It is the foundation, the rock, always there, patiently being itself, always available if we only choose to seek it out.

Which brings us back to the Horn of Africa, during a horrific drought, with armed *morani*, having just patrolled the perimeter to protect those inside the *boma*. They stand silently in front of the village, announcing their presence, but asking for nothing. These men are hunters, warriors, herders, spiritual monks and hard-core pragmatists. They are about as young, strong and fit as human beings can be. I have trusted my life to them in the event we bumble into a small war or insurrection.

To find their Power, they have buried their wants and expectations, and learned to sacrifice and contribute. Every day, guarding their cattle or their tribe, they rely on the wisdom of Wilderness. And they wear feathers on their heads so they can fly toward the Other World.

CHAPTER 14

A TALL WOMAN
IN A WHITE DRESS

Dipa drops me off back at the Motel at the End of the World, and heads home. I join Tina at the small table, with the ever-present clean white tablecloth, by a cheery campfire, and she asks about my day. I'm not sure what to say, so I answer in broad generalities, without mentioning the rock-climbing adventure, the proposed tomato garden or the fact that we crossed lion tracks and didn't follow them.

Tina pauses, her face tightens, and she tells me about a big shoot-em-up at Archers Post. The assailants drove through the small town in a pickup truck and pumped one or more bullets into every single house. Several people were murdered.

"Tina? What's going on here?" I ask for the umpteenth time. "Who is shooting who, and for what reason? Who are these mysterious assailants?"

"Well, we don't really know. There is so little information. But our best guess is that it relates to a government attack, perhaps related to the election, but maybe really an attempt at real or threatened genocide against the Samburu people."

"You mean there's a small war going on out there and you don't know who is pulling the trigger [or why] on the other side of those guns."

"Well, as far as I can tell, the shoot-em-up is part of government-sponsored, pre-election terrorism. The opposition leader is a Bernie Sanders-type guy who is advocating taxation of the rich to provide more and better services to the poor. And the government doesn't like that, so they are trying to warn the poor people to stay away from the polls."

If that is true, it seems a heavy-handed way to discourage a tiny handful of voters in the inconsequential village of Archers Post. I suspect that the underlying explanation – pure, ugly, racism and tribal animosity – is a big part of what is happening. But it's all conjecture on my part.

"Tina. I really appreciate the opportunity to be here, all these weeks, as your guest. I've had some deeply transformative experiences and adventures. But this whole security scene is way too crazy. The information we get is so fuzzy and mixed with innuendo. I hear what you tell me, but I don't feel that I have a firm grasp on who is perpetrating these shootouts, how great the present or future threat is, or how widespread the violence might become. I don't like being in the dark, like this, especially when my life could potentially be on the line. I'm sorry, but I really have to leave."

"Jon. I told you. The road is too dangerous. Anthony won't drive up from Nairobi."

"I understand. I've been thinking about this. Some weeks ago, when Jawas and I were on the summit plateau of Mt. Sabache-Ololokwe, I saw an airstrip down in the valley, just north of the game park. I'd like to charter a bush flight to come get me."

"Okay then. Actually, I've been thinking about leaving myself. I don't think you need to charter a flight. A twin-engine plane is coming the day after tomorrow to transport hotel guests back to Nairobi. I believe there is an extra seat, so I'll check and book a ticket for you. But it will cost more than a ride with Anthony."

I think, "Why didn't you give me the information about the airstrip and the scheduled flight before?" But all I say is, "How much?"

"Three hundred dollars."

I reach into my pocket, take out my wallet and hand her three crisp US hundred-dollar bills. "Thank you. I'd appreciate it if you would book me a seat on that plane."

She tells me she will buy my ticket tomorrow when she is in town.

Then, I ask, "Will you be joining me?"

"Soon. I'll head home in a day or two. Right now, I have a little business remaining while I'm here."

Tina throws a farewell party for me the night before I leave. The fire in the dining area glows brighter than usual. In place of our cozy table for two with the white tablecloth, the young men have laid out a long plank table, supported on sawhorses. The cooks have roasted a goat, and Tina has bought one soda for each person.

The partially Westernized motel staff intermingle with the *morani* warriors in their elaborate headdresses and still-painted faces. A few of the women from the village join us. We feast, drink our sodas, dance the *adamu*. I jump as high and straight as my 71-year-old legs will jump, holding my head and back erect, my mind focused clearly on the darkness of the African night, one more time, one last time. Jump, breathe, jump higher. Laugh with the others at my own frailness. There are lions out there, and black mamba snakes, and bad guys with guns. But none of that matters. I am dancing the *adamu* with my tribe. Well, not my birth tribe, or my death tribe, but my traveller's tribe of the moment. Nevertheless, safe within my tribe.

I walk among the gathered humanity, shaking hands and thanking everyone, from the bottom of my heart, for their generosity, the adventures we have shared, the wisdoms I have learned, and the fun. Drinking vodka with the Russians, doing doughnuts in the sand, riding a reluctant camel I call Lightning Bolt; fun, play, laughter. Humanity at its best.

There is nothing more I can do or say. I have spent a lifetime in international travel, making dear friends to then leave forever, holding on only in memory. Maybe in my end of days, I need to concentrate on my own tribe. A White Man from the Northern Rockies. My ski buddies. My mountain bike companions. My dear wife Nina. It's time to go home.

The morning of our departure, Dipa shows up with four *morani* to guard me on the journey to the airport: the three men I went rock climbing with, plus a fourth I recognize from the wedding. They are all dressed in full warrior garb, freshly painted with red ochre dye and wearing headdresses and the usual lavish, beautiful, almost gaudy adornment of beadwork. They are all carrying *rungus*. No spears. No AK-47s.

My first reaction is: "No, no. Bad idea. If the government is out to commit genocide against the Samburu people and Samburu culture in general, let's go to the airport with as little fanfare as possible. Please, if you are concerned about my safety, don't surround me with an obvious, colourful, in-your-face flamboyant parade of honour guard warriors with Stone Age weaponry. There must be some historical precedent for this. Marching proudly into the machine guns, adorned with feathers, carrying clubs."

I try to be analytical. Given enough water, I could walk to the game park and one of the fancy hotels, alone, in a long day or a day and a half. "Would that be safer?"

"No, no. Again. Bad idea. I watched those *morani* stand in front of the village, asking for nothing, giving everything. I am honoured that these men have come to guard me, to lay down their lives, if necessary, to protect me, and yes, to honour me with their presence. It would be such a dishonour to charge off on my own into the bush. And perhaps stupid as well. All things considered, I am safer under Dipa's care than I would be wandering around the savannah, willy-nilly, by myself. Your strength is within your tribe. In my arctic expeditions, partners share an unspoken promise to one another: If a polar bear attacks one person, the person attacks the bear with whatever weaponry is available in his hand. A gun, a knife or, if neither is available, a rock. Or you whack the bear across the snout with your camera. Under no circumstances do you abandon your buddy. Yes, honour is on the line. And honour is real here; it is one of the foundations of our Power. Honour can become distorted by stories, myth and mass movements. But this is real, person to person, friend to friend, rock climbing buddy to rock climbing buddy honour." I smile at my guards, with two emphatic thumbs up. They are here without their guns, honouring me with their lives. We are Team Samburu and we have made it into the Final Four. I will not and cannot slink into the savannah by myself on some ill-thought-out theory that I might be safer. It doesn't work that way.

I slide into the middle of the back seat. Two of the *morani* flank me, one on either side, and two climb up onto the roof. Dipa slips into the driver's seat and Tina sits in the passenger seat. Two thumbs up and broad smiles all around. We are off to war, or off to display our identity, our courage and our honour. Or off to the airport. We are not intimidated or defeated. Two thumbs up all around.

Dipa revs the old and reluctant engine into life, slips the transmission into gear, and we ease across the wash, bounce out to the A-2 Road, turn south, and accelerate onto the smooth tarmac. After about five minutes, we approach a minibus on the side of the road, leaning onto a flat tire. Ten clean, young tourists are standing outside, while the driver is loosening lug nuts. The tourists are cheerily doing their morning yoga, spinning their arms to form La-La Land windmills.

"Who is crazy? Who is normal? What is normalcy? Is there really a clear and imminent threat or is this just a story? And if there is a threat: Who is vulnerable? What is going on around here?"

I don't know the answer to any of these questions. And it doesn't matter anymore. I have my plane ticket in the top flap of my green pack. Would I be safer if I tapped Dipa on the shoulder and asked him to let me off here, and joined forces with the windmill arm-spinning tourists? No, I've already thought through that scenario. And rejected it. Dipa shows no emotion. The *morani* by my side show no emotion. I remind myself, once again, that these warriors have left the relative security of their canyon stronghold and are riding into the vicinity of yesterday's shoot-em-up, to protect me, so I can climb into the aluminoscape tube of the airplane to fly back to the safety of my home in Montana. At this instant in time, this is my tribe. There is no way I am going to jump ship. No way.

Dipa's cellphone rings. He listens briefly and says nothing, but slams on the brakes, and hangs a quick right. The Land Rover lurches into the ditch beside the road and sways menacingly. As the wheels spin in the soft sand, and the vehicle lurches, the three of us in the back seat sway back and forth, bumping into each other, rubbing shoulders. I look up through the skylight and watch the two men on the roof, hanging on, cowboy style, like Major T.J. Kong riding the hydrogen bomb down into oblivion in *Dr. Strangelove*. We churn up the other side of the ditch and take off through trackless, roadless, desert savannah. No one shows any emotion, not even Tina.

We are back in the scrub, reminiscent of the landscape where Dipa and I tracked the lion that had eaten the cow such a short-long time ago. Except we are moving too fast now, in this Land Rover, to peer meaningfully into the lacework of branches. The Aboriginal

Australians sing Songlines that aid in navigation by describing specifics of the landscape such as waterholes, rocks, small hills or other subtleties that might otherwise be missed. The Songlines are also 'dreaming tracks' because they represent the routes of creator-beings during the ancestral Dreaming. You can't effectively sing Songlines from a moving vehicle, because the vehicle moves so quickly that the landscape becomes a blur. You lose the animistic personality and spirit of every rock and gnarled tree. You are too distanced from the wholeness of it all to enter the Dreaming. The Luxury Trap giveth and taketh away.

After half a mile we intersect a dirt road that leads to the airstrip, cutting an unnatural straight line through the scrub.

We drive up to a gazebo-type structure with a concrete floor, a thatched roof and unforgiving concrete benches. Dipa brakes the Land Rover to a stop, and everyone climbs out. I grab my green day pack and look around. Two thumbs up to the warriors, a warm handshake with Dipa, a brief hug for Tina, and they all climb back into the vehicle and drive away. I am alone now in this spartan airport-sort-of-place with the great empty-full stillness of the savannah. I am drained of emotion; there are no reflections, no analyses, no stories in my head. The stories will come later when I sit at this computer and write this book.

A late model washed and polished Land Rover with no rust and a smooth-running engine and good tires drives up and disgorges its passengers. Money changes hands. If this violence or threat of violence is real, and if it is about elections and racism, I am now protected by the money in these people's wallets and faraway bank accounts. I feel funny about it, incomplete, as if I'm cheating in the game of life, because I was born with an ace of spades up my sleeve. I feel safe, but not uplifted.

As Harari writes in *Sapiens:*

> When trust depends on anonymous coins and cowry shells, it corrodes local traditions, intimate relations and human values, replacing them with the cold laws of supply and demand.
>
> Human communities and families have always been based on belief in 'priceless' things, such as honor, loyalty, morality, and love.... Money has always tried to break through these

barriers.... Although money builds universal trust between strangers, this trust is invested not in humans, communities or sacred values, but in money itself.... As money brings down the dams of community, religion, and state, the world is in danger of becoming one big and heartless marketplace.[122]

I share a commonality with these folks from the luxury hotel in that we were all born with that ace of spades up our sleeves. My parents weren't hedge fund billionaires; my father was a chemistry professor, and my mother was a school psychologist, but we always had food in the refrigerator, and we lived in a comfortable house with toilets that flushed and electricity and all that stuff. And enough left over to give me an education and a healthy start in life. I was raised with the confidence to succeed, at whatever I attempted to do. So I share the same culture with these Europeans who are waiting with me for the airplane. But there is a disconnect between us. We have experienced different realities out here on the Horn of Africa, and this difference hangs in the air, bolstered by not-so-subtle clues such as the cleanness or lack thereof of our clothes, how recently our hair has been combed and how much luggage we are carrying. Everyone must feel it because we nod casually in each other's direction, but no one initiates a conversation. There are no lions or elephants in the immediate field of view, there is nothing to photograph, so all the tourists spontaneously decide that the best game in town right now is to stare at a screen. No one talks; no one looks around. I miss the Motel at the End of the World and the cadence of daily life in the savannah. I get up and walk out into the scrub one last time. A Samburu woman shows up to sell some beadwork, but no one even acknowledges her existence. I buy an ankle bracelet for Nina. She probably won't wear it, but that's not the point.

The plane arrives on time, with a spinning of props and a whirr of well-tuned precision machinery. I stand in line with the others, hand my ticket to the pilot with a vague smile and a nod, and find a seat. The plane takes off, a boat in the air.

I had only been in Samburu for a month. Based on tangible, observable, recordable events, I had no physical adventures. I went

122 Yuval Noah Harari, *Sapiens: A Brief History of Humankind* (New York: HarperCollins, 2015), pp. 186–87.

for a walk with Dipa and we didn't see a lion. I went for a walk with the *morani* and no one hassled us, shot at us or tried to kidnap me. That type of non-event happens all the time. Ski a big, potentially lethal backcountry couloir or bowl and it doesn't avalanche. No adventure? Misadventures occur when you make a huge mistake or get unlucky. But misadventures and adventures are not the same. An adventure is a journey into the unknown, where you encounter unforeseen events that trigger unforeseen insights – or failures. I had journeyed into a world ruled by myth and wilderness, and now, as I sit in that airplane, alone in a crowd of others, I marvel at the adventures I had experienced, and feel deep sadness, mixed with relief, upon parting Samburu.

Mount Kenya comes into view. From the perspective of the airplane window, as we float across the sky, rocking gently in the thermals, life seems so pastoral and peaceful down there, with green plants growing in lush agricultural fields and villages tucked in among the foliage. I'll never understand what happened these past weeks. Even if I spent a lifetime here, I wouldn't be able to quite put my finger on all the details, but in my mind's eye I see the little girl with the white dress holding her daddy's hand on the way home from church, and the men with the AK-47s, and the bloody figures twitching and bleeding in the dust in Tina's grainy iPhone video. All part of the collage. My whole life I have somehow managed to float above Big Trouble. Sometimes it's been skill, but all too often I have squeaked by relying on blind, old-fashioned luck. But behind this mysterious mixture of skill and luck, it's always helped to know that at any time I could reach into my wallet and casually hand over those crisp hundred-dollar bills, which are only a mythology after all, but which have worked well enough all my life to secure me the real or metaphorical airplane flight, to carry me to safety.

Soon the pollutant haze of Nairobi darkens the sky, and we begin our descent.

I had texted Nina the day before, and she's booked me a room in a bed and breakfast. I have a one-day layover before my flight home. The cab driver has trouble finding the address. We bumble around through a slum and past an industrial area of small fabrication shops. Life in the streets proceeds peacefully, at least today, and I don't see any evidence of heavy-handed police with their armoured vehicles and machine gun stations. We reach a gated community, with high concrete walls topped with razor wire. We stop at the gate, where an armed guard with a clean, pressed uniform checks the taxi driver's licence and business permit. I hand him my passport and show him the text confirming my reservation at the B & B. The guard takes photos of all the documentation with his phone and gives the driver directions. As we wind our way through narrow, clean streets, a group of wealthy Kenyan boys and girls hold up our progress when they zoom past on skateboards, smiling and laughing. We reach the address, and the driver tells me he will wait to be sure we are at the right place.

I walk up to a massive wooden door set into a high wall, a fortress within the fortress of the gated community, also topped with razor wire. I ring the bell. And wait. The door creaks open to reveal a tall, erect, exquisitely beautiful woman in a spotlessly clean white dress. From her bearing and facial features, I speculate she is Maasai, or perhaps Samburu.

"You are Mr. Turk?" she asks.

"Yes."

"We are glad you have chosen to stay with us," she tells me in carefully articulated, grammatically perfect English. "May I make you comfortable Mr. Turk? Are you hungry? I can fix you something to eat?"

If you had asked me this morning, I would have told you that I was fond of my simple camp in the thicket. I was enjoying the secretive solitude of the place, the boyhood fort-like ambiance, the emotional embrace of the chaotic canopy of overhanging thorns, and even the silliness of the rodeo cowboys imprinted on the musty old sleeping bag. I had learned to accept the leaky Therm-a-Rest that deposited me onto the soft sand more or less precisely at midnight, like clockwork. If you had asked me this morning, I would have told you that I was deeply appreciative, thrilled even, at my colourful *morani* honour guard on the drive to the airport. But, in a flash emotional about-face, a traitorous abandonment of all my lofty thoughts, standing here in front of the tall woman in a white dress, I have a deep and sudden longing for clean sheets, geometrically square walls and a copious warm shower. And security. Like the palace in the heart of a medieval walled fortress city state, I am protected by walls within walls. I understand that our society is perched precariously on so many fallacious concepts, understand that, long-term, money is a flimsy form of protection, and certainly it is morally corrupt, but right now the loftiest idea in my head is to strip off all my sandy, sweaty clothes and stand naked under a torrent of hot water flowing out of a pipe that doesn't leak.

I hang out the next day in Nairobi doing tourist stuff and then call my cab driver for a ride to the airport. I run through all the normal routines, board the big jet headed for Frankfurt, buckle my seatbelt, and soon enough, the pilot pulls the Big Stick back and, in a roar, we accelerate down the runway.

Within that roar, tons of jet fuel conflate with tons of air to produce tons of carbon dioxide to enhance the already formidable Greenhouse Warming of our planet.

I don't need to do this anymore. I don't need to ride jet planes off to remote locations to find enjoyment and adventure, to gain insight into the world I live in. Yes, I have spent most of my adult life as a world traveller, built my writing career and my personal self-image around adventures in foreign lands, amid cultures and people so different from those in my youth in suburban Connecticut. My past journeys with Moolynaut in Siberia and on the arctic sea ice, and my current journey to Samburu, have formed me and changed me more positively than I can conveniently put into words. When I said those words to myself and resolved to eschew international airplane travel, I felt a sense of sadness. My brain is filled with so many fond memories of tea with Mongolian herders, storms at sea, ski lines on remote mountainsides, all enveloped within a sense of wonder and adventure. I have made deep and lasting friendships during my travels with people whose wisdom and love have uplifted and will continue to uplift me. I have used vignettes of experiences in exotic landscapes as examples and guidance in this book and in my life. Perhaps it is unfair that I suddenly decide to break my lifelong addiction to travel after I have done so much of it, now that I am sliding into old age, and so many doors are closing anyway.

When I fly round trip from Missoula to Nairobi, I am personally responsible for spewing about three metric tons of carbon into the upper atmosphere. As a comparison, the average Canadian uses 15.12 metric tons in a year. In those two days of flying, I am using 20 per cent of your yearly allocation *for a Canadian*. But wait a minute: the average European uses only 6.4 metric tons per year, so my flight emits nearly half the yearly carbon footprint of a relatively affluent person in London or Paris. And, moving down the line, that three metric tons for my jaunt across the ocean is undoubtedly more than a decade, or perhaps a lifetime, of consumption for a *moran* whose grass is withering under the ravages of climate change-induced drought.

I've been an environmental science writer since 1970, and for the past 50 years I've known that our profligate use of fossil fuels is rocketing our planet toward cataclysmic climate change. Time to 'fess up: I'm guilty. Because time and time again, I've rationalized it all off, loaded carabiners in my carry-on to avoid overweight charges and hopped on that plane – to Kathmandu, Lima, Urumqi, Nairobi or Resolute. And those years of globe-trotting adventure have been wonderful. But I can't do it anymore.

It dates me as an old hippie, but the timeless words of an old Dylan song have been on auto play in my head for *55 years* even as times have, in fact, changed and the modern message of those lines is now aimed at a new and perhaps even more urgent target:

> There's a battle outside and it is ragin'
> It'll soon shake your windows and rattle your walls
> For the times they are a-changin'[123]

I can no longer sit on a small stool by a low campfire and drink a cup of fresh, warm goat milk and look into the eyes of that woman beside me and figuratively tell her, "Sorry. My transcontinental flight, complete with seatside movies and airplane cuisine dinner and breakfast, is contributing to the global warming that is withering your grassland and killing your livestock. Or contributing to flooding and locust plagues that further kill your grass and livestock. Sorry if you don't have enough to eat. But it sure is cool to visit your remote homestead."

But now, here's another aha moment in addition to the socially responsible Green-Think that is so mandatory in today's world. There's no big altruistic sacrifice here. I'm happy playing in my

---

123 Bob Dylan, "The Times They Are a Changing," Columbia Records, January 1964.

backyard, or near backyard. If you can imagine all the ranges, rivers, seas and deserts, from the Rockies to the Pacific, from northern British Columbia to the Mexico border, you will be imagining some of the most wild and beautiful landscapes anywhere on the planet. And even if I narrow the scope and draw a circle within a 500-kilometre radius of my home, or a 100-kilometre radius, or a 25-kilometre radius, there is a lifetime of high-quality wilderness recreation available. As a bonus, within these imaginary arcs, the natives are generally friendly. No days on the computer applying for visas, no sleep-deprived layovers in Frankfurt followed by cramped nine-hour sit-a-thons, no institutional violence or threat of institutional violence.

As the magical aluminoscape tube lifts into the air to eventually carry me back across the ocean, I resolve that all of my future recreational energy will be concentrated into riding my mountain bike, skiing cool lines, backpacking and every now and then rock climbing or kayaking, all close to home. Because what I really love, and have loved all these years, is the beauty and solitude of wild places. And yes, I also love the inexorable pull of gravity, the compression of the turn, that feeling as your skis arc and your quads burn, snow flying in your face. It's in my DNA, as part of my Paleolithic survival strategy, to cherish the act of movement itself, that gave our ancestors the skill and fortitude to escape a lion or chase a gazelle.[124] And as for the wisdom and wonder I have experienced on my travels, it's been quite a ride, but wisdom and wonder are in front of my face anywhere and anytime I choose to open my eyes.

— — —

Five million years ago, too long ago to comprehend in any meaningful way, a random sequence of improbable events initiated an evolutionary experiment by endowing certain primates with slightly larger brains than their contemporaries on the African savannah. With all the mixed bag of advantages and disadvantages of a big brain, the

----

124 Borrowed and adapted from an article I wrote: Jon Turk, "The Compression of the Turn," *Mountain Life, Coast Mountains*, Winter/Spring 2020, p. 67.

outcome was tenuous and uncertain, but, in fact, these large-headed primates did well enough to survive, proliferate and branch into several different species.

This evolutionary experiment teetered on a knife edge and came within a squinch of failing. Then, about 70,000 years ago, and continuing right up to today, people began a curious journey of sidestepping a direct path to pragmatism, and instead filtering and interpreting their actions through music, song, dance, symbols and myth as expressed through carvings, paintings and later the spoken and written word. Think of the ancient artists, squatting in the sand, bashing rock against rock, chipping away in the bowels of the Earth, crystal by crystal, to create the Great Serpent who guards the entry or leads us into the Other World. And then, these stories, myths, statues, holy places, paintings, songs and Great Books gave us Power as individuals and as a tribe.

Power. A slippery devil of a word. No matter how many times we roll the word over, like a giant rock, to marvel at the ants crawling underneath it; no matter how many times we break the word down with our physics, statistics or philosophy; no matter how many times we attach fancy explanations or analysis of this Power so we can pat ourselves on the back because we now believe we understand it; no matter how many "no matters" we conjure out of our imagination, Power is just a word, squiggly sprays of ink on a piece of paper or vibrations in the air. And a word is a representation of the thing and not the thing itself. All I can suggest for certain is to tell your think-too-much-know-it-all-brain to get out of the way and don't try to interfere with what is happening right NOW, in front of your eyes.

Power to love, to share, to sacrifice, to support, to show compassion, to endure, to be stronger than you have strength to be, to find peace within yourself.

The Power of Nature to soothe and comfort, to transfer Power from the soil, sky, trees and atmosphere into us feeble humans who all too frequently fail to appreciate, who denigrate and rape the source of life.

The Power of science to help us when we need help, and to stand out of the way when other approaches become necessary.

But then, as in the plot of some *Lord of the Rings* novel of adventures in Middle Earth, or of a post-apocalypse science fiction tale of life after the Great Bombing, the dark armies of evil set out to steal the Stone or hack into the Facebook account that holds the Power.

Somewhere in the great sweep of human history, these dark armies of evil learned that they could hijack myth to change the meaning, direction and concentration of Power. These new stories were modelled after the stories of unity sung in the Great Caves, but the Power became something focused on owning, controlling, buying and killing.

Those bastards stole the Power Stone from the people. They hid it in great vaults locked away deep inside their castles where the Stone cried out in anguish as its magic was subverted to create division, anger, hatred, theft, selfishness, cheating, murder, rape, genocide, war, intolerance, destruction of Mother Earth. And they stole the Talking Stick, as well, so only they could dominate the ring around the campfire, the bully pulpit and the airwaves.

This is no secret.

But we don't have to let the dictators and the Donalds in this world get away with this shit. We can take back the Talking Stick and the Power Stone.

Science assures us that the human brain is plastic. Even mature adults can form new synapses and adapt to new situations – and cultural change is orders of magnitude faster than biological change. We can teach an old dog new tricks. Despite all the obviously horrible violence and inequality going on today, despite all the despots and would-be despots, despite starvation in the face of plenty, despite airplanes flying into the World Trade Center, gang rape as a calculated tool of warfare, someone shooting the water engineer at the Motel at the End of the World for no good reason, babies dying for lack of clean water, there is less overall violence, less inequality, and more prosperity and health now than ever before in human history. Yes, it might be a sad form of hope to compare awful human behaviour today with even more awful behaviour in the past, and yes, we have a long way to go, but at least we're on the upswing.

The frontal cortex is the part of the brain least affected by our genes and most malleable by culture. As a result, there is no universal or inevitable reason why humans must continue to harm one another and our planet. Within this reality, every person has the opportunity and responsibility to understand the genetic and cultural foundations of our actions and to channel his or her brain into positive thinking.

Maybe each one of us is going to have to do some hard pulling on our own.

> I don't know but I been told
> If the horse don't pull you got to carry the load
> I don't know whose back's that strong
> Maybe find out before too long.[125]

There is no unambiguous guideline to this elusive goal, 'positive thinking.' But there are signposts. I set out on this journey with the poorly articulated quest to find guidelines within the ancient wisdoms that had endowed our ancestors with the power to survive. Along this journey – through the savannah with real and metaphorical lions in the bushes, and then through a historical passage into the Cognitive, Agricultural, Industrial, Scientific and Computer revolutions – I glimpsed the realities and mythologies that bind people together, but also the mythologies that people kill each other and the planet for. It becomes terrifying to see how societal forces for good can so easily morph into rationales for evil.

Whenever I face this terror, I feel the imperative to Stop. Calm down. Focus. Recalibrate.

If I ignore grand generalizations about humankind and concentrate instead on who I am and what I have control over, I open the floodgates of my brain to find uncomplicated sensual awareness – without mythologies of any kind. Yes, humans are hard-wired to follow the pathways of myth. But we don't have to go there. We are hard-wired for violence as well, but we can journey through life without killing anyone if we choose to. Each one of us has a plastic cerebral cortex and it is imperative, in this modern world, teetering on the brink, to do our best to crank that cortex into positive action. One good place to start: We can know and trust ourselves well enough not to journey too far into imaginary worlds. We don't need to listen to stories someone tells us or stories we tell ourselves. We don't need to follow mass movements. There are too many pitfalls along that pathway. Presence in the NOW is sufficient. Presence in the Real World is sufficient.

Kei supat oleng oleng. Thank you very, very much for joining me.

---

125 The Grateful Dead, "New Speedway Boogie," on the *Workingman's Dead* album. Written by Jerry Garcia and Robert Hunter.

ACKNOWLEDGEMENTS

Fifty years ago, I co-authored my first book, *Ecology, Pollution, Environment*, with my father, Amos Turk, my sister, Janet Wittes, and my brother-in-law, Robert Wittes. That project launched my writing career; I have no idea how my life would have unfolded if we hadn't written that book and found a publisher, John Vondeling, willing to take a chance on it. So I start my thank yous in that long-ago time. In the 1990s, I launched into adventure writing, and I wish to thank Richard Parks for being my loyal and faithful agent for 25 years, before he retired.

Moving into this book, my first thanks is to Tina Ramme, who invited me to Kenya and supported my stay while I was there. Deepest gratitude to my Samburu friends, Jawas, Ian, David, Moses, Tiepe and Dipa, and all the other Samburu who made my time in Samburu fun, informative, safe and memorable.

In the early stages of this manuscript, several writer-friends lent advice and moral support. I thank them (in alphabetical order): Jack Christie, Marni Jackson, Henry Pollack, Chris Smith, Peter Stark, John Vaillant and Jon Waterman.

Writing is essentially a lonely job. It's so easy to wander astray. Special thanks to my dear wife Nina Maclean, who has been my dearest and best friend and invaluable bullshit meter throughout, calling me down gently when I, all too frequently, charge off on useless tangents.

As the manuscript began to take shape, Don Gorman saw a future in *Tracking Lions, Myth and Wilderness in Samburu*, and I would love to thank him for giving it a wonderful home at Rocky Mountain Books. Peter Enman, my careful editor, read the manuscript with a fine-toothed comb, and found more errors and inconsistencies than I would care to admit. He turned a rough manuscript into the finished product you hold in your hands. Thanks also go to everyone at Rocky Mountain Books – Chyla Cardinal, Colin Parks, Jillian van der Geest, and Grace Gorman – for all of their work in bringing this book into being.

Finally, I'd like to thank Skip Horner, a dear friend and international guide/outfitter, for encouraging me to take an active role, from afar, in sending aid to the Samburu villages. The effort has enriched me, and helped people who are just hanging on, at the edge of the abyss.